Wyndham Lewis and the Avant-Garde

Wyndham Lewis and the Avant-Garde

The Politics of the Intellect

TOBY AVARD FOSHAY

McGill-Queen's University Press
Montreal & Kingston • London • Buffalo

PR
6023
.E97
Z595
1992

© McGill-Queen's University Press 1992
ISBN 0-7735-0916-X

Legal deposit fourth quarter 1992
Bibliothèque nationale du Québec

∞

Printed in Canada on acid-free paper

This book has been published with the help of a
grant from the Canadian Federation for the Humanities, using funds provided by the Social Sciences and
Humanities Research Council of Canada.

Canadian Cataloguing in Publication Data

Foshay, Toby Avard, 1950–
    Wyndham Lewis and the avant-garde
    Includes bibliographical references and index.
    ISBN 0-7735-0916-X
    1. Lewis, Wyndham, 1882–1957 – Criticism and inter-
    pretation. 2. Modernism (Literature). I. Title.
    PR6023.E97Z6 1992   828'.91209   C92-090237-5

This book was typeset by Typo Litho composition inc.
in 10/12 Palatino.

28675678

To my parents, Shirley Fairn Aston and
Avard Woodman Foshay.

Contents

Acknowledgments

This study originated as a Ph.D. dissertation in the Department of English, Dalhousie University, under the supervision of Rowland Smith. The manuscript was revised and prepared for publication while I was a Post-doctoral Fellow at the Calgary Institute for the Humanities. I would like to thank Rowland Smith for encouraging and overseeing my interest in Lewis, William H. Pritchard, for his contribution as external reader, and also Harold Coward (Director of the Calgary Humanities Institute) for intellectual and institutional support, and for his recommendation of McGill-Queen's University Press to me.

At McGill-Queen's, thanks are due to Peter Blaney and Joan McGilvray, editors, and to Käthe Roth for her insightful and comprehensive copy-editing. I am especially grateful to the readers for McGill-Queen's and for the Canadian Federation for the Humanities. Their responses to the manuscript were receptive to my argument and productive of suggestions that substantially improved the text. Sincere thanks also to the CFH Aid to Scholarly Publications Programme for a subvention that made publication possible.

Portions of this text have previously appeared as "Wyndham Lewis: Between Nietzsche and Derrida," *English Studies in Canada* 16 (1990): 339–53, and "Wyndham Lewis' 'Physics of the Not-Self': Reason and Representation in Literary Vorticism," *Enemy News: The Journal of the Wyndham Lewis Society* 30 (Summer 1990): 4–12. The latter essay gave rise to a helpful exchange with Paul Edwards in issues 31, 32, and 33 of *Enemy News*. My thanks to these two publications for permission to include this material here.

Finally, a necessarily inadequate expression of gratitude to Ann Wetmore, whose interest and support were crucial during the most difficult stages of my work on Lewis.

Wyndham Lewis and the Avant-Garde

Introduction

In a 1986 collection of essays on modernism, the editor makes the observation: "The reader will be visited by the strong sense of an ending, a sense, made more acute by the growing number of attacks on Modernism's 'negativity,' its self-replicating mode of infinite regress, that this extreme self-reflexiveness, as particularly shown in its later manifestations, is a sign of its own undoing."[1] Yet, as recently as 1980, the prominent French critic Marcelin Pleynet asserted, "The process of an overall reevaluation of the problems raised by 'modernity' is barely starting."[2] It is within this climate of "the sense of an ending" and of a "barely starting" that the present study of Wyndham Lewis situates itself. The attacks on modernism's "negativity" by its current reassessors shed an interesting light on Lewis's marginal status in the Modernist pantheon. As Fredric Jameson says of Lewis, "A consistent perversity made of him at one and the same time the exemplary practitioner of one of the most powerful of all modernistic styles and an aggressive ideological critic and adversary of modernism itself in all its forms."[3] It is to the consistency of Lewis's perverse opposition to modernism that this book addresses itself, in an attempt to elicit a reading of his development which presents, for this least read and understood of significant modern English writers, a revised estimation of his role in the modernist movement, and through him of the movement itself. Such a re-estimation of Lewis's significance in relation to modernism is intended to contribute to Pleynet's proposed process of "overall reevaluation."

This study traces the interdependence in Lewis's career between his criticism and his fiction. Lewis was among the most aggressively intellectual of British novelists, and his criticism provides an effective access to the philosophical milieu evoked in his novels. Three hitherto largely ignored works – *The Caliph's Design, Enemy of the Stars,* and "Physics of the Not-Self" – provide the basis for my claim that Lewis represents a strain of post-aestheticist writing that differs significantly from what has come to be defined as "modernist." The socio-economic and political isolation of art and art practice in modernity gives rise, according to Peter Bürger, to two alternative responses: the formalist and stylistic experimentalism of canonical modernism, and a more politically aware and thematic experimentalism, which Bürger terms the avant-garde.[4] *The Caliph's Design,* the most consistent and forceful critical essay of Lewis's early career, clearly articulates his opposition to what he sees as the empty formal experimentation of modernist painting and presents his understanding of the need for a more socially and politically aware art practice. Lewis's struggle to realize such an avant-garde practice is traced through *Enemy of the Stars,* "Physics of the Not-Self," and his first novel, *Tarr.*

Lewis called the First World War his "political education,"[5] and it is clear that he took a significant departure in the 1920s from his prewar vorticist concerns. From looking at the psychological, social, and political worlds from the point of view of art, he turned toward looking at art from the point of view of its role – or, rather, lack of role – in a society which valued it, as he saw it, wrongly or not at all. *The Revenge for Love* is the novel in which this stage of Lewis's career finds its mature expression. It is the fullest realization of his gifts as a satirist, and the context in which his political concerns become the vehicle for a new perception of the interaction of social-political environment and individual consciousness, leading him back toward the questions of self and identity that had preoccupied him in his vorticist period. But, as his autobiographical *Blasting and Bombardiering* demonstrates, interiority has become more personally problematic than it was in *Enemy of the Stars, Tarr,* or *The Revenge for Love.* Though less polished than *The Revenge for Love,* the late novel *Self Condemned* radicalizes and interiorizes the Nietzschean psychodynamics that had, from the beginning, been at the basis of Lewis's understanding both of modernity and of the artist's role within it.[6]

Wyndham Lewis's avant-gardisme, arising as it does from a Nietzschean vision of modernity as a nihilism, entails not an intellectual politics – that is, some kind of interior polity – but a "politics

of the intellect," a grasp that intellectual positions and artistic prac-
tices have social-political as well as personal implications. His pursuit
of a political understanding of art practice in modernity was circuitous; it produced, as it did among his more typically modernist
contemporaries, eccentric, wilfully naïve, and at times repellent political views. But Lewis's peculiar aesthetic and political education
led him through politics as such into a personal encounter with the
interior roots of both political thought and artistic practice, forcing
from him a critical response that clarifies our understanding of modernity.[7] As an artist shaped, as this study argues, by the Nietzschean
critique of metaphysics, Lewis's criticism and art are the scene of a
confrontation between reason and representation that anticipates
and illuminates central issues in poststructuralist and postmodernist
debate.[8]

1 Where is Your Vortex?
The Caliph's Design

In *The Caliph's Design: Architects! Where is your Vortex?*,[1] Lewis offers the most sustained and considered of his early critiques of the art scene of the early twentieth century. Published in 1919, it is a work of the immediate post-vorticist period and a product of Lewis's chastened sensibility following his service in the Great War. In the commentary to the reprint of his art criticism in *Wyndham Lewis the Artist, From 'Blast' to Burlington House* (1939), Lewis described his frame of mind at this time: "We all of us went over into the War, and lost our 'Vortex' in it. When we came back into art out of life – desperate life – again, we had no appetite for art-politics. At least I had not. I had tried the 'group' game, in the art-racket: I had found it more trouble than it was worth. And in *The Caliph's Design* ... it was not as a part of a rather bogus battalion, but as *a single spy*, that I was speaking."[2] Lewis is expressing himself for the first time as an individual art critic in *The Caliph's Design*, rather than as part of an art-political group movement. But the change in delivery of the message is not intended as a radical change in its content. Lewis became "a single spy": "Yet *The Caliph's Design*, written just after the war, was another *Blast*, and it continued the criticism of *Blast* (No. I) and *Blast* (No. II)."[3] We see in *The Caliph's Design* the full force of Lewis's critical intelligence as it was formed by his bohemian apprenticeship in Paris, Madrid, and Hamburg, his leadership in the only modern art movement original to Britain – vorticism – and the sobering experience of his active service, both as soldier and as painter, in the Great War.

In *Rude Assignment*, Lewis describes the combination of the ardent and the tentative that was vorticism: "It was, after all, a new civilization that I – and a few other people – was making the blueprints for … A rough design for a way of seeing for men who as yet were not there. At the time I was unaware of the full implications of my work, but that was what I was doing. I, like all the other people in Europe so engaged, felt it to be an important task. It was more than just picture-making: one was manufacturing fresh eyes for people, and fresh souls to go with the eyes. That was the feeling."[4] The idea of designing a fresh civilization and shaping the changed sensibility that might inhabit it is precisely embodied in Lewis's vignette of the Caliph's design which opens the book and acts as a parable for which the remainder is commentary.

As Lewis describes it, the Caliph arises one morning "dissatisfied with the shape of his city" and feverishly tosses off a "design for a new city, or rather of a typical street in a new city." This little "vorticist bagatelle" is presented to his chief engineer and his architect, who are instructed to produce by the following day (on pain of death) the requisite plans for execution of the design. "After a half-hour of complete paralysis of their intellectual faculties," they rally and appropriately comply, and "within a month a strange street transfigures the heart of that cultivated city."[5]

The main point to be observed about the parable is its emphasis on art as total environment, as an encompassing design blending all media into a unified vision, localized in the figure of the Caliph, who "negligently" and "facetiously," though with an underlying artistic seriousness, "executes" his vision. In a preface, Lewis anticipates the Caliph's design by interpreting a parable with another parable, likening the contemporary art scene (of 1919) to a bull-fighting arena. This scene is first described as one in which "you get this contradiction of what is really a very great vitality in the visual arts, and at the same time a certain sceptical discouragement, a misuse of that vitality," in which the "pleasant amateur … drops down into the arena from among the audience, flourishing a red handkerchief. By his pranks … he adds to the general confusion."[6] "Contradiction" and "confusion" plague modern painting, "which stands to our revolutionary epoch as a legitimate offspring of great promise" but which suffers from "weakness" and "fatigue": "The spirit that pervades a large block – cube if you like – of the art of painting today is an almost purely art-for-art's-sake dilettantism. Yet you find vigour and conviction: its exponents, Picasso, Matisse, Derain, Balla, for example are very considerable artists."[7] It is Lewis's diagnosis, then, that modern painting, despite its "great revolutionary promise," still has not sufficiently freed itself from aestheticism, that last flower of romanticism, which he describes as "art-for-art's-sake dilettantism." For Lewis, cubism has not broken free of the *ancien régime* of aestheticism; it is simply not revolutionary enough.

The confusions underlying a half-revolutionary painting provide an opening for "the pleasant amateur (the vindictive failure of more settled and splendid ages)."[8] Thus the amateur multiplies confusion in the bullring of modern art, already inhabited by "crowds of degenerate and dogmatic Toreros" (the professional artists), viewed by an audience made up largely of women who "hurl expressionist javelins torn from their hats, and transfix the bottoms of the buffoons and the billy-cocks of the bandilleros!" Art, the object of this charade, is a "little bull, at first amused," who finally drops "with boredom, goes quickly aside and falls asleep": "Is this not a fairly accurate picture of the bloody spectacle that we, Public and Performers, present?"[9]

Both the public and the artists are to blame, Lewis implies: the public for not demanding a more substantial bull – a better type of art, or at least "some fine animal from Nineveh, or ... the Nile Valley."[10] A return to the classical art expressive of all aspects of a civilization – religious, political, social – would at least be an acceptable substitute. The artists too are responsible, but what of the architect, "this strange absentee ... this Ghost of the great Trinity, Sculpture, Painting, and Architecture ... *why does he not cheer us up by building a New Arena*? – around the new Bull we are breeding, our new very active Art – a brand new and most beautiful Arena?"[11]

The engineers and architects, however, have not responded to the challenge of the artistic revolution, so that "the Cubist painters of Paris, the quantity of ponderous painters to be found cubing away in that city, are the best fitted for this role."[12] This would be a great gain, but, significantly, Lewis implies that the need is not only to fill the void left by architecture itself, but to bring painters into a more serious engagement with art: "The energy at present pent up (and much too congested) in the canvas painted in the studio and sold at the dealer's, and written up with a monotonous emphasis of horror or facetiousness in the Press, must be released. It must be used in the general life of the community. Thence, from the life outside, it will come back and enrich and invigorate the Studio."[13] Modern painting is a "revolutionary oasis," artificially contained by the institutions of studio, gallery, and press. A hothouse effect produces the contradiction of a weary and languid revolution. Impressionism, Lewis says, suffered the same fate, so that both cubism and impressionism have remained in thrall to romantic aestheticism, "art-for-art's-sake dilettantism": "Listlessness, dilettantism is the mark of studio art. *You must get Painting, Sculpture, and Design out of the studio and into life somehow or other*, if you are not going to see this new vitality desiccated in a pocket of inorganic experimentation."[14]

The Caliph's Design is Lewis's blueprint for breaking out of the institutional greenhouse of studio art by occupying the void left by architecture and attempting an overall *Design*[15]: "Let us divide up this ramshackle empire of Architecture. We could even dispense with a Caliph. There need not be any bloodshed. It is a not quite irrational world!"[16] Lewis is explaining in the preface, then, that what he is calling for in *The Caliph's Design* is in the nature of a bloodless coup. The "bloody spectacle" of the modern "art racket" can give way to a revolutionary transformation of civilization, supplanted by an art capable of transforming consciousness by first transforming sensibility. *The Caliph's Design* is a parable of such a transformation, which in classical civilizations (such as that of Baghdad, Nineveh, or the Nile Valley, in Lewis's view) would proceed, as it were, from divine decree, at the facetious but deadly whim of a son of heaven. But the age of reason, the eighteenth century, the high-water mark of civilization for Lewis,[17] has intervened: it is no longer "a quite irrational world." Bloodshed and Caliph can be dispensed with. By breaking out of its institutional thraldom, art can achieve an *organic*, living experimentalism, and so transform culture as to lead to the emergence of a new form of humanity.

Under what may at first appear to be an arbitrary and eccentric parable lurks Lewis's aesthetic politics. In evoking primitive aesthetic wholeness, he is careful at the same time to adjust the Caliph's absolutist powers from the perspective of the age of reason. His combative desire to inhabit the arena of modern life with a real artistic bull requires him to defend modern art from being co-opted by modern ideologies of either right or left, reactionary or revolutionary. Lewis's revolution would place art *in control of* politics.

In *The Caliph's Design*, Lewis is severely critical of the direction taken by the contemporary movement toward abstraction in painting, whether cubist, expressionist, futurist, or vorticist. It has been overtaken by what he calls a nature-mortism, a mere studio art which is formally and technically experimental but which, in its content, involves a mere play of variations on the objects of its immediate environment – objects which have become, he says, trite in the extreme. Art must break out of this passivity of content and bring its technical prowess to bear on a transformation of the experience of our whole environment, of life at large:

Well, then, what I propose is that as much attention might be given – it would end by being as concrete – to the masses and entire form-content of life as has been given by the Nature-morte school to the objects upon the studio table. If architecture and every related – as we say, applied – art were drawn in – were woken up, then the same thing would be accomplished upon a big scale as is at present attempted upon a small scale. All the energies of art would not be centred and congested in a few exasperated spots of energy in a few individual minds. But the individual, even, would lose nothing as a consequence! the quality of his pictures would not suffer. And a nobility and cohesion would be attained that under present conditions it is difficult to visualize. [18]

Lewis expresses the highest possible regard for the abilities of Picasso, but, because of his position of leadership in the art scene, Lewis places at his door much of the responsibility for the para-doxical malaise of the visual revolution. [19] Picasso, he says, is a technical wizard who plays on an immense range of styles with unmatched dexterity, but whose preoccupation with form is trivialized by his lack of attention to content. Picasso's greatness has led the whole contemporary art world astray: "Braque and Picasso have *changed*, indeed, the form-content before them … But it has only been the debris of their rooms. Had they devoted as much of their attention to changing our common life – in every way not only the bigger, but the more vital and vivid, game – they would have been finer and more useful figures." [20] The public, too, is to blame for giving its sanction to such art: "Two things, then, have made this indifference displayed by most artists to their form-content come to be regarded as a virtue. One is the general scepticism and dis-couragement, the natural result of the conditions of our time. In-tellectual exhaustion is the order of the day; and the work most likely to find acceptance with men in their present mood is that work that most vigorously and plainly announces the general bankruptcy and their own perdition." [21] Thus, the chief artists and their public are locked in a symbiotic reinforcement of decadent and dispirited experimentation, in which formal inventiveness is an act of cynical despair over the lack of significant content in life or art. Lewis sides with a faithful and heroic remnant: "A number of younger painters are embarked upon an enterprise that involves considerable sacri-fices and discomforts, an immense amount of application, and an eager belief. This effort has to contend with the scepticism of a shallow, tired and uncertain time. There is no great communal or personal voice in the Western World of today, unless some new political hegemony supply it, for art to build on and to which to relate itself."

Lewis identifies himself here with a serious and committed belief in the possibility of vital art civilization, against scepticism, flaccidity, despair over the fate of the West. His expression of hope that there might emerge some "great communal or personal force in the Western World" is a product of his faith in art as an expression of a full humanity, within which resides an unsatisfied need to affirm and believe that will later give an uncritical welcome to the stirrings of Nazism as a possibly constructive, unifying hegemony. We can observe in *The Caliph's Design* the healthiness of Lewis's opposition to a lifeless trend in the revolutionary art movement that he had himself helped to create. That he was deceived by the vitality of the Hitler Youth Movement is perhaps a commentary on the degree to which his desire to affirm an organically experimental art had been frustrated and starved in what he saw as the attenuated and devitalized cultural environment of the postwar period.

Lewis attempts, in *The Caliph's Design*, a utopian vision of a culture in which "all the energies of art would not be centred and congested in a few exasperated spots of energy in a few individual minds."[22] Lewis sees culture in a condition of fragmentation in which the wholeness of vision, the cohesive nobility of the classical ages of art, is hardly imaginable, so far has individualism eroded sensibility. The whole phenomenon of individualism is, for Lewis, the fragmentation of a cultural unity within which art achieved an organic wholeness of expression. In his view, it was the aim of the post-aestheticist visual revolution to break out of the art-for-art's-sake ghetto of the studio and to restore contact with experience, with *experimental life*. When he was a vorticist and still a participant in the mainstream of the movement, Lewis put it thus: "The painters have cut away and cut away warily, till they have trapped some essential. European painting today is like the laboratory of an anatomist: things stand up stark and denuded everywhere as the result of endless visionary examination. *But Life, more life than ever before, is the objective* ... When they say LIFE, they do at least mean something complete."[23] In *The Caliph's Design*, Lewis has taken up a solitary critical position outside partisan movements because he has begun to see that the prevailing current of the revolution has stopped short of a complete break with the bourgeois institution of art and its bureaus of studio, gallery, and press. Rather, it had perpetuated the decadent aestheticism against which it reacted, through a similar preoccupation with form to the neglect of content, with technique rather than with life-renewing, organically whole creativity. Lewis emerges in *The Caliph's Design* as a highly original critic of the overall trend of art and culture in the modern period. The breakdown of classical civilization and emergence of bourgeois individualism in the eighteenth century was, for Lewis, expressed chiefly in the ideology of romanticism, a creed of artistic individualism that ran to seed in the narcissism of turn-of-the-century aestheticism and decadence. By 1919, Lewis had discovered the worm in the rose of his own revolutionary experimentation. The visual revolution, his own included, had not been conceived on a large enough scale. Not only painting but the whole environment needed to be redesigned in a new canon: *Architects! Where is your Vortex?* For the sensibility of isolated *individuals* to become that of integrated *persons*, a new culture on a classical scale had to be conceived, one in which art defined social and economic relations, rather than vice versa.

In the afterword to his edition of *The Caliph's Design*, Paul Edwards notes that Lewis's call for the "fusion of life and art" in this work is a significant about-face from his earlier position. In *Blast*, Lewis had asserted, "We do not want to change the appearance of the world, because we do not depend on the appearance of the world for our art."[24] From this statement in 1914 to his position in *The Caliph's Design* in 1919, we can see a development in Lewis's thinking that exactly parallels the distinction between the modernist and the avant-garde put forth by Peter Bürger in his *Theory of the Avant-Garde*.[25] For Bürger, the modernist artwork is characterized precisely by its aestheticist autonomy from its social context in democratic-capitalist culture: it is formed within the development of artistic style and genre exclusive of the objective role of art in social, political, and economic life. What Bürger terms the avant-garde, however, explicitly addresses the role of art in contemporary social-political life. It criticizes the autonomy of art as an isolation from the praxis of life, and calls for a breaking down of the institutional barriers that structure the role of art in modern society.

Bürger's theoretical stance takes as paradigm Marx's explication of the category of "labour," in which the presence of the category and the awareness of its significance depend on the development of the economy into more explicit industrial conditions. Bürger applies this principle to aesthetics within the modern period:

It is my thesis that the connection between the insight into the general validity of a category and the actual historical development of the field to which this category pertains and which Marx demonstrated through the example of the category of labor also applies to objectifications in the arts. Here also, the full unfolding of the constituent elements of a field is the condition for the possibility of an adequate cognition of that field. In bourgeois society, it is only with aestheticism that the full unfolding of the phenomenon of art became a fact, and it is to aestheticism that the historical avant-garde movements respond.[26]

It was only with the rise of the aestheticist movement at the end of the nineteenth century that art achieved the development possible to perceive its own characteristic role in modern society, as a separate, autonomous "aesthetic" realm within experience, divorced from the vital interests and identity of the mainstream of bourgeois life. It was because aestheticism allowed art to be seen in its separateness from bourgeois life that the avant-garde could assert itself in opposition: "It is my thesis that certain general categories of the work of art were first made recognizable in their generality by the avant-garde, that it is consequently from the standpoint of the avant-garde that the preceding phases in the development of art as a phenomenon in bourgeois society can be understood, and that it is an error to proceed inversely, by approaching the avant-garde via the earlier phases of art."[27]

It is this principle of seeing aesthetic categories and movements in their immanent historical relation that gives Bürger's approach its claim to consistency, yet enables it to forgo assertions of absolute truth that would place it outside the very historical conditions that it describes. That we are ourselves still so discernibly within the historical continuity of the modern period, along with Wyndham Lewis, and therefore so much a part of the conditions we seek to understand, undermines any possible claim to a naïve scientific objectivity for our analysis. Bürger shows how we can grasp modern art movements from within our shared historical perspective with them, so that our own ideological anticipations, whether Marxist, conservative, or liberal historicist, can be manifest – at least at the level of presuppositions.[28]

Until the appearance of Bürger's study, the avant-garde had been treated as a sub-category of, or even a synonym for, modernism.[29] The underlying assumption was that, like modernist experimentation with style, "avant-garde literature derives from the dichotomy between conventional, cliched language and experimental linguistic forms that dislodge those cliches,"[30] an explanation common to the treatment of the form-content relation in all artistic media. For instance, in his well-known study *The Theory of the Avante-Garde*, Renato Poggioli sees the tendency of "avant-garde" writing to concentrate on linguistic creativity as a "necessary reaction to the flat, opaque and prosaic nature of our public speech, where the practical end of quantitative communication spoils the quality of expressive means." The experimental nature of avant-garde style, then, is a response to the "tensions of our bourgeois, capitalistic, and technological society,"[31] within which art has felt it necessary to adopt a critical or corrective stance. Jochen Schulte-Sasse points out, however, the lack of historical specificity in this explanation. Such a critical relation of art to society has clearly been in evidence throughout the bourgeois era, so that "the term avant-garde would have to be stretched to apply to the late eighteenth century and would become an empty slogan, no longer able to help us distinguish romanticism, symbolism, aestheticism, the avant-garde, and postmodernism from each other."[32]

Bürger defines modernism as a purely aesthetic revolution, with its roots in the nineteenth-century move away from content to form. As such, it does not warrant the radical claims made for it by modernist artists and theorists. Bürger feels that the turn toward form was a development implicit in the autonomous status of art from its beginning. As Schulte-Sasse explains,

Even if the autonomous art of bourgeois culture in the late eighteenth century criticized society through its contents, it was separated by its form (which includes the institutionalization of the commerce with art) from the mainstream of society. According to Bürger the development leading to Symbolism and Aestheticism can be best described as a transformation of form into content. As art becomes problematic to itself, form becomes the preferred content of the works ... In other words, the development from the autonomy of art in the eighteenth century to the aestheticism of the late nineteenth and early twentieth centuries is in Bürger's perspective an intensification of art's separation from bourgeois society.[33]

Modernism, then, finding its own origins in symbolist and aestheticist concern with technique, is not a radical break with the role of art in our era, but rather its fullest realization as isolated and socially ineffectual. Modernism is, for Bürger, a negative phenomenon. The increasing sensitization to aesthetic form, to the neglect of content, leads modernism to a "semantic atrophy": "Means become available as the category content withers."[34] A characteristically modernist definition of the avant-garde is given by Clement Greenberg in just such terms: "In turning his attention away from subject matter of common experience, the poet or artist turns it in upon the medium of his own craft."[35]

For Bürger, however, the true avant-garde consisted in a wholly different and more radical response to aestheticist emphasis on pure artistic experience. The latter, in fact, in being the full development of the implications of the autonomous mode of art in bourgeois society, was the necessary, if negative, precondition for the emergence of the avant-garde. As Schulte-Sasse describes it,

Aestheticism's intensification of artistic autonomy and its effect on the foundation of a special realm called aesthetic experience permitted the avant-garde to clearly recognize the social inconsequentiality of autonomous art and as the logical consequence of this recognition, *to attempt to lead art back into social praxis*. For Bürger, then, the development of the avant-garde has nothing to do with a critical consciousness about language; it is not a continuation of tendencies already present in Aestheticism. Rather, for him the turning point from Aestheticism to the avant-garde is determined by the extent *to which art comprehended the mode in which it functioned in bourgeois society*, its comprehension of its social status. The historical avant-garde of the twenties was the first movement in art history that turned against the institution "art" and the mode in which autonomy functions. In this it differed from all previous art movements, whose mode of existence was determined precisely by an acceptance of autonomy.[36]

Bürger's radical claim for the uniqueness of the avant-garde as distinct from modernism, then, consists in its social, political, and economic *self-consciousness* – its perception that the institutional role of art in modern society and the free-enterprise economy was the determining factor in its inability to influence society in a creative and concrete way, in a way that would expand its audience's experience of life.

Inherent in the achievement of artistic "self-criticism" by the avant-garde, Bürger says, was a correlative "objective understanding" of the development of art up to that time:

The self-criticism of the social subsystem, art, which now sets in, makes possible the "objective understanding" of past phases of development. Whereas during the period of realism, for example, the development of art was felt to be in a growing closeness of representation to reality, the one-sidedness of this construction could now be recognized. Realism no longer appears as *the* principle of artistic creation but becomes understandable as the sum of certain period procedures. The totality of the developmental process of art becomes clear only in the stage of self-criticism.[37]

Like realism, avant-gardisme makes it possible to gain a perspective on the very idea, as well as the actual phenomena, of period styles as products of their historical conditions:

Up to this period in the development of art, the use of artistic means has been limited by the period style, an already existing canon of permissible procedures, an infringement of which was acceptable only within certain bounds. But during the dominance of a style, the category 'artistic means' as a general one cannot be seen for what it is because, *realiter*, it occurs only as a particular one. It is, on the other hand, a distinguishing feature of the historical avant-garde movements that they did not develop a style. There is no such thing as a dadaist or a surrealist style. What did happen is that these movements liquidated the possibility of a period style when they raised to a principle the availability of the artistic means of past periods.[38]

It would be difficult, in my view, to overestimate the importance of this point regarding the nonexistence, in the usual sense, of a specifically avant-garde style. That avant-gardisme was a movement of artistic self-criticism and institutional self-consciousness, which "raised to a principle the availability of the artistic means of past periods," gave to its employment of styles a theoretical force specifically directed to the undermining of the aestheticist, and consequently of the modernist, experience of "style." The radical nature of modernist style, used in its most exemplary fashion in works such as Joyce's *Ulysses*, was to marshal a vast repertoire of period styles to the creation of a new kind of aesthetic experience, one which transcended history and periods by seeing them as aspects of a single day, an "eternal now." Since it has an "aesthetic" goal, and is concerned with totalizing the aesthetic experience in the moment, modernist experimentation with style, even in its iconoclasm, can be properly termed a period style of its own (as indeed it is seen in the light of postmodernism). From Bürger's point of view, avant-garde use of period styles is more radical in that it seeks to undermine "aesthetic experience" as such. It is fully "critical" because it is directed toward a dismantling of the very experience of "style" as something distinct and autonomous. It seeks to rediscover an experience of "life in the round", in which "art" and the "beautiful" are not a sphere apart, but rather aspects of the whole panorama of experience. The difference between modernist and avant-garde stylistic iconoclasm is the latter's *critical* edge, its "raising to a principle" the critical notion of style. The character of avant-garde "style," then, is its parody of style itself.[39] However, as Lewis was to discover in *Enemy of the Stars*, anti-style is no more necessarily liberating than the totalizing style of modernism.[40]

The analogy between Bürger's *Theory of the Avant-Garde* and Lewis's position as presented in *The Caliph's Design* will already have become apparent. What Lewis sees as the prevalence of an aestheticist dilettantism in the development of the visual revolution precisely bears out Bürger's contention that modernism and aestheticism were continuous phenomena. Lewis pointed to the utter triviality and passivity of content and to the promiscuous nature of the endless formal experimentation in the work, for example, of the most talented painter of the time, Picasso. It is this elevation of form over content that Bürger sees as the essence of aestheticism. Far from being a revolutionary break with tradition, then, modernism, as Bürger describes and Lewis berates it, ends in slavishly perpetuating that most ambiguous and problematic feature of art in the previous century and a half: its autonomy, its separation from the mainstream of modern life. As Lewis points out, the modernist revolution had allowed itself to be contained within the bourgeois institutional straitjacket of studio, gallery, and press, which mediated it to the public in the palatable form of "bohemian naughtiness." At a deeper level, formal inventiveness hid a cynicism and despair in artist and public alike over modern life, and the capacity of art to materially affect that life for the better. As Lewis baldly puts it, "Intellectual exhaustion is the order of the day; and the work most likely to find acceptance with men in their present mood is that work that most vigorously and plainly announces the general bankruptcy and their own perdition."[41]

What has to be acknowledged, however, is that, despite Lewis's commitment to the avant-garde deautonomization of art and its involvement in the stream of contemporary life, his motivation, political as it genuinely is, is not egalitarian or leftist in sympathy with movements, such as surrealism and dadaism, which Bürger identifies as avant-garde. As we have seen, Lewis calls in *The Caliph's Design* for a "great communal or personal voice in the Western World ... for art to build on and to which to relate itself," but the source from which he expects such support is "some new political hegemony."[42] The only means that he sees for art to overcome its marginal and ineffectual role in modern society is to be aligned with a strong power base, whether communal or personal. His conservative and rightist tendencies are clearly visible here, as are the roots of his later unguarded susceptibility to fascism.

In his important book *Fables of Aggression: Wyndham Lewis, the Modernist as Fascist*, Fredric Jameson focuses on the contradiction of Lewis's modernism in its combination with his sharp criticism of the movement and its representatives. Jameson describes Lewis's criticism of modernism as "sterile and cranky oppositionalism, his cranky and passionate mission to repudiate whatever in modern civilization seemed to be currently fashionable."[43] Lewis's perverse practice of combining modernist style with anti-modernist polemics produces, Jameson says, a "grinding contradiction between his aggressive critical, polemical and satiric impulses and his unwillingness to identify himself with any determinant class position or ideological commitment."[44] Lewis's central theoretical position, his critique of modernist subjectivism and empty formal experimentation, and his promulgation of his alternative objectivist and content-significant visualism, Jameson sees as an "untenable squaring of the circle" that enables Lewis to mask what Jameson sees as the central, though unconscious, motivation of his work. Lewis's critical stance, Jameson says, "allows him to repress the structural center of his work, which lies not in the position of the observing subject, but rather in his implacable lifelong opposition to Marxism itself."[45]

In response, however, I would emphasize that Lewis's persistent attacks on collectivist mentality – from the early Cantelman "Experiments with a Crowd" through *Enemy of the Stars* and *The Art of Being Ruled*, to his satire of leftist fellow-travelling in *The Revenge for Love* and open attacks in *Left Wings Over Europe*, *Rude Assignment*, and *The Writer and the Absolute*[46] – hardly constitute "repressed opposition" to Marxism. The notion that anti-Marxism is the "structural center," whether conscious or unconscious, of Lewis's work misses the point. Lewis opposed all egalitarianism and collectivism, whether democratic or socialist. His classicist and rightist sympathies were rooted in a commitment to *fundamental difference*, to the irreducible uniqueness of the artist in society, the mind in the body, the genius among the common run of humanity. He opposed democratic mass collectivism, socialism, feminism, homosexuality, primitivism, historicism (the "time cult"), and modernist subjectivism in its aestheticist reduction of significant content to experimental form. He opposed all erasing of distinct lines of demarcation between objects, social classes, races, sexes, states of mind, categories. Dualism, the tension of opposites, was an instinctive and visceral response of Lewis's in every sphere of life, a response which he

deliberately cultivated and theoretically and polemically promul-
gated. So basic an impulse would have unconscious elements to it,
no doubt, though Lewis's aggressive, energetic, and variously gifted
nature left him little inclined to ethical self-analysis. Indeed, his
objectivist aesthetics precluded searching self-reflection, for which
during much of his career he had a positive antipathy. But to locate
a structural centre of his work in "repressed" anti-Marxism is too
distant from Lewis's primarily aesthetic and philosophical concerns.
The present study will emphasize, rather, his "politics of the intellect," an at once more interior and more problematic crux for his
work: an indebtedness to and difference with Nietzschean nihilism
and devaluation of values in which he explores the structure of the
will to power and *ressentiment*, first in psychological and philosophical terms; then, admittedly, for a period in historical, political, satirical fashion; but finally in later years in a penetrating and
disturbing self-criticism, as his life and work uncomfortably con-
verge, during blindness, in the theatre – or, rather, the "bull-fighting
arena" – of his mind.

Lewis's call in *The Caliph's Design* to "get Painting, Sculpture, and
Design out of the studio and into life,"[47] in its ideological opposition
to modernism and its political attack on the bourgeois institution of
"Studio, Gallery, and Press," is, then, avant-gardiste in Bürger's
sense, but it is not egalitarian. Lewis's aim was not to give art into
the hands of the people, but to "manufactur[e] fresh eyes for people,
and fresh souls to go with the eyes."[48] It was to be a collaboration
of artists in all media to offer a unique vision of the range and
richness of life, which would not be attainable by the ordinary person's unaided efforts. Lewis conceives the artist as the romantic
genius, the secular priest, Shelley's "unacknowledged legislator,"
who in the late, decadent, and enervated state of culture of the early
twentieth century he described needed "some new political hegemony" to supply the power base to build on. Thus, the Caliph's
design, as an exercise in social transformation through art admin-
istered by political authority, is not an arbitrary parable on Lewis's
part. The embodiment of artist as avant-garde agent of social change
in the reactionary figure of the Caliph represents Lewis's aesthetic
politics, his view of artists as a natural and cultural élite who thrive
in a hierarchical social milieu in direct alliance with political power.

Lewis is just as anti-democratic as he is anti-socialist. His roman-
ticist identification of the artist as the spiritual locus of his secular
vision of culture commits him to on élitism rooted both in natural
capacity and in cultural facility. Lewis is fundamentally at odds with
bourgeois culture, in both its isolating individualism and its deper-

sonalizing collectivism. What sets him off from his fellow modernists, especially in England, is his rejection of the aestheticist ineffectuality of mere stylistic experimentation in its absorption in subjectivism – in individual, isolated consciousness. In the thirties, he became equally at odds with the leftist political allegiance then in vogue, since it led to a similar loss of structuring borderlines on the social-political plane. His visualist objectivism, rooted in his firm commitment to mind/body dualism, opposed modernism and socialism alike.

Lewis's unique profile and itinerary, describable only in oxymoronic terms as reactionary avant-gardisme, provide an invaluable perspective on the cultural milieu within which he pursued his problematic career as artist and critical savant. The task of the present study is to trace Lewis's critical and creative development in the light of the foregoing analysis of his orientation to the dominant cultural tendencies of his times. The coherence that will emerge in this exploration of Lewis's peculiar career will provide the basis for a valuable perspective on the forces at play within the disputed realms of the historical "modern" and aesthetic "modernism."

2 Agon of the Intellect:
Enemy of the Stars

The Caliph's Design is the key theoretical statement of Lewis's early career. Published in 1919, it is his reflection on the heady prewar artistic experimentalism in which he was immersed as a bohemian student and which, in his person, provided the leading impetus behind the vorticist phenomenon. The First World War was a turning point for Lewis, for the other vorticists, and indeed for the utopian ferment of the experimental art revolution throughout Europe. Lewis's reaction to the demise of *Blast* (after only two issues) and to his experience at the front as an artilleryman was to withdraw and to re-evaluate the overall trend of the movement. The forceful personal vision that placed him at the head of the vorticist phalanx turned, in the light of sober wartime reflection, into a unique voice of dissent, protesting the aestheticist self-indulgence of modernist self-involvement in the midst of a social-political environment which called for real and not merely imaginal transformation. The seeds of the Enemy persona he had adopted in the twenties are easily discernible here. It is in *The Caliph's Design* that his critical consciousness first achieves the unity and coherence of a cultural vision, a vision which is shaped by the modernist revolution, but which denounces what it sees as the failure of the deeper and more radical aims of that revolution. In *The Caliph's Design*, Lewis launches himself on the avant-gardiste career that made him the pariah of English modernism for almost forty years.

With the exception of Geoffrey Wagner, no Lewis critic has given serious treatment to *The Caliph's Design* as a central early Lewis statement.[1] Even Wagner classes *Design* as "a destructive pamphlet," while at the same time acknowledging it as "one of the least strident and most impressive of all Lewis' critical works, [and one which] seems to have received the best press of any of his books."[2] Such favourable press was short-lived, while the subsequent critical oversight is companion to the more significant neglect of a work that incorporates in its two versions the disparate elements of Lewis's literary career, and into which he poured the full force of his creative energy. The play *Enemy of the Stars* was the first full-length literary work of Lewis's to be published, appearing in the first issue of *Blast* in 1914.[3] Lewis described himself as having "restored passages ... and added new ones"[4] for a much longer and more readable version published in book form in 1932.

The critical neglect of *Enemy of the Stars* is both more and less understandable than that of *The Caliph's Design*. Particularly in the terse 1914 version, *Enemy of the Stars* is, at every level, an extremely difficult work to penetrate. Written as a vorticist literary experiment, its style is highly abstract and telegraphic. The action is sparse and the setting surreal, throwing greater weight on the dialogue of two characters, who are polar opposites in personality and belief. This version is opaque on first reading, and easily discourages further effort. The appearance of the 1932 version, coming, however, as it did after *Hitler* and in the midst of three other highly controversial Lewis books,[5] failed to lift the work out of the obscurity into which it had plunged in 1914, and from which it has begun to emerge only in recent years.[6]

What is less understandable about the neglect of *Enemy of the Stars* is its position both at the inception of Lewis's literary career and at the close of its most vital period eighteen years later. Following the 1932 version, Lewis entered a dark tunnel of illness, critical boycott, and financial duress from which he emerged a different writer. The extensive work that went into the revised version shows that he not only felt very strongly about the play but was still sufficiently preoccupied with the issues it addressed to rewrite it almost completely.[7] The presence of *Enemy* in his mind throughout the intervening years between the two versions is attested to by the appearance in 1925 of an essay, "Physics of the Not-Self," which he described as "in the nature of a metaphysical commentary upon the ideas suggested by the action of *Enemy of the Stars*."[8]

A detailed comparative study of the two versions of *Enemy of the Stars* has yet to be made, but the most cogent observations on their relation are made by Wendy Stallard Flory, who remarks, "Most significantly, we find that his changes do not correct the earlier version so much as amplify it, making clear that after eighteen years his concern was not to modify or qualify what he originally wrote, but to present the same characters and the same basic ideas as forcefully, dramatically and accessibly as possible."[9] Accordingly, it is the 1932 text upon which the following discussion is based, bearing in mind that it represents at once Lewis's revolutionary vision in all of its vorticist intensity, and also the considered reflection of the most productive later years of his literary career.

It is instructive to chart the critical reception of *Enemy* in its uniform concern with form and style and its rejection of the work's thematic significance. The almost caricatural opposition of the two leading characters, Arghol and Hanp, along with the experimental style, has led to the criticism that *Enemy* is too static and abstract. A representative treatment of the work is that of Timothy Materer, who, in suggesting undeveloped depths in *Enemy*, is content merely to draw a parallel to what he considers Lewis's more substantial works: "From this viewpoint, *Enemy of the Stars* becomes a monodrama, like Beckett's *Endgame*, and Lewis's characters seem less simplistic. If Hanp is an aspect of Arghol, Lewis's hero must then realize that he is not merely the object of mindless attacks and so must take a more responsible and ironic view of Hanp. Although the play only hints at this theme, the action it suggests – the hero ironically suffering from his own failings embodied in others – recurs throughout Lewis's fiction."[10] This sums up Materer's brief treatment of the characters and action of *Enemy*, and he proceeds to discuss, with an even more negative verdict, Lewis's experimental vorticist style: "Despite what Pound called its 'abundance of conceptual hustle,' Lewis's vorticist style never gathers dramatic momentum ... The action of *Enemy of the Stars* ... is not powerful enough to shine through the thick layers of static images."[11]

In *The Literary Vorticism of Ezra Pound and Wyndham Lewis*, Reed Way Dasenbrock argues on the other hand, for the seminal importance of *Enemy* precisely as stylistic experiment: "*Enemy of the Stars*, with its paratactic concatenation of phrases anticipated the subsequent stylistic direction of Pound, Eliot, and Joyce," and "announces a central theme of modernism."[12] Dasenbrock accords high importance to vorticism, and to *Enemy* as its premier literary document: "If the Vorticist movement was not exactly the vortex of modernism, it is its seedbed or laboratory."[13] But Dasenbrock, while acknowledging *Enemy*'s stylistic importance, has nothing positive to say about its thematic significance: "To focus one's discussion of *Enemy of the Stars* on the sense that it makes is to miss Lewis's point altogether. The real significance of the play is as a gesture. Lewis wanted to start a revolution in literature ... and he conceived of *Enemy of the Stars* as a gesture that would show writers the path."[14] Thus, he accuses Lewis of "programmatic modernism," of innovating merely "from his own desire to be in the artistic vanguard."[15]

In her pioneering essay, Flory cuts through this tendency to dismiss *Enemy* with a challenging thesis:

Enemy of the Stars has not been taken as seriously as [Lewis] hoped it would – as seriously as it deserves ... If we read this primarily as a play about the fate of Arghol, it is likely that we will find it unsatisfactory – the action too predictable and the characters too artificially stylized and obviously symbolical. Yet once we realize that Lewis's presentation of the agon of these two characters is a means to an end, rather than an end in itself, we can see *Enemy of the Stars* for what it is: a serious, eloquent and complex piece of self-analysis in which the power and grandeur of the style is commensurate with the intensity of the author's personal involvement with his subject.[16]

Flory's conclusions about *Enemy*, moreover, reflect her critical approach: "Lewis's decision to externalize and objectify his own state of mind by making the two conflicting drives within him into two characters and by creating for them their own surreal world which would be proof against his own authorial intrusion *enabled him to be self-analytical with a steadiness of gaze that he did not try to achieve again.*"[17] She goes on to observe, "Frequently after this he would describe the repulsiveness of his characters as though the cause of his revulsion lay entirely in their shortcomings rather than largely in his own nihilistic and claustrophobic view of the human condition."[18] Behind Flory's apparent commendation of *Enemy of the Stars* is a sharply negative view both of Lewis's vision as an artist and of his artistic insight. *Enemy* is given a positive reading in that Lewis achieves in it an insight into his own psyche – that is, into his own "nihilistic and claustrophobic view of the human condition." His depressing vision is redeemed, in Flory's eyes, only by virtue of his acknowledgement that it is his own and not that of others, that it is not an objective human condition. Flory has successfully broken through the earlier superficial readings of *Enemy*, but her negative judgement about the *content* of the play has led her to place emphasis on the form – on reflexivity, the involvement of the author with his own subjectivity.

Flory's modernist reading of *Enemy* is managed at the considerable cost of dispensing with Lewis's message to his audience, and indeed with any audience at all for the work itself: "Lewis's main object is to create this 'close atmosphere of terror and necessity', to explore for himself and create for his reader the harrowing state of mind that is not only Arghol's but ultimately, and much more urgently, that of the author himself. Acutely aware of the constant struggle between his own interior 'Arghol' and 'Hanp', Lewis on the first page of the play reminds his readers, 'It is our 'agon' too. Remember that it is our destiny!'"[19] Flory reads the "our" here as a royal "we," but this is explicitly contradicted by the passage. After describing the two main characters in the opening lines, the narrator addresses his audience:

['*Yet you and me!' I hear you* – What of you and me? '*Why not from the English metropolis?' But in this mad marriage of false minds, is not this a sort of honeymoon? We go abroad. Such a strange place too for the initial stages of our intimate ceremonious acquaintance. It is our 'agon' too. Remember that it is* our *destiny!*][20]

The narrator steps out of role here (note the brackets) to address the audience in his voice as author or teller, in order to prevent a sense of foreignness which would result in the audience's seeing the action as external to it. It is because of the inherent "strangeness" of the "intimate ceremonious acquaintance" of artist and audience that a foreign setting is dictated. The foreignness of the intimacy points to its status as allegory. The agon and destiny are that of both the artist and the audience, both *within* each and *between* them, since Arghol and Hanp represent the polarities both within human nature (mind/body; thought/action) and in society (intellectual/man of action; artist/public; individual/collective).[21] Flory's attempt to see the agon as interior to Lewis is valuable in uncovering a dimension of the work so far overlooked, but it is somewhat less than half the story. Lewis was not only well aware of this personal dimension of *Enemy*, he specifically designed the interiority of the work as an exploration of *both* the personal and social dimensions of life and thought. Self-reflection is evoked not only in the author but in his audience: "It is our 'agon' too. Remember that it is *our* destiny!"

Arghol's agon, his exchange with Hanp, is an allegory of the artist's relation to his audience, and specifically of Lewis's to the readership of *Enemy* and vice versa. This is the full complexity and import of the reflexivity that Lewis consciously embeds in the work, but, contrary to Flory, what is most conspicuous is its *objective* quality. Far from being a mere exercise in "self-analysis," *Enemy of the Stars* addresses an alienation inherent to modern art and to experience at all levels: interior alienated from exterior, personal divided from social, subjective cut off from objective.

The uniform tendency, then, in the comparatively scant attention accorded *Enemy of the Stars* has been to emphasize the formal and stylistic experimentalism of the work, and therefore to measure its success as a modernist text in aesthetic terms. Flory is a partial exception in her attempt to valorize *Enemy* 's reflexivity, but, again, the yardstick is modernist in its attention to purely subjective, and therefore autonomous, artistic values, which in this case would entirely dispense with Lewis's need to communicate anything of interest to his audience. But we have seen that Lewis was clearly under the conviction that he was addressing matters of objective importance, that his main character's agon was also his own and that of his readers. It is thus the *thematic substance* of Arghol's agon that is focused on in the analysis to follow. It is argued that Lewis's attention in *Enemy* to content is in fact the *origin* of the formal and stylistic experimentalism of the work. This view allows us to discover the motivating interests of Lewis's career as writer, and so to offer an account of how this motivation served, in this first of his full-length works, to move him from the abstract vorticist style of *Enemy* toward the more conventional form of the realist novel in his next work, *Tarr*.

As a conscious vorticist work, *Enemy of the Stars* revolves, literally, figuratively, and conceptually, around the central character, Arghol. The image of the vortex is meant to convey the tension between dynamism and stasis, between rapid circular motion and its fixed centre. As Lewis defines him in *Blast*, "The vorticist is at his maximum point of energy when stillest." The image includes energy not only in space but also in time: "The new vortex plunges to the heart of the present."[22] Arghol is the still point and focus of all action and attention in *Enemy*. The play as his agon makes of him a "foredoomed Prometheus," a propitiatory sacrifice to the forces both human (historical, temporal) and cosmic (eternal, spatial) that are ranged against him. As the narrator describes the beginning of the action,

THE RED WALLS OF THE UNIVERSE NOW SHUT [POSTERITY] IN, WITH THIS FOREDOOMED PROMETHEUS. THEY BREATHE IN CLOSE ATMOSPHERE OF TERROR AND NECESSITY, UNTIL THE EXECUTION IS OVER AND THE RED WALLS RECEDE – THE DESTINY OF ARGHOL CONSUMMATED, THE UNIVERSE SATISFIED. (143–4)

Prior to this, the narrator had turned to his audience with the pointed notice that Arghol is a type of modern humanity, that his struggle and inevitable propitiatory sacrifice typify our own, that his agon is our agon too. As an experimental attempt at vorticist literature, *Enemy of the Stars* reconstructs spatial and temporal coordinates in order to evoke in the audience awareness of a crisis, of a dramatic physical and spiritual challenge at the heart of modernity.

Enemy of the Stars (as not a play at all, but a kind of novel)[23] is a narrative about a play set in a surreal universe, in a time dimension called the "Thirtieth Centuries," in which the audience comprises the whole of humanity. Called, simply, "Posterity," it includes representatives of all generations. The visionary nature of the setting extends to scenes, properties, and costumes, which change and shift of their own accord. There is a necessarily heavy dependence on the narrator, who describes and extensively interprets characters, action, and fantastic setting.

There is a series of parallels in the work with classical tragedy: the action is an *agon*; Arghol is a Prometheus figure; the characters, as in classical drama, wear masks designed to amplify their voices: "THE MASKS FITTED WITH TRUMPETS OF ANTIQUE THEATRE – WITH EFFECT OF CHILDREN BLOWING AT EACH OTHER WITH TOY IN-STRUMENTS OF METAL" (144). At a significant point early in the principal section of the narrative, the action stops and the focus of attention becomes the masked face of Arghol:

(*The aloof master of this arc-lit vortex is Arghol. His mask has been designed to represent the magical function ... But abruptly everything flicks out ... In the momentary blank a close-up of the chief player's head is conveyed, in a breathless upward rush, to the distant watches ... then the fact stands out for all to see – a pallid mask ... All gaze upon it as upon a spectacle of awe.*) (160–1)

Arghol's mask is foregrounded as the still point of the "arc-lit vortex"; "snatched up to be scrutinized by the busybodies in the remotest galleries of Time" (161), it is the locus where the dynamics of space and time meet.

Etymologically, our word "person" is derived from the Latin *persona*, "a mask, especially as worn by actors in Greek and Roman drama," and by extension the "role, part, character, person represented by an actor."[24] The problem of personality, of self and of identity, is the central theme of the long dialogue between Arghol and his companion Hanp, who represents the sensuous man and who identifies with the collective mind of modern mass man. Arghol at one point declares, "When mankind are unable to overcome a personality, they have an immemorial way out of the difficulty. They become it. They imitate and assimilate that Ego until it is no longer one – that is what is called success. As between Personality and the Group, it is forever a question of dog and cat. These two are diametrically opposed species. Self is the ancient race, the rest are the new one. Self is the race that lost" (155). The formal centrality of Arghol's mask, then, points to and reinforces the thematic locus of the play, the problem of human identity, represented by Arghol and Hanp. Arghol is the Self, "the ancient race," "the race that lost" to the likes of Hanp, whose "black bourgeois aspirations undermine that virtuosity of self." Hanp is "a violent underdog ... put at the service of Unknown Humanity, our King." This "new race" of mankind is the headless mob, whose "boundless royal aversion for the great Protagonist ... finds expression in the words and expressions of this humble locum tenens [Hanp]" (143).

Following up the allusions, Arghol as the "foredoomed Prometheus" has stolen his figurative fire, not from the gods for mankind, but from mankind in an attempt to assert a god-like sovereign identity, a Self. The classical allusions in *Enemy* function as pointers to the inversion of values that has taken place in the modern displacement of the classical world-view. Within modernity, the battle is not the attempt of mankind to capture a heroic, god-like identity from the transcendent realm. It is, rather, the need to deny the very existence of a world beyond nature and any necessity to assert a heroic identity in contradistinction to the material conditions of life. Arghol is an inverse Prometheus – his persona is not heroic; instead, the masks give the ludicrous effect of "two children blowing at each other with toy instruments of metal." We are told that the set for the main scene is "SUGGESTED BY CHARACTERS TAKING UP THEIR POSITION AT THE OPENING OF THE SHAFT LEADING DOWN INTO MIME'S QUARTERS." Arghol and Hanp, "GIDDILY MOUNTING IN [the] OPENING" formed from the mime's stage entrance, as if from "THE UNDERGROUND" (144), are mimicked or parodied by the setting, which associates them not with the Olympian but with the spirits of the underworld. They become parodies of the heroes of Attic tragedy, and, as two employees of a provincial wheelwright, are the farthest thing from Aristotle's aristocratic tragic heroes (*Poetics* 1453a, 10).

Enemy of the Stars, in addition to its syntactic experimentation, is conceived on the formal level as a vorticist universe operating under its own laws of space and time. But, more fundamentally, the formal vorticist design of the play is explicitly enlisted as support and emphasis in the unfolding of a fully developed – indeed, a determining – thematic content. As already mentioned, *Enemy* is an unperformable play; it is the *story* of a surrealistic drama that takes place within a fantastic spatio-temporal realm. The formal, vorticist structure of this universe finds its physical axis in Arghol, literally in his face – that is, in his mask, or persona. (Hanp later partially decapitates Arghol, a further physical correlative of the mind/body conflict taking place between himself and Arghol and within Arghol himself.)

Just as the formal (spatial) structure of the play incarnates the theme of Arghol's sacrifice, so the temporal, narrative structure of the work is more than simply a medium. As a narrative of a play, it has itself a thematic content. The lack of an objective polarity between man and a transcendent realm against which he struggles to define himself robs the theme of the essential ingredients of drama, at least in the classical terms against which Lewis is defining vorticist man. The agon of modernity is not an objective contest, man measuring himself against the ideal of the gods in a struggle full of the pathos, the pity and fear, of tragic human limitations. It is, rather, an internecine warfare of man with himself, represented in the confrontation between Arghol and Hanp, between individualism and collectivism. Hanp is the man of the people, of purely material and pragmatic concerns, who mocks Arghol's preoccupation with Self, with a higher identity and purpose which leads to his excepting himself from common-sense expectations. Hanp is the man of the body, Arghol the man of the mind. The "plot" of *Enemy* is Arghol's gradual discovery that his conflict with Hanp is really a conflict internal to himself, between his own mind and body. It is Lewis's attempt to point to the source of the modern agon as a dividedness of man from himself, within himself, which reduces him to the bathos of a pure self-involvement, a state of confusion rendering him incapable of action, either positive or negative. As Arghol says, "To make it worthwhile to destroy myself there is not enough there to do it with and that's a fact!" (169).[25]

By rendering *Enemy* as the narrative of an unperformable play, Lewis is pointing his audience in on themselves in the privacy of their reading: "*It is our 'agon' too. Remember that it is our destiny!*" By breaking up the syntactic continuity and flow of his sentences, he tries to bring about a formal vision of a static world, which will presumably serve the recognition by his readers of the vorticist condition of modern life. We have also seen how the vorticist formal design of *Enemy*, in focusing on Arghol's mask, tries to fix the reader's attention on the graphic representation of the thematic axis of the work. Along with its status as a narrative of a play, all the formal elements of *Enemy of the Stars* are consciously designed to contribute to the thematic content of the work, and are motivated and informed by Lewis's vision of the modern agon. A second passage of the work reveals what Lewis sees as the source of the problem.

The long dialogue that forms the centrepiece of *Enemy of the Stars* results in Arghol's realization that the basis of his conflictual relationship with Hanp is a projection of himself onto Hanp: "That's it! I find I wished to make of you … the animal to me! … I wished – I've just found out – to make you myself you see. But every man who wishes that – to make out of another an inferior Self – is lost. He's after a mate for his detached ailment – we say self, but mean something else. For without others – the Not-Self – there would be no self" (175–6). Arghol, having realized that he was merely using Hanp as an antidote to his own inner contradictions, attempts to banish him. Hanp will not be dismissed so peremptorily; a fight ensues, and afterward both collapse into unconsciousness. The narrative follows Arghol as "he rolls heavily into sleep. Now a dark dream begins valuing, with its tentative symbols, the foregoing events" (180).

Arghol dreams that he has returned to Berlin, and to the room he had occupied there as a student before he had abandoned the city. He picks up an open book, Max Stirner's *Der Einzige und Sein Eigentum*: "Stirner. Well! That bad offshoot of the master of Marx in his prime. That constipated philosopher of action. One of the seven arrows of his martyr mind! Poof! he flings it out of the window" (181). Moments later, someone arrives at the door, having retrieved the book from where it had fallen into the midst of a funeral procession. The figure at the door is first seen as "an undergraduate," but then, in dream-like fashion, is transformed, first into Hanp, then into Stirner himself, and finally into "a middle-aged man … evidently a philosopher. Self-possessed, loose, free … Stirner, in fact, as he had first imagined him" (182).

At the beginning of *Enemy of the Stars*, Arghol is presented as being "in immense collapse of chronic philosophy" (143). The action of the narrative has reached a climax in Arghol's recognition of his exploitation of Hanp and Hanp's retaliation at having been sent packing. The post-pugilistic dream is Arghol's unconscious, instinctual narration of the events leading up to the traumatic fight with Hanp, a fight that will shortly lead to Hanp cutting Arghol's throat while the latter snores in exhaustion. That is, the reader, so far given Arghol's intellectual commentary on what the narrator describes as philosophic collapse, now receives the commentary of Arghol's unconscious perceptions of his experience. However tentative and symbolic the dream version is, it is also more direct, more concrete. It is the commentary by his "Hanpness," "the Animal" in Arghol, of the physical and finite side of his experience with which he has been unable to come to terms.

The dream reveals that Arghol's philosophical collapse is typified in his reading of Stirner's book, which is left open – that is, being actively read – at his collapse. Arghol's attempt to rid himself of Stirner is foiled by a figure which is transformed from Hanp into Stirner himself, into the mature, free, and self-possessed ideal philosopher of Arghol's imagination, a figure he had once identified with Stirner. First translated into English in 1907 as *The Ego and His Own*,[26] Stirner's single major work presents his neo-Hegelian supreme egoism. In opposition both to Christianity and to Hegel's transcendental Absolute Mind, into which all mere individuality must eventually pass, Stirnerian egoism champions the absolute, uncategorizable uniqueness of the individual self: "God and mankind have concerned themselves for nothing, for nothing but themselves. Let me likewise concern myself for *myself*, who am equally with God the nothing of all others, who am my all, who am the unique one" (41). The universality of spiritual and philosophical absolutes, in Stirner's view, eclipses, swallows up the particularity of individual existence. Identity lacks all specificity from a Christian or Hegelian point of view, and is therefore a "nothing," empty of any explicable significance. Stirner turns the tables on the tradition, drawing out the logical corollary that, from his own point of view, all else *but* his specificity and uniqueness is a nothing.[27]

The Stirnerian ego is *sui generis*: "To be a man is not to realize the ideal of *Man*, but to present oneself, the individual. It is not how I realize the *generally human* that needs to be my task, but how I satisfy myself. *I* am my species, am without norm, without law, without model, and the like" (55). It is hardly surprising that Stirner did not write another book of comparable force or originality. Where can thought go from the principle of its own uncategorizable uniqueness? Equally explicable is Arghol's philosophical collapse following his apprenticeship to Stirner. More to the point, however, is the dream's revelation of Arghol's virtual identification with Stirner as philosopher and of the philosopher as such with Stirner. That is, Arghol's dream reveals that the philosophical collapse into solipsism that had unfolded in the dialogue with Hanp is internally inconsistent. Stirner's doctrine of individual uniqueness is still a doctrine; it is the universalized *model* of specificity. As a disciple of Stirner, Arghol had not only embraced solipsism, but in the very act of doing so had undermined the apparent logic of egoistic self-sufficiency in becoming the follower of a doctrine which itself rejects the notion of any ego patterning itself after another. Where can Arghol go when he is barred even from entering a cul-de-sac?

The attempt to explain such a condition to his erstwhile disciple issues in Arghol's "enlightenment," his realization that all action, from his passivistic return to his rural home and submission to the physical abuse of his employer-uncle even to his mere attempt to explain himself to Hanp, is pre-empted by this nihilistic quandary: "We say self but mean something else. For without others – the Not-Self – there would be no self." The very ground of supposed uniqueness and authenticity is an illusion, and the "self" is merely the locus of an aporia, a contradiction in terms, a self that, in its dependence upon others as "Not-Self," is equally a self and a not-self – or, rather, neither in any absolute sense. We are earlier told that "SITTING" is the "POSE [that] BECOMES HIM BEST – THE AFFINITY WITH THE BUDDHA" (145). Lewis indicates that Arghol is in fact beyond the Western polarity of self/not-self in its implication in romantic, transcendentalist interpretations. Arghol is beyond the polarity self/mankind as a secular romantic equivalent of the more classical God/mankind opposition. He is Buddhist in his rejection of absolutes, whether of individual ego or of collective humanity, and in his embrace of *anatman*, no-self, the relativity and transience of ego identity.[28]

Arghol's unconscious valuation of his fight with Hanp is able to be precise with its "tentative symbols" in a way that Arghol's discursive explanation to Hanp of his post-philosophical condition is not. Just as the structure of the narrative finds its symbolic axis in the foregrounding of Arghol's mask, so the thematic content achieves symbolic form in his dreamt return to his Stirner apprenticeship. The figure that returns *The Ego and His Own* in the dream appears first as Hanp, then as Stirner, then as Arghol's own ideal philosopher. Arghol's actual experience had been in reverse order, from a philosophical ideal, to Stirner, to Hanp. That his discipleship of Stirner should lead him to annex to himself in turn such a quotidian disciple as Hanp is the problem around which *Enemy of the Stars* revolves (so to speak). The narrative motivation is provided by Hanp's need to push Arghol for an explanation of his behaviour (which will, in turn, provide Hanp with an understanding of his own role), an explanation which, in the very effort to provide it, disabuses Arghol of his need for Hanp's companionship. Because of the internal inconsistency of Stirnerian solipsism (the *principle* of egoistic uniqueness), Arghol's immense philosophical collapse has put him beyond the capacity to provide a rationale for either his condition or its consequences. Arghol has become an embodiment of self-contradiction, something in itself offensive to the pragmatic consciousness of Hanp, driving him to rid nature of the Argholian anomaly. Hanp murders Arghol in his sleep, and so "THE DESTINY OF ARGHOL [is] CONSUMMATED, THE UNIVERSE SATISFIED!"

After the "something distant, terrible, and eccentric" that Arghol embodies has been "forever banished from Matter" (190), "a galloping blackness of mood overtakes the lonely figure" of Hanp, and he quickly jumps in the canal: "He sinks like a plummet ... heavy with hatred and nothing left to work it off on – so quite certain to go to the bottom and stop there" (191). Having expelled the representative of Personality, of self, there is nothing against which Hanp can define himself as mankind, as not-self. He merges himself with undifferentiated matter; then there is nothing: "A black cloud enters and occupies the whole arena, immediately everything is blotted out ... Then there is no sound in particular and only the blackness of a moonless and unstarlit night" (191). Stirner is the thematic axis of *Enemy* in the way that Arghol's mask is its formal axis.[29] As philosophical model, Stirner embodies the discrepancy that on the formal level is revealed between the origin of persona in dramatic character (i.e., imaginative construct), and (via Christianity) its modern, romantic transmogrification into identity, self-present completeness – that is, into Stirnerian uniqueness. *Enemy of the Stars*, then, is perfectly coherent on both the formal and thematic levels as a representation of the crisis of modernity. It can be seen primarily as a radical philosophical vision, which in its urgency and extremity requires a sufficiently striking and revolutionary form and style.

In the light of my reading of *Enemy of the Stars*, it becomes impossible to see Lewis's evolution as a writer as primarily a question of stylistic or formal design. Our approach must be informed by an appreciation of the more complex thematic concerns of *Enemy*, concerns that, rather than being motivated by a desire primarily for revolutionary *style*, can be clearly seen to be the *origin* of the demand for stylistic and formalistic experiment in this work. Yet the tension within the play between thought and self-representation emerges in Lewis's own relation to this text in its two versions.

The period between the 1914 and 1932 texts was punctuated by an essay, "Physics of the Not-Self," first published separately in 1925,[30] but included (slightly revised) in the 1932 edition of the play. Symptomatic of the neglect of *Enemy* itself, the essay has never been accorded more than the most cursory analysis, despite the striking declaration of its opening lines: "This essay is in the nature of a metaphysical commentary upon the ideas suggested by the action of *Enemy of the Stars*. Briefly, it is intended to show the human mind in its traditional role of the enemy of life, as an oddity outside the machine" (195). But "Physics" is as difficult to follow on first reading as is *Enemy* itself, as it conducts a very oblique argument on mind as "enemy of life," and never comments on how it is to be seen as functioning in the play itself. Despite the explicit announcement of his intention, Lewis is ill-inclined to make the commentary easy for his readers.

"Ethics," rather than "Physics of the Not-Self," might be a more appropriate title, since the essay focuses on the question of "goodness" in the light of the problematic of self at work in *Enemy of the Stars*. The argument has two phases. First, Lewis looks at the problem of "truth" inherent in the self/not-self opposition, and the ethical notions implicated in it. Second, he turns to what he calls "the old status of 'goodness'" (199), to what he claims is a more objective tradition of morality, which he identifies with the Greeks and particularly with Socrates. The essay is a polemical manipulation of the dialectic of truth and goodness as involved in that of self and not-self. The truth of the self (called by Lewis "catonic," presumably after the pragmatism of Cato the Younger) is that which immediately serves the practical ends of the man of action, the "man of his word," who knows what he, and life, are about. In contrast is the truth of the philosopher, who is chronically uncertain about what is genuinely true: "His scruples brand him as a liar from the start," his affirmations "so beset with reservations that [they remain] a particularly offensive sort of lie for those who prefer the will's truth to that of the intellect" (196).

The truth of the self serves its own interests. In contrast, the truth of the intellect is so uncertain as to disabuse its devotee of all easy certainty, even of the knowledge of who he himself is: "The *not-self* established in the centre of the intellect betrays at every moment its transient human associate" (196). Because it brings with it this uncertainty, this dedication to the objective and counting of oneself at naught, philosophic truth is greeted by pragmatists as an anti-social principle. The philosopher is the "enemy," "in league with the diabolical principle of the *not-self*" (198). Such a "giver" cannot be trusted: "A gift that *expects no return* is not a human gift ... If you are respectable, then you can only accept things from a person who evidently benefits more than you do as a consequence of his bounty" (199). The irony is palpable, Lewis appearing to feel justified in his counter-polemic by the inherent bias of conventional utilitarianism.

It is in the second part of the argument that Lewis turns from polemics to logic, presenting a serious ethics of the not-self rooted in the Greek notion of "goodness." Relying on the historian of philosophy John Burnet, and his *Greek Philosophy*,[31] Lewis argues that the term used by Socrates to designate the highest philosophical and artistic attainments was arete, of which "'goodness' in its modern sense is, as a translation, misleading."[32] After Burnet, Lewis maintains that goodness as arete "had no ethical significance ... 'it was, in fact, what we call efficiency.'" Lewis cites Liddell and Scott on arete: "'Goodness, excellence of any kind; excellence in any art'" (200). His argument, then, is for the non-ethical significance of the Greek notion of "goodness," and he goes on to bolster this by identifying the Greek and Hindu notions of goodness as knowledge of the eternal (*episteme* as opposed to *doxa*, belief): "This epistemological absolute is much the same as Brahman; and the inferior knowledge of the world of temporal experience is much the same as the upanishadic *avidya* [ignorance, delusion]" (201).

Lewis seems to be relying here on Paul Deussen's *The Philosophy of the Upanishads*: "The conception of *avidya* was developed from the negative idea of mere ignorance to the positive idea of false knowledge ... This is a very noteworthy step in advance. It is the same which Parmenides and Plato took when they affirmed that the knowledge of the world of sense was mere deception, *eidola*."[33] Lewis is clearly referring to the Hindu ("upanishadic") notion of *avidya*, rather than (as Munton suggests [224]) the Buddhist one.[34] However, as revealed by his immediately following citation of Yajnavalkya on the unknowability of the self ("thou canst not know the knower of knowing" [201]), apparently gleaned from Deussen (80), Lewis is concerned with the notion of the non-essentiality of self which perhaps derives from merely perspectival differences between Hinduism and Buddhism.[35] The point that he is trying to establish in connecting Greek and Indian philosophy is the epistemological and cognitional rather than the ethical and affective character of our relation to the highest reality. Lewis is consistent in his comparison of two monist systems, the Greek and the Indian, but he then brings in Near Eastern Manicheism as support: "The fusion of the idea of goodness with that of knowledge we see in the teaching of Mani, for that matter ... he taught that as the mind of a person contains increasingly more light, so it contains correspondingly more goodness." He compares this to Socrates' notion "that it was impossible for a man to *understand* and to be evil" (202). Lewis seems unaware of the inconsistency in claiming an equivalence between the monism of Platonism and (advaitic) Hinduism and the dualism of the war of the powers of light and darkness in Manicheism.

As a secondary comparison in support of the point that goodness is, in Burnet's words, "'something that belongs to the very soul that possesses it'" (202), Lewis's assimilation of dualism and monism here is a mere oversight. But the underlying inconsistency in Lewis's thinking emerges into a full-blown contradiction in his treatment of the implications of his purely epistemological ethics for the affective life. The object of the pursuit of the "epistemological absolute," he says, is a Stoic *apatheia* (203): "It is the philosopher's business to dispose of all desire" (202), "to avoid suffering, or the turbulent 'intoxication' of action or feeling" (203). The objective character of his philosophical "ethics of the not-self" then results not simply in an impersonalism, but in a depersonalization: "You cannot, logically, 'love' or admire, either, if you *fully* understand" (203). But Lewis cannot eat his cake and have it. In describing the character of the "not-self" in the earlier, polemical phase of the argument, he noted the resentment with which the "enemy principle" is received by the self-interested: "Since, again, by its very nature it awakens love, that is not in its favour either. Love being the thing that is most prized by men, the individual who (in league with the diabolical principle of the *not-self*) appears to be attempting to obtain it by unlawful means is at once without the pale" (198).

While an argument could be made for a difference between the detached "awakening" of love in others and the interested pursuit of it for oneself, in effect Lewis fails to make this distinction good. This is demonstrated in the concluding argument of the essay. The implications of the cultivation of the "not-self" are typified for Lewis in the figure of Socrates and the practical form taken by his philosophical detachment. He quotes Alcibiades' speech in the *Symposium* commenting on "'how passionately Socrates affects the intimacy of those who are beautiful, and how ignorant he professes himself to be.'" Alcibiades claims that the real Socrates "'despises more than anyone can imagine all external possessions, whether it be beauty, wealth or glory ... He esteems these things, and us who honour them, as nothing, and lives among men, making all objects of their admiration the playthings of his irony'" (204). In his concluding paragraph, Lewis emphasizes the archetypal stature of Socrates as man of the not-self and as the ironist of "'external possessions ... and us who honor them.'" For Alcibiades, Socrates' irony is a matter of objective principle, an undervaluing of secondary things and of others in their attachment to them. Lewis's characterization is much more ambivalent. Is Socrates' detachment irony or cynicism? Socrates is "a supreme market-place performer (properties ironically chosen, ironically handled, and ironically displayed, but also ... his celebrated language of love ... [was] ironical ... Was not the language of love the *cynical* gilding of the pill?" (204; my emphasis). Is Socrates instructing, or administering a personal, and therefore an ethical, reproof? Lewis's Socrates sounds more like a satirist, despairing over persons rather than over objective principles. His Socrates may or may not be objective, but he is not ethically detached.

In "Physics," we can trace the contradiction of Lewis's treatment of love and affectivity, through his ambivalence about irony, to what can only be called an error of interpretation bearing on the crux of his argument. In describing, after Burnet, goodness as arete, Lewis mentions the Socratic distinction between *philosphike* and *demotike arete*, between philosophical goodness depending on intellect and "popular" goodness depending on habit. Socrates' "highest philosophical goodness," Lewis says, "is the one identified with knowledge, and which can be taught, like a trade" (200). This description of the highest arete as a technical skill is clearly an error on Lewis's part. As Burnet says, "But though goodness in the full sense of the word is knowledge, it is not an art, that is to say, an external accomplishment that may be acquired by anyone, and which he may exercise or not at his pleasure."[36] This misinterpretation of the degree of control inherent in our relation to arete leads Lewis to a further misconstruction of a point made by Burnet. It has to do with the emergence of the doctrine of forms in Socrates' thinking and its relation to earlier schools, particularly to Pythagoreanism. Based on a sharp distinction between objects of thought and objects of sense, the theory attributes true being only to the objects of thought in their greater proximity to the pure form or idea of the thing. Burnet notes the Pythagorean influence on this notion of pure form, but observes, "Where it differs from anything we can reasonably attribute to the Pythagoreans is in the systematic inclusion of what we should call moral and aesthetic forms on an equality with the mathematical."[37] As a result of his bias toward a notion of arete that is subject to technique, Lewis applies this point of Burnet's to his reading of Socratic goodness and its practical implications: "If it is in the introduction of ethical and aesthetic forms upon a footing of equality with the mathematical that the originality of Socrates, as the successor of the Pythagoreans, reposes, then in a sense ethics is only introduced to be disposed of; for the *skill-cum-knowledge-goodness* of Socrates, or the approximation to perfect knowledge, are very mathematical conceptions, when compared with those of more emotional ethics ... There is, in short, no emotional value attached to 'goodness' ... whatever" (202).

Lewis reads Burnet's point about the relation of Socrates to the Pythagoreans in precisely the opposite sense to that intended. The equal footing of moral and aesthetic forms with the mathematical is meant by Burnet to denote the *expansion* of logic beyond mathematics into ethics and aesthetics – that is, the raising of merely technical thought to the level of philosophy. Lewis reads it, rather, as the assimilation of the less precise notions of morality and aesthetics into the greater precision and beauty of pure mathematics, a kind of purification of goodness and beauty of their "emotional value," as he derogatorily conceives it. Lewis's Socrates becomes a worthy "successor of the Pythagoreans" in their attempts to determine numerically such things as opportunity, justice, and marriage;[38] Socratic "goodness," as "skill" as well as knowledge, is a "very mathematical conception" and therefore not merely detached from emotion but essentially unrelated to and actually above it: "If you know or understand *fully* you no longer desire" (202).

In this divergence from his sources, we find the origin of Lewis's rationale for the notion of a "physics" of the not-self. But this "very mathematical conception" is also an ambiguous one. Lewis implies that the not-self has a necessary relation to the "physics" of the (wild) body; however, this relation is not a corporeal one, but, in the nature of a scientific physics, a mathematical and clinically logical one, of the mind as "the enemy of life, as an oddity outside the machine" (195). Lewis inscribes in his title the ambivalence inherent in his mind/body dualism. Is arete the spiritualization of emotions and senses, ethics and aesthetics, or the purification of the intellect from a gross affective and sensuous life? We can locate here the locus of the inherent ambivalence between irony and cynicism in the conclusion of "Physics." Alcibiades describes a gentle monistic irony, in which Socrates holds to the objective priority of the higher goodness over the lower immersion in the life of habit and desire. For Lewis, Socratic irony is more critical, more conscious of the essential incompatibility of – indeed, the opposition to and violent confrontation between – intellectual and bodily life. For him, irony partakes of cynicism, of a contest with a diseased bodily life for which it seeks the cure of the intellect, and for which the sharp goads of satire seem more appropriate than the wry observance of inconsistencies that is irony. Lewis emphasizes this dualism: "We cannot be surprised that this peculiar and very rare sense of fun should have brought [Socrates] at last to a violent end" (204).

If an ethics of the not-self is a "physics," a quasi-scientific technique of "excellence," in which the virtue of clear and consistent thinking triumphs over emotions and senses, then Lewis himself is in breach of his own ethical code in "Physics of the Not-Self." His divergence from Burnet, on whom he relies as an authority, is, as we have seen, not a matter of legitimate difference of interpretation. He clearly gets Burnet, and Burnet's Socrates, wrong on a point crucial for his argument. In viewing goodness (arete) as a matter of technique, Lewis brings it within the orbit of volitional control and out of the transcendental realm of objective principles to which we can appeal for standards of judgement in matters whether of physics, ethics, or poetics. The ambiguity in Lewis's position on the nature of Socratic irony in the conclusion of "Physics of the Not-Self" is a product of the desire for an objective criterion of evaluation in arete, coupled with his unwillingness to grant to transcendental principles the autonomy and freedom from human control that would make them genuinely authoritative. "Physics of the Not-Self" illustrates how ardently Lewis was attracted to classical principles of objective order and authority and, yet, how essentially captive he was to the modern conviction that such transcendental principles are in the end merely arbitrary conventions, determined by rather than determinant of human conscious or unconscious choices.

Dasenbrock uncovers this inherent classical/modern ambivalence in the context of Lewis's vorticism: "The image of the vortex offers one representation of this separation [of life and art], as the artist and art work attain the still point, leaving the flux of the external world behind them. But the nature or status of that still point remains unclear, partly because it remains unclear to what extent Lewis endorses the Idealist and transcendental philosophy implicit in his aesthetic formulations."[39] Though an invaluable expression and guide, visual vorticism by its very nature cannot settle for us these questions of Lewis's philosophical convictions and temperament. As the embodiment of the purely objective relations between time and space, dynamism and stasis, the image of the vortex is not an adequate representation of the central principles at issue in Lewis's aesthetic, simply because, as an objective correlative, it takes no account of consciousness and of subjectivity. The vortex cannot represent the central dichotomy in Lewis's work: mind/body dualism. As Dasenbrock acknowledges, vorticism remains unclear about the status of the still point, but that is because it cannot represent it visually as consciousness, as mind. Vorticism is not the key to *Enemy of the Stars*. *Enemy* and its "metaphysical commentary," "Physics of the Not-Self," as Lewis's most comprehensive explorations of mind/body dualism and the clearest revelations of his early mind and work, are crucial to our understanding of his artistic and intellectual development.[40]

Lewis's misreading of arete as technique in "Physics" reveals his almost instinctive bias toward the modern, his tendency to privilege consciousness over objective order even in the midst of his attempt to erect the classical notion of arete into an "ethical" criterion for modernity. As a "metaphysical commentary," "Physics" is itself a paradoxical technique. Why did Lewis feel that it was necessary? The obvious answer is that the sheer obscurity of *Enemy* required a sense of conviction that the struggle of reading it would repay the effort. But the fact remains that "Physics," precisely as "metaphysical" commentary, is in clean contradiction to *Enemy of the Stars* itself.

On the verge of the main sequence of *Enemy of the Stars*, "The Dialogue Begins," Arghol hesitates in the doorway of the hut in which Hanp has laid their meal: "*Shall he or not bar the barbarian* [Hanp] *from him for the future? Shall he go in now and deny him all rejoinder? Shall he disallow this mockery of organic speech? But* shall he – *he was half a mind!*" (150). Arghol is indeed of half a mind, saying one thing even while he does another. Hanp calls him on this: "All the talking you do does not seem to bear out your pretensions. For what you pretend you are, you talk too much, Mr. Arghol" (172). Arghol responds, "Let me do a lot of extraordinary talking … Men possess a repulsive deformity, it is generally referred to as 'Myself' … Promiscuous rubbing against their fellows is responsible for it. As to the activity you call in question, namely *talking* – why that is just such an unsuitable rubbing and contact too" (172). There is only one cure, Arghol says, for "this abominable ailment – namely Self … the classical stoic operation, namely – emptying an artery into the bath" (172). But he has already admitted, "To make it worthwhile to destroy myself, there is not enough of myself there to do it with and that's a fact!" (169). In this state of philosophical prostration, it is easy for the quotidian mind of Hanp to catch Arghol in his own contradictions. "Why do I talk to Nobody – is that the question before the meeting now? Well, it is not to you, really. It is to myself" (174), says Arghol. This realization, that Arghol wished to make of Hanp "my inferior nature – to be The Animal to me" (176), an extension of himself that makes it possible not to see in himself his own dividedness, facilitates the crisis of the play.

"Talking," then, is the "promiscuous rubbing against their fellows" that produces the "repulsive deformity" of Self: "For without others – the Not-Self – there would be no self" (176). Talking, for which Arghol only had "half a mind," is an activity of the Wild Body: "But it is a physical matter too – simply to make use of one's mouth and stretch one's tongue" (174). Language is a point of "promiscuous rubbing" between body and mind, a medium for creating the illusion of a self that is unique and autonomous. The contradiction of Arghol's position is that he must employ language, the vehicle of identity, in order to explain his rejection of the very notion of a self. But the point is that no one forces Arghol to talk. Hanp merely has to goad him. But the goading only enlightens Arghol as to his self-contradictory condition: that he is the perfect solipsist, that to be entirely empty of self is to be the self-complete egoist, and vice versa. Hanp is driven, by his sheer sense of nothingness in Arghol's presence, to physical retaliation. He awakens the Wild Body of Arghol and gets a sound trouncing. Half-measures are not enough, and he cuts Arghol's throat, severing mind from body, and performing the office for which Arghol himself lacked the wherewithal.

The irreducible tension between mind and body is made concrete in language. Arghol's attempt to resolve this tension through logic is self-contradictory (insofar as he has himself already rejected philosophy by abandoning his student life in Berlin), and merely aggravates the conflict within himself and with Hanp. Hanp's attempt, as the representative of nature red in tooth and claw, to resolve it by violent action is simple nescience. *Enemy of the Stars* maps a nihilistic condition in which the tension of polar opposition cannot achieve Hegelian dialectical sublation in a higher unity, and the attempt to resolve it into autonomous wholes merely brings about the "blackness of a moonless and unstarlit night."

Lewis's attempt to provide a "metaphysical commentary" on *Enemy of the Stars* is distinctly Argholian, an effort to apply logic and technique to a sphere and a condition that he has already represented as irresolvable in those terms. In the very act of outlining it, he abandons the virtue of Socratic *apatheia* that he claims for himself at the end of *Enemy* in the character of Sfox, with his "faceless helm, with a mask of inexpressive clay" (191).[41] In "Physics," Lewis argues divine indifference while at the same time asserting a "metaphysical" consistency which *Enemy of the Stars* clearly repudiates. Far from the work of a "programmatic stylist," as Dasenbrock asserts, *Enemy* has an artistic integrity that is violated, in fact, by "Physics of the Not-Self." We would rather accuse Lewis of programmatic criticism, an attempt to employ logic and technique to capture the attention of readers for artworks that themselves demonstrate the limits of logic and technique.

Lewis allows the *apatheia* of Arghol's Buddhist no-self to be undermined by the "wild body," by Arghol's physical retaliation to Hanp's attack. This pulls Arghol back into the infinite alternating regress of dualistic oppositions within himself and therefore between himself and Hanp. Thus, the nihilistic void that closes the work. Lewis himself abandons the artistic *apatheia* of Sfox in the "metaphysical commentary" of "Physics," and so is himself pulled back into the agonistic play of opposites: artistic detachment versus artistic engagement and critical objectivity versus critical polemics. But what is certainly clear is that Lewis finds no way out of or beyond this infinite regress, either in *Enemy* or in "Physics."

"Physics of the Not-Self" demonstrates that Lewis was fully aware of the ethical implications of his chief vorticist work. "Physics" argues, as we have seen, for an "ethics of the not-self," but Lewis's valuation of the "still point" of the not-self is arete, the *"skill-cum-knowledge-goodness* of Socrates." Lewis calls, in fact, for a Nietzschean "transvaluation of values," an attempt to go "beyond good and evil" to the stability of an "epistemological absolute." In its specific contradiction of the deeper insights of the artwork on which it is a commentary, "Physics" is a commentary indeed on the crisis of discourse and representation which *Enemy of the Stars* addresses, a crisis in which Lewis himself is deeply implicated and in relation to which he is far from achieving his own ethic of arete, of an intellectual and logical *apatheia*, that would make of him as an artist the "indifferent god" in dispassionate contemplation of the world.

The invocation of Nietzsche here is not without purpose. He is the silent antagonist and foundational intellectual influence on Lewis's early career.[42] The argument for a non-ethical, intellectual ideal in "Physics," in its appeal to Socrates as model, is an attempt to turn Nietzsche's call for a "revaluation of values" against him. Socrates was himself the antagonist of much of Nietzsche's thought, but particularly so in *The Birth of Tragedy*, where he is cast as the villain, "the type of the *theoretical man*," and source of "the profound *illusion*" of a victory of reason over intuition: "This illusion consists in the imperturbable belief that, with the clue of logic, thinking can reach to the nethermost depths of being."[43] It is this Apollonian belief in logic that Nietzsche sees as undermining the "tragic perception" that achieved its highest realization in the Dionysian art of Aeschylus. In choosing Socrates as model in "Physics," Lewis champions an Apollonian, logical transvaluation of values in contrast to Nietzsche's Dionysian apotheosis of the self as will to power. The preoccupation with classical dramatic motifs in *Enemy* itself now appears less arbitrary and recondite. *Enemy of the Stars* is Lewis's Apollonian answer to Nietzsche's call for a renewed Dionysian tragic art.[44] In fixing on Stirner, Lewis goes directly to the precondition for Nietzsche's own analysis of the crisis of nihilism,[45] in an attempt to clearly extrapolate and represent its ramifications for a genuinely modern art. Lewis's contention in *Enemy* that "drama," particularly tragic drama, is inappropriate to modernity is perhaps an attempt to push nihilism to even more radical conclusions than did

Nietzsche. The conclusion of *Enemy of the Stars* is that discourse is itself a compromise with temporality and with pragmatic nescience (Hanpness). Language can no longer be the vehicle of a logical "thought content," a pure signified, but must be a performative act, a symbolic gesture, a verbal dance in which signification is a function of the total work of art, rather than of any "truth" which it may be said to contain.

A thematic, formal, and stylistic unity and seriousness in *Enemy of the Stars* derives from its attempt to represent bathos. Lewis's ambivalence is the ambivalence of modernity, so vividly announced by Nietzsche, a questioning of the very grounds and possibility of both truth and goodness in a post-classical world. Lewis was caught on the horns of ambivalence, in a dualistic response to Nietzsche's invocation of Dionysian tragedy and will to power, which took the form of the Apollonian *Enemy of the Stars* and its "metaphysical commentary," "Physics of the Not-Self." We can be rightly critical of Lewis for not sustaining the virtue which he enunciated in "Physics," the excellence of intellect, which he is himself offending in attempting a "metaphysical commentary" that is demonstrated in *Enemy of the Stars* itself as no longer appropriate to modernity.

Lewis effectively embodies, if he does not successfully resolve, the ambivalence of the modern era (challenged as it is in particular by Hegel's declaration of the end of the essential usefulness of art): metaphysical thought has come to dominate our conception of the world and to define the limits of art; it is somehow only through art that we can articulate the limits of metaphysics. Lewis addresses the first problem in *Enemy of the Stars*, and then falls victim to the second in "Physics of the Not-Self." The fuller implications of Lewis's development as artist and critic centre on his relation to Nietzsche, his attempt to answer and to circumvent him, a relation which sets him within the wider context of European modernism, and which through him can bring to our appreciation of English modernism an understanding of its place in the larger crisis of modernity.

3 Harmonious and Sane Duality: *Tarr*

In *Rude Assignment*, Lewis recalls his state of mind during the *Blast* period in 1914:

My literary contemporaries I looked upon as too bookish and not keeping pace with the visual revolution. A kind of play, 'The Enemy of the Stars' ... was my attempt to show them the way. It became evident to me at once, however, when I started to write a novel, that words and syntax were not susceptible of transformation into abstract terms, to which process the visual arts lent themselves quite readily. The coming of war and the writing – at top speed – of a full-length novel ('Tarr') was the turning point. Writing – literature – dragged me out of the abstractist cul-de-sac.[1]

As the writing of a primarily visual artist, *Enemy of the Stars* is an attempt to shape the linguistic and literary medium in accordance with criteria developed within the visual arts. In *Tarr*,[2] on the contrary, we find Lewis coming to terms with the exigencies of language and of literary genre:

The writing of 'Tarr' was approached with austerity. I clipped the text to the bone of all fleshly verbiage. Rhetoric was under an interdict. Even so, it soon became obvious that in order to show the reader character in action, with all its attendant passion, there was no way of reducing your text to anything more skeletal than that produced by an otherwise normal statement, even if abnormally abrupt and harsh.

In the course of writing, again, I grew more interested with every page in the life of my characters. In the end … 'Tarr' turned out a straightforward novel.[3]

The operative terms in the above passage are "character in action," "passion," and "life." In Lewis's mind, these are the characteristics that distinguish the medium of language and the genre of the novel from the art of painting. The art of prose fiction imposes a concreteness, the straightforwardness of "normal statement," which "dragged [Lewis] out of the abstractist cul-de-sac."

As the work of an abstract artist, *Enemy of the Stars*, particularly in its highly condensed *Blast* version, makes few concessions to the demands of narrative continuity or dramatic plot. Its vorticist structure and technique lean heavily on long descriptive passages packed with elliptical metaphors and analogies: "Harsh bayadere – shepherdess of Pamir – with her Chinese beauty – living on from month to month, in utmost tent, with a steppe-gypsy, a solid vagrant, lean and lewd … summon those images, to fatten this solitary encounter of two ill-assorted fellow workmen …"[4] The action of the play consists primarily of the ideological clash between the two main characters and the resultant "enlightenment" of Arghol, an insight into the truer implications of his own, fundamentally intellectualist, dilemma. *Enemy* is not only visually abstract, it is abstract in the conceptual sense as well, centred as it is on the implications of Arghol's "immense collapse of chronic philosophy."

What Lewis, in *Rude Assignment*, labels the "abstractist cul-de-sac" is graphically inscribed in *Enemy of the Stars* as a nihilistic void, what the closing line of the play describes as the formless "blackness of a moonless and unstarlit night."[5] Abstraction was not only an artistic but also, in a real sense, an intellectual dead-end. Abstract technique and form had an accompanying abstract content for Lewis, and that form/content led directly into a vortex whose "still point" was less an immovable, timeless content than a bottomless void.[6]

Lewis's inversion of the genre of drama in *Enemy of the Stars* is a representation of the relation between form and content in the play. *Enemy* is, after all, an *unperformable* play, a "play" which is not a dramatic *action* and which must in fact be read like a novel. That it is presented as a play (rather than as a novel) gives it a generic orientation which is fundamentally abstract and conceptual. The "audience," which is itself generalized and represented in the work as "posterity," is in reality the private reader, who is drawn into complicity, along with the author, in the real drama of the play, the awakening of Arghol to his inescapable isolation. Arghol's agon becomes "ours too" in that the *personae* of the narrator and reader can experience the play only through the privacy of writing and reading. The paradoxical sharing of the author's and reader's isolation is the sharing of a *nihilum*. The medium operates by overturning, inverting, and, in fact, denying itself. Drama, an essentially social and shared experience, can only survive, Lewis seems to be suggesting, as a "dramatic" encounter with one's own ego. With the advent of modern solipsism, common experience is no longer possible, and neither, therefore, is the traditional experience of drama. Characters thus become representatives of ideological positions, and the action consists of a necessarily futile exchange of ideas. Arghol's awakening is to the necessity of this futility, an awareness that unleashes the only logical fulfilment of intellectual solipsism and aggressive egoism: a murder/suicide in which the roles of aggressor and victim are interchangeable.

In 1935, Lewis wrote an essay on his beginnings as a writer, opening with a discussion of the relation between his performance as a visual and a literary artist: "Beginning with pen and brush, the penman and the painter are apt to clash; but in my own case this did not occur, when at a very early age these two personalities first came on the scene. Indeed, they made their appearance arm-in-arm, as though they had always cohabited and neither could quite conceive of life without the complementary presence of the other. Indeed, at first, until the fact was pointed out to me, I swear I did not notice that they were two familiars instead of one."[7] Lewis, of course, is speaking from hindsight here, and his description of the harmony of the two media in his own person is idealistic, to say the least: "With me, I am inclined to claim, the equilibrium was practically perfect. My best picture, I believe, is as well done as my best book."[8]

In relating the actual circumstances of his first becoming a writer, Lewis reveals more precisely the grounds for his experience of "equilibrium" between the two arts:

It was the sun, a Breton instead of a British, that brought forth my first short story – *The Ankou* I believe it was: The Death-God of the Plouilliou. I was painting a blind Armorican beggar. The "short story" was the crystallization *of what I had to keep out of my consciousness while painting*. Otherwise the painting would have been a bad painting. That is how I began to write in earnest. A lot of discarded matter collected there, as I was painting or drawing, in the back of my mind – in the back of my consciousness. As I squeezed *everything* that smacked of literature from my vision of the beggar,

it collected in the back of my mind. It imposed itself on me as a complementary creation. That is what I meant by saying, to start with, that I was
so *naturally* a painter that the two acts, with me, have co-existed in peculiar
harmony. There was no mixing of the *genres*. The waste product of every
painting, when it is a painter's painting, makes the most highly selective
and ideal material for the pure writer.[9]

Lewis is talking throughout this essay of the external role these two
media have in his overall artistic ethos. They are complementary,
he asserts, as revealed by the emergence of the one from the concentrated pursuit of the other. In his discussion of *Tarr* in *Rude
Assignment*, however, the relation between the abstract visual concerns of the painter is described as resulting in a dead end from
which he emerged only when he turned to writing. When discussing
media and form, he speaks of harmony and complementarity. When
discussing content, he speaks of struggle and competition.

Most striking in Lewis's description of his first short story is the
clarity with which the two activities, painting and writing, distinguish themselves as visual image and narrative action: "Technically,
then, the short story, as we call it, was the first literary form with
which I became familiar; and I think I may say that the dramatic
necessities of this form of art were immediately apparent to me –
namely, that *action* is of its essence."[10] It appears that the contrast
which constitutes the complementarity for Lewis is between the
immediacy and static presence of the visual image and the temporal
extension of a significant series of events in narrative – between a
timeless present *Being* and a coming-to-be, a *becoming*.

Strictly speaking, from the point of view of content, it is not the
case, as Lewis claims that there is no "mixing of the *genres* " of
painting and literature in his work. As he himself admits, *Enemy of
the Stars* was the writing of a visual artist, but the static quality of
Enemy stems not only from its abstract, visualist prose style but from
the *abstract conception* of the play as a work of literature. The inversion
of literary genre and the primarily philosophical nature of the central
concerns of *Enemy* are abstract in both the visual and the conceptual
senses. Arghol's agon stems primarily not from any *action* of his in
which he becomes something he is not already. The agon is Arghol's
station, his static becalming in a pure Being: "I am that I am. No
progress is possible from that." Part play and part novel, half stylistic
tour de force and half philosophical debate, the play is very much the
"mixing of genres" that Lewis later preferred to overlook in the
interests of an imaginatively (or imaginarily) integrated artistic persona.

Lewis's inability to resolve the dualism in *Enemy of the Stars* resulted in a personal vorticist manifesto, published in the second issue of *Blast*, significantly entitled "BE THYSELF." The reference to the Socratic dictum is doubly ironic:

There is nothing so impressive as the number TWO.
You must be a duet in everything.
Why try and give the impression of a consistent and indivisible personality?
Hurry up and get into this harmonious and sane duality.

In the light of the dead end of *Enemy*, Lewis is compelled to openly embrace inconsistency: "You must talk with two tongues, if you do not wish to cause confusion."[11] Lewis thus abandons the classical requirement of the artist to present an organically unified work of art, backed by an integrated artistic persona.[12] This newly asserted inner freedom coincides with the writing of *Tarr* under rather extraordinary conditions, described by Lewis in "Beginnings:"[13]

Tarr was my first published book. It is a novel ... and I wrote it during the first year of the war, while I was ill for six months, off and on and preparing for the worst ... When the last coccus took itself off, I knew I should then become a soldier ... and already my late companions were dying like flies. I naturally assumed that it was quite on the cards that I should take the same road as they ... It was very much with this in mind that I took up my pen one day to write my first novel – perhaps my *only* novel, I said to myself. I wished to leave behind me a little specimen of my hand, that was the idea – upon the big scale, in a great literary form, to show the world – should I in my turn succumb – what a great writer it had lost! A romantic consideration! But the war, as it descended upon us, made romantics of us all ... I had, however, in the back of my head a great accumulation of that matchless literary material, that waste product I have mentioned (flung back in his toil of uncompromising painter.)[14]

In other words, the final stages of the composition of *Tarr* were accompanied by an inward letting go of the traditional demand for a unified artistic persona, driven by ill health and, in particular, by the imminent prospect of death. "It was very much with this in mind," namely death, "that I took up my pen to write my first novel." Just as his first short story "imposed itself upon [him] as a complementary creation,"[15] Lewis was in a remarkably fluid and susceptible state when completing *Tarr*, sufficient to be responsive to the exigencies of language and the demands of literary genre. But Lewis's mind was also fertile ground in another sense. *Enemy of the Stars* was a prolonged and serious exploration of isolation, nothingness, and death. What were issues emerging from visual abstraction and philosophical reflection for the writer of *Enemy* became existential facts for the author of *Tarr*. What had been theoretical questions became immediate concerns, but not in the sense of a preoccupation with physical survival alone. Lewis wanted the perdurance that only a significant work of art would provide. In order to achieve this artistic survival, however, the problem inherent and apparent in the nihilistic ending of *Enemy of the Stars* had somehow to be *artistically* overcome.

In *Tarr*, as in *Enemy of the Stars*, Lewis constructs the work around two principal characters, in this case Otto Kreisler and Frederick Tarr. In *Enemy*, the dual characterization is a concretization of a primary and abstract dualism, interior to Arghol as main character. Hanp is rather too transparently a mere foil to Arghol and a concession to the mechanics of literary representation. Given the conceptual nature of the problem addressed in *Enemy*, this skeletal dramatic context is appropriate. The problem, as a philosophical one, is prior in both conception and importance to its literary embodiment. Insofar as the issue is precisely the irreconcilability of mind and body, idea and activity, a true incarnation of this idea in dramatic form cannot by the very nature of the case be achieved. This is the motivating factor in Lewis's conceptual inversion of genre in the work.

In *Tarr*, however, no such abstract dualism controls either characterization or action. Tarr and Kreisler are not preoccupied with one another. They are related by the respective and, for a while, collaborative involvements with two women, Bertha Lunken and Anastasya Vasek. Although they are secondary characters, each of these women has a much more independent role than does their counterpart in *Enemy*, Hanp. (This is particularly the case with Anastasya, as will be explored below.) Because of the autonomy of Tarr and Kreisler, the novel is structured with a parallelism of characters rather than as a dualism of concepts. *Tarr* is based on an acceptance by Lewis of literary character, action, and genre; herein resides the "turning point."[16]

At the same time, Lewis's version of the realistic novel is not traditional in that it attempts an avant-garde concern with the inherent dualism of modern culture. The autonomy and isolation of the modern artist that divide him irrevocably from the existential conditions of his audience require a strategy to achieve the "realism" that is traditionally assumed to be immediately accessible to both artist and audience. In *Enemy*, Lewis had explored the conceptual and abstract dimensions of this dualism and failed to find a resolution. The manifesto "VORTEX: BE THYSELF" indicates that he had not rejected dualism itself; indeed, he had embraced it systematically, while at the same time acknowledging the need to render it more concrete, more "harmonious and sane": "You must give the impression of two persuaders, standing each on a different hip – left hip, right hip – with four eyes vacillating concentrically at different angles upon the object chosen for subjugation."[17] This particular form of duality is rendered "sane" because it is irreducible. The "four eyes vacillating concentrically" do not meet and coalesce. The "two persuaders" exist independently. Tarr and Kreisler, for instance, are "left hip, right hip" in *Tarr*, each with his own pair of eyes. Their parallel peregrinations around Paris are concentric vacillations around the "object chosen for subjugation" in the novel. The interesting question is what Lewis's "object" *is* in *Tarr*. Since there is no longer a question of traditional realistic imitation and representation (which is itself far from simple), but one of dualistic "subjugation" and control, the strategy of a "harmonious and sane" over a supposedly ordinary and divisive duality becomes itself Lewis's artistic "object."

The novel opens with an encounter on the streets of Paris between two Englishmen, Frederick Tarr and Alan Hobson. Hobson is less a friend to Tarr than an acquaintance, and a particularly galling one. A Cambridge graduate and amateur artist, he is for Tarr the quintessence of aestheticist inauthenticity – he affects the bohemian appearance of an artist while undertaking none of the labour. As such, he muddies the clear, hard distinction between art and life that so exercises Tarr:

'The Cambridge set that you represent is, as observed in the average specimen, a hybrid of the Quaker, the homosexual and the Chelsea artist ... You represent, my good Hobson, the *dregs* of Anglo-Saxon civilization: there is absolutely nothing softer upon the earth. Your flabby potion is a mixture of the lees of Liberalism, the poor froth blown off the decadent Nineties, the wardrobe-leavings of a vulgar bohemianism with its headquarters in the suburb of Carlyle and Whistler. You are concentrated highly-organized barley-water: there is nothing in the universe to be said for you: any efficient state would confiscate your property, burn your wardrobe – that old hat and the rest – as infectious and prohibit you from propagating.' (25)

The over-refined and under-committed Hobson is too flaccid to take offence at Tarr's ridicule, but is rather flattered to be party to Tarr's agonizings over the relation of the refinement of art to the raw energy of life as sexuality.

Hobson becomes a sounding board for Tarr's sexual involvement with another "bourgeois-bohemian," Bertha Lunken: "'Half of myself I have to hide. I am bitterly ashamed of a slovenly common portion of my life that has been isolated and repudiated by the energies of which I am so proud'" (22). Tarr points to the "character" of his art to explain his conflict over Bertha. In his art, he is fastidious: "'You may have noticed that an invariable severity distinguishes it. Apart from its being good or bad, its character is ascetic rather than sensuous, and it is divorced from immediate life. There is no slop of sex in *that* … Very often with an artist whose work is very sensuous or human, his sex instinct, if it is active, will be more discriminating than with a man more fastidious and discriminating than he in his work. To sum up this part of my disclosure: no one could have a coarser, more foolish, slovenly taste than I in women'" (21). The ascetic character of Tarr's art, its "invariable severity" (he supports Cubism [18]), contrasts with his sexual drives, which are "slop." Conventional sex and sexual expectations are part of the quagmire of life which art tries to avoid:

'In this compartment of my life [day-to-day sexual relations] *I have not a vestige of passion*. That is the root reason for its meanness and absurdity. The closest friend of my Dr. Jekyll would not recognize my Mr. Hyde, and vice versa … But consider all the *collages* marriages and affairs that you know, in which some frowsy or foolish or some doll-like or log-like bitch accompanies everywhere the form of an otherwise sensible man … Oh sex! oh Montreal! How foul and wrong this haunting of women is! – they are everywhere – confusing, blurring, libelling with their half-baked gushing tawdry presences! It is like a slop and spawn of children and the bawling machinery of the inside of life.' (23)

Tarr's artistic pride and sexual shame, his Jekyll-and-Hyde existence, have left him "divorced from immediate life" without a "vestige of passion." He is clearly driven by this divided condition, in a state of inner siege, unleashing his frustration on Hobson and Bertha, who are the visible signs of his tendency to associate with superficial bourgeois substitutes for both art and life: "As to Hobson, he had shocked something that was ready to burst out: he must help it out: Hobson must pay as well for the intimacy. *He must pay Bertha Lunken afterwards*" (22). It is at this point that the narrator intrudes in the dialogue with a passage from Tarr's diary that leaves no question as to the nature of his diatribe:

'A man only goes and importunes the world with a confession when his self will not listen to him or recognize his shortcomings. The function of a friend is to be a substitute for this defective self, to be the World and the Real without the disastrous consequences of reality. – Yet punishment is one of his chief offices. The friend enlarges also substantially the boundaries of our solitude.'

This statement was to be found in Tarr's diary. The self he had rebuked in this way for not listening was now again suffering rebuke by his act of confession with the first-met, a man he did not regard as a friend even. Had a friend been there he could have interceded for his ego. (22)

Tarr's confession to Hobson, his intellectual repudiation of Bertha, and his verbal attack on Hobson himself are, then, a disguised rebuke and humiliation directed at a self which would not "listen to him or recognize his shortcomings." That Tarr would not seek out a real friend "to be a substitute for his defective self" is a further self-rebuke arising from his uncompromising artistic aspirations, their "invariable severity and asceticism."

There is a vicious circle at the core of Tarr's personality. As he reveals it to Hobson, it is his *tragic* conception of art that places him in an irreconcilable conflict with himself:

'Also I do not mean that sex is my tragedy, but only art.'

'I thought we were talking about sex?'

'No. Let me explain. Why am I associated with that irritating nullity? First of all I am an artist. With most people, who are not artists, all the finer part of their vitality goes into sex if it goes anywhere ... The artist is he in whom this emotionality normally absorbed by sex is so strong that it claims a new and more exclusive field of deployment. Its first creation is *The Artist* himself. That is a new sort of person; the creative man ... One by one his powers are turned away from the usual object of a man's personal poetry or passion and so removed from the immediate world. One solitary thing is left facing any woman with whom he has commerce, that is his sex, a lonely phallus.' (20)

The ascetic and tragic quality of Tarr's aesthetic theory is that sex is in the end not fully integrated into and sublimated by art. One by one, his powers of discrimination are deflected from their "usual object," a woman, until the merely sensual aspect of sexuality remains, the "lonely phallus." Tarr does not allow for a sublimation of sexuality in which it would find expression in art; rather, he sees in art a redirection of as much energy as possible in such a way as to exclude sexuality. His artistic asceticism therefore sets up a dualism between creative and sexual energy such that the latter persists in all that is most antagonistic to the "refinement" of art, remains crude and altogether negative. Women "haunt" artists. They confuse, blur, and libel with their "half-baked gushing tawdry presences," as Tarr puts it. But, of course, it is not women at all who do this, but Tarr's own alienating concession to his "lonely phallus." His view of the artist as the "complete" (20) and self-created man, as "a new sort of person" whose primary artistic act is "The Artist" in his wholeness, is rendered tragically unattainable by his diagnosis of his own unredeemable sexuality. Tarr is lacking the "vestige of passion" in both his artistic and his sexual lives because he melodramatically insists on opposing them to one another. His "defective self" will not listen to him because he refuses to accept himself as artistically *and* sensuously creative. His berating of Bertha and Hobson for inauthentic bourgeois-bohemianism is a veiled libel on himself: "After all it is chiefly myself I am castigating" (24).

Despite Tarr's state of inner siege, he is a working artist meeting with a measure of success. Tarr's counterpart, on the other hand, the German Otto Kreisler, is a dark and brooding pseudo-artist, without a vestige of talent, but with an overweening measure of passion. Kreisler has refused an order from his father to "give up art" and take up a post in business, provoking reductions to and a threatened ending of his monthly subsidy: "How near was the end? This might be the end. So much the better! Kreisler's student days – a life-time in itself – embracing a great variety of useless studies of which painting, the last, was far the most useless – had unfitted him, at the age of thirty-six, for practically anything" (79). Kreisler's increasingly determined passivity feeds his fund of negative passion, producing in him a further "rapid deterioration of the will" (91).

Kreisler had followed his financially solvent friend Ernst Vokt to Paris, only to find that he had been supplanted in Vokt's favour by Louis Soltyk. Soltyk is precisely what Kreisler is not, an art-businessman making a (somewhat too) shrewd living from the sale of paintings and art objects. With Vokt's pocket out of reach and his father's retreating, Kreisler becomes dejected and anti-social, until he encounters Anastasya Vasek, newly arrived in Paris. Kreisler's hope is revived: "The one great optimism of Otto Kreisler was a belief in the efficacity of women ... There they were all the time

– vast dumping-ground for sorrow and affliction ..." (100). Women were "Kreisler's Theatre, they were for him art and expression: the tragedies played there purged you periodically of the too violent accumulations of desperate life" (101):

In this manner 'woman' was the aesthetic element in Kreisler's life. Love, too, always meant *unhappy* love for him ...

A casual observer of the progress of Otto Kreisler's life might have said that the chief events, the crises, consisted of love affairs ... But, in the light of careful analysis, this would have been an inversion of the truth. When the events of his life became too unwieldy or overwhelming, he converted them into love; as he otherwise might have done, had he possessed a specialized talent, into some art or other. He was a sculptor – a german sculptor of a mock-realistic and degenerate school – in the strange sweet-hearting of the 'free-life.' (101)

Love is for Kreisler a means to the "gold of the human heart and any other gold that happened to be knocking about" (100). His primary interest in life is money; he had earlier married off his fiancée to his widowed father, presumably to place himself more firmly in favour. In his present financial straits, the figure of Anastasya, advertising herself as "*lousily* rich" (100), presents a much-needed "theatre" in which Kreisler can perform his only art, the purging of the "violent accumulations of desperate life."

Anastasya, a powerful and exotic woman, is more formidable than Kreisler expects. Instead of alleviating it, she accelerates his "rapid deterioration of the will," producing a resentful state of inner panic: "This is the phenomenon of the imagination, repressed and as it were slighted, revenging itself" (103). Kreisler becomes obsequious: "He would be her dog! Lie at her feet! He would fill with a merely animal warmth and vivacity the void that *must* exist in her spirit. His imagination, flattered, came in as an ally: this, too, exempted him from the necessity of being victorious" (103). Kreisler's "imagination," his creativity, first rebels against neglect by undermining him, then leads him farther into his network of self-deception. But Kreisler's groping breaks the flow of the conversation: "Her attitude, suggesting 'Yes, you *are* funny, you know you are, I'd better go, then you'll be better' was responded to by him with the same offended dignity as the drunken man displays when his unsteadiness is remarked. Sulkily he repudiated the suggestion that there was anything amiss: then he grew angry with her. His nervousness was all her doing. All was lost: he was very near some violence. But when she stood up he was so impressed that he sat gaping after her ... Anastasya – Otto! – it was though he had just become aware of the fact" (104). Completely mastered by Anastasya's commanding presence, Kreisler is embarrassed, as if he had been caught muttering to himself aloud in public. With someone as self-willed and determined as she is (she gained her independence by feigning insanity [103]), Kreisler's "theatre" is revealed as a mere fantasy, a passive dream, unrelated to his real circumstances. His continued pursuit leads from one mortification to the next. He acts the buffoon at a formal party, arriving in disheveled street clothes because his "frac" is in pawn, only to receive an amused and indifferent reception from Anastasya. Two things, however, emerge from this event. First, he has an amorous encounter with Bertha Lunken, who has been made vulnerable by Tarr's recent breaking of their engagement. Second, he observes Anastasya in the company of Louis Soltyk, now become a double rival.

Kreisler's treacherous befriending of Bertha and his challenging of Soltyk to a duel are the agonized expression of his resentment at Anastasya's superiority. His well-tried tactic of working off his frustrations and financial crises on unsuspecting females is blithely ignored by her. This brings to the surface his simmering anger, and Bertha becomes the even more brutalized victim. More and more desperate at the discontinuance of his allowance, Kreisler rapes Bertha and vindictively challenges Soltyk to a duel as a way of getting at the serene Anastasya. He bungles the duel, first reconciling with Soltyk and then shooting him by accident. Finally, Kreisler hangs himself in a provincial jail.

Both Kreisler and Tarr use women as scapegoats for their inability to cope with themselves either financially or sexually. Kreisler operates from the assumption that *all* women are even more passive and helpless than himself. Far from susceptible to his bullying masculinity, Anastasya demonstrates her financial and sexual autonomy in hiring Soltyk to sell some of her jewelry. Bertha, however, is more susceptible, a typical bourgeois-bohemian affecting a taste for art in order to gain a husband. As Tarr reflects, she has so thoroughly sentimentalized her passivity (seeing it as sacrificial love) that she can appear noble in her own eyes: "She does nothing it is the man's place to do: she remains 'woman' as she would say. Only she is so intensely alive in her passivity, so maelstrom-like in her surrender, so exclusive in her sacrifice, that very little remains to be done. Really with Bertha the man's position is a mere sinecure'" (68). Bertha is so uncompromising in her stance as martyr that she evokes a kind of respect for her sheer determination. The two women demonstrate a consistency absent in the elaborate self-justifications indulged in by Tarr and Kreisler, whose respective machinations work the destruction of the hapless Bertha. Cut loose by Tarr, she duly prostrates herself in Kreisler's path. He is only too happy to oblige her sentimental notion of herself, with Tarr fostering the liaison as a means of gaining his freedom and so participating in the violence done her. Each of the three uses the other as a substitute: Bertha uses Kreisler to get at Tarr; Kreisler uses Bertha to work off his resentment toward Anastasya; Tarr uses Kreisler to engineer his separation from Bertha. Pathetic and vindictive, Kreisler's sordid end evokes little regret, but Tarr's manoeuvrings excite interest, and are in fact the living centre of the novel.

Having contrived his escape from Bertha, Tarr isolates himself in a new studio (appropriately, a former convent) in order to paint. After a week of lonely work, he is in trouble. "The day's work done, his depression again grasped him, like an immense gloomy companion who had been idling impatiently while he worked: he promenaded this personality in 'Montmartre-by-Night,' without improving his character. Nausea glared at him from every object he met: sex surged up and martyrized him" (206). This other "personality," an "immense gloomy companion," is the self to which he would not listen. It "martyrizes" him because he treats it as "mere" sex, yet he rejects the "relief and pleasure" of the night streets "mainly because of his besetting fear of the pox" (206). But "sex" has more in store for Tarr. His restlessness draws him back to his old haunts with Bertha, under the guise of a nostalgic purgation. He meets Anastasya Vasek and, like Kreisler, underestimating her, takes a patronizing interest. He begins to be dimly aware that his rejection of Bertha and "mere sex" is a devitalizing loss of passion and of "Life" in its wholeness:

His sensual nature had remained undeveloped: his Bertha ... had not succeeded in waking his senses ... But he had never wished for that sort of reality: his intellect had conspired to the effect that his senses never should be awakened, in that crude way ... When he was on heat, it turned his eyes away from the highest beauty ... so that he had nothing but rudimentary inclinations left.

But perhaps that chapter was closing: in the interests of his animalism he was about to betray the artist in him ... 'Life' would be given a chance.

Anastasya's highly artistic beauty suggested an immediate solution to him. (213)

Just as Tarr's "intellect had conspired that his senses never should be awakened," it now conspired with his senses that he should "betray the artist in him." From justifying art as life itself, his intellect turns to a justification of "life" itself as art, in the form of Anastasya's "artistic beauty." In both instances, Tarr's intellect conspires and betrays as a "substitute for his defective self" when "his self will not listen to him." Intellect, for Tarr, is substituting here for the more fundamental creative will, whose "first creation is *the Artist* himself. That is, a new sort of person; the creative man." Tarr's intellectual substitution of "life" for art remains a failure to activate that unified creative will that would forge "a new sort of person."

The dualism avoided by Lewis in the basic structure of characterization in *Tarr* is at work within the main character. Marked by the alienation of intellect from senses, Tarr is estranged from his own deeper creative will. The intellect, which at first defended the will from the "heat" of the senses, eventually betrays it to an all-out pursuit of sensuous "life" in the form of Anastasya. To see her as "life" on the basis of her "artistic beauty," as if she somehow integrated (instead of merely suppressing) the dichotomy between art and sex, is not only an intellectual betrayal of art but *a self-betrayal of the intellect itself*. An intellect that conspired to protect the creative will from mere sensuality ends by betraying it to a sensuality to which it is completely subordinate, a mere refinement of the sexual drive. The "emotionality" that is the shared drive of art and sex (20) has found an object in Anastasya, but the intellect has betrayed its own position of control. Henceforth Tarr's energies, channeled into the higher sensuality of sensuous "life," are no longer free to pursue the integration of creative will, whose object is the creation of "*the Artist* himself." Tarr has become like those he had earlier scorned.

Hobson's musings early in the novel sound this note of uncertainty about the workability of Tarr's position: "Tarr looped the loop and he looked on. A droll bird! He wondered, as he watched him, if he was a *sound* bird. People believed in him: his exhibition flights attracted attention. What sort of prizes could he expect to win by these a little too professional talents? Would this notable *ambitieux* be satisfied?" (18). Tarr's "looping the loop" exactly describes his imprisonment in the vicious circle of the art/sex self-division. Given his self-involvement, how indeed *could* his ambitions be satisfied?

Tarr's character is the "object chosen for subjugation" in the novel, the representation of a struggle for the transformation of an abstract into a "harmonious and sane duality." Lewis's attempt to enshrine a sane dualism in a structural parallelism of characters, despite its promise, suffers from an incommensurability. Kreisler's ambitions are only derivatively sensual, his main focus being mere survival.

The dynamic of his personality has too little in common with Tarr's for an effective harmony to occur (except in the negative form to be discussed below). It is not altogether surprising to observe the duality at the core of Tarr's character to be precisely that which Lewis had ascribed to himself. Tarr is a painter in an "abstractist cul-de-sac," producing interesting but apparently somewhat directionless Cubist "flights" and indulging in a solipsistic, intellectual looping the loop which is in reality a form of self-castigation. The question as to Tarr's ability to satisfy his ambitions is precisely the same for Lewis himself in *Tarr*: *can* the greater concreteness of language in the realistic novel accomplish the required transformation of abstract into concrete dualism when Lewis clings so inveterately to a conceptual art/sex dualism at the core of his characterization?

Tarr is not an autobiographical novel in the ordinary sense, but it has a reflexive dimension. The aims of the main character, his attempt to create "*the Artist* himself," are precisely those of the author. Tarr's struggle to become "the creative man," to transform his divided self into an integrated artistic persona, are a direct reflection of Lewis's aim in turning from the abstraction of *Enemy of the Stars* to the concreteness of *Tarr*.

After Kreisler works his own destruction and is cleared from the scene of the novel, the final section of the book, entitled "Swagger Sex," is devoted to Tarr and Anastasya. On first meeting Anastasya, Tarr had decided that "'Life' would be given a chance" (213). By their "tenth meeting" (303), Tarr had still not advanced beyond formalities, but on this occasion he was determined to initiate intimacy: "The backwardness of his senses was causing him some anxiety: his intellect now stepped in, determined to do their business for them. He put his arm around her waist and planting his lips firmly on hers, began kissing" (303). For so long the ascetic artist, Tarr has to make a conscious decision to act sensuously: "He was committed to the role marked out by reason" (304). Tarr's stilted love-making fails to arouse Anastasya: "Mature animal ardour must be set up then: he had the sensation of embracing a tiger, who was not unsympathetic but rather surprised" (303). Clearly, Tarr's approach is inept, and it is only because the "tiger" decides to take the lead that matters proceed. The main obstacle is Tarr's "rational" approach, and Anastasya begins skilfully to disarm his intellect by affirming its independence from sexuality: "'We agree in the most marvellous way Tarr. These things, all things that are stamped feminine gender, is not a thing that bears cold print, unless it is to be read by madmen'" (306). She subtly challenges Tarr's virility, and his ability to be both sensual and intellectual at the same time: "'A high-brow girl like me must be sexually ... an abomination: I am convinced that with me a man would become impotent within a month at the outside, I mean it'" (308). She then challenges his intellect, his understanding of the relation between mind and senses, imagination and sensation, and Tarr resorts to more and more sophistic defences of intellect: "'In the case of the sucking-pig' said Tarr, magisterially, flinging his flushed face up for air toward the ceiling 'it is the tongue. The thing seen is merely disgusting to the eye, but it is delightful to the tongue: therefore the eye passes beneath the spell of the palate, and it is not an image but a taste – much more abstract, in consequence – that it sees – if one can say that it sees. The body of the sucking-pig is blotted out'" (309). Tarr is responding to Anastasya's analogy of the female body to food. He had claimed that it is the "imagination" that excites sexual desire, but when Anastasya challenges him he backs down, acknowledging that "it is not an image but a taste" in the case of both food and sex. He saves himself, however, by asserting the "abstract" and therefore intellectual nature of sensuous involvement, because visual contact with food or partner is "blotted out." By failing to defend the imagination's role in sensuous life, Tarr enacts the "betrayal of the artist in him" (213) that had for so long resisted the sway of both palate and phallus.

Anastasya has gained the upper hand. Her analogy between food and sex is literally pursued over dinner, where she continues to press her advantage, leading Tarr to submit to his senses:

They ordered oysters: they would be his first, he had never before dared to eat an oyster, because it was alive.

When he told her that it was his first oyster she was exultant.

'You perfect savage – your palate is as conservative as an ox's. Kiss me Tarr – you have never done that either properly.' (310)

Having led Tarr to associate food with herself, she continues to undermine his intellectual aestheticism by pressing the issue of life and death. For Tarr, what distinguishes art from women is that the latter in practice mix art and life up, while art is "'Life with all the humbug of living taken out of it ...'" Life is "'everything that is not yet purified so that it is art,'" while "'*Death* is the one attribute that is peculiar to life,'" the "'*motif* of all reality: the purest thought is ignorant of that *motif*" (311). Death, then, is the "humbug of living" extracted by art: "'Death differentiates art and life. Art is identical with the idea of permanence. Art is continuity and not an individual spasm: but life is the idea of the person'" (312). Such is Tarr's confusing and dualistic aesthetic, in which life, "with the elasticity of movement and consciousness" (312), is death because it is impermanent and individual ("personal"). Art has the permanence and the stability of pattern and continuity.

Anastasya leads Tarr to tie himself up in the static and essentially unworkable dualism of his intellectual aesthetic: "She had been driving hard and inscrutable Art deeper and deeper into herself: she now drew it out and showed it to Tarr. '... I wish intensely to hear about life'" (313). She manoeuvres the ground out from under Tarr's intellect – "Their third bottle of wine had put art to flight" (315) – and, turning the conversation to sex, elicits from him the confession "'I want a woman ... badly, that's all!'" (317). Anastasya has become the friend to which Tarr can confess what his self would not listen to. His deeper desire is not art but a woman, and *that's all*. Anastasya exults:

'This is something that can die! Ha! Ha! we're in life my Tarr: we represent *absolutely nothing* thank God!'
  'I realize I'm in life, but I don't like being reminded of it in that way.'
(317)

Tarr's disgruntlement at having betrayed himself into Anastasya's hands leads to a quarrel. They part, and Tarr returns home alone, only to find her awaiting him – in the nude: "'Forgive me, Tarr, my words belied me, the acidulated demi-mondaine was a trick. It occupied your mind – you didn't notice me take your key!'" (320).

Anastasya's words belied her, but her actions are a direct representation of her argument. She "crossed into the moonlight and faced him," her "hands placed like a modest statue's." Her invitation is ironic: "Will you engage me as your model sir?" (320). Anastasya is inviting Tarr to take her as the model not for his art but for his new life. She is that living representation of the self to which he would not listen. She had to distract and preoccupy Tarr's intellect in order to "take his key," to possess his "lonely phallus," and to present herself, within his studio, in all her "highly artistic beauty." Her nudity is indeed a form from which all the "humbug of living had been removed," her coy modesty an ironic comment on the humbug of an art that could not frankly admit to its sensuality. Anastasya "models" for Tarr a new art form. She enters into his own psyche, behind his intellect, and mocks its tragic pose, its melodramatic dualism of art and life: "This tall nudity began laughing with a harsh sound like stone laughing" (320). Anastasya embodies a living, comic art deeper than the superficial humour with which Tarr had approached Bertha.[18]

To Anastasya's parodic request to be engaged as Tarr's model, his reply is typically humourless: "But I don't require a model thank you, I never use nude models for my pictures" (320). Anastasya turns to dress and go, and Tarr capitulates: "'I accept, I accept!'" (320). Next morning, Anastasya is pleased with her conquest, but is careful to adore Tarr's masculinity:

'Thank you Tarr for being so nice to me just now. It was perfect.'
   Tarr drove the smoke away from his face and wiped his eye.
   'You are my efficient chimpanzee then for keeps?'
   'No. I'm the new animal; we haven't thought up a name for him yet – the thing that will succeed the Superman.' (321)

Tarr's egoistical invocation of the Nietzschean Superman at the end of the seduction scene sets in context Hobson's query in the opening chapter: "Would this notable *ambitieux* be satisfied?" (18). Tarr's dualistic cultivation of ascetic artistic refinement and bourgeois sexual indulgence (with Bertha) clearly could not satisfy him. But his discovery of and conquest by Anastasya involves a "betrayal of the artist in him." It is unclear how it can thereby fulfil Tarr's ambitions such that he not only attains the level of Nietzsche's Superman but surpasses and even supplants him. This is an ambiguity at the centre of Tarr's characterization and therefore at the centre of the novel, and needs to be explored further.

In an interesting essay, entitled *"Tarr*: A Nietzschean Novel,"* Alistair Davies argues that *Tarr* has been consistently misread as a traditional realist novel, resulting in a strong preference for the tragic character of Kreisler and a consequent "negative assessment" of the work as a whole. Davies opposes this reading: "*Tarr* is not, as critics have suggested, an incoherent work in which the final apotheosis of Tarr destroys the emotional and moral focus of the novel in the tragic action of Kreisler. The unconventional structure is that of the Nietzschean novella, which presents the development of the central hero, Tarr, marked out by his superior vigour and vitality, as he breaks through and transcends the sick and destructive forces which surround him. This process, rather than Kreisler's tragic fate, forms the central adventure of the novel."[19] Davies's treatment of Tarr as a Nietzschean hero suggests that, instead of tragic pathos over Kreisler, "our response, as readers, to *Tarr*, and to the final stage in particular, must be one of metaphysical gaiety": "We must not attribute to Tarr that inner spiritual depth, that moment of tragic insight, that glimpse of resolution or immortality with which classical or Christian fiction concludes ... We understand him, from his appearance, from his surface, as a true Self, who has been able to release his sexual energies into modes of human and creative response which, on the one hand, fashion enduring works of art, and, on the other, surmount the banality and inauthenticity of the culture which surrounds him."[20]

Little swayed by the tragic pathos of Kreisler, the present reading wholly concurs with Davies's emphasis on the centrality of a Nietzschean perspective at work within *Tarr*. However, the lyricism with which Davies interprets Tarr's apotheosis into a "true Self" seems to pass over the considerable ambiguity inherent in Tarr's union with Anastasya. In Davies's eyes, "Anastasya releases Tarr's full, masculine and formative instincts, for, in his subsequent sexual relations with other women, he fathers three children. He becomes a literal source of formation and regeneration. From Anastasya, Tarr learns a lesson which he can apply to his art."[21] Davies overlooks the fact that for Tarr the pursuit of Anastasya means "the betrayal of the artist in him." It is true that Tarr fathers three children in a subsequent relationship. However, not only is there no mention of any artistic activity post-Anastasya, from the time of his first date with her Tarr not only stops painting but falls into a Kreisler-like "rapid deterioration of the will":

Painting languished in the Montmartre studio, which was no longer anything but an inconvenient address, requiring a long bus or taxi ride at the end of the day. At this time Tarr's character performed repeatedly the following manoeuvre: his best energies would, once a force was started, gradually take over the business from the play department, and continue the farce as a serious line of its own. It was as though it had not the go to initiate anything of its own accord: it appeared content to exploit the clown's discoveries. But as for painting he ceased almost to think of it. (249)

There is no evidence for Davies's claim that Tarr is able to achieve transcendence, whether artistic, social, or sexual. We have very little more to go on than Tarr's own egoistic assertion that he is "the thing that will succeed the Superman." Tarr has gone from intellectual conspiring to betraying, and thence to manoeuvrings of his "character" in which he has not only "almost ceased to think" of painting but has lost "the go to initiate anything of his own accord." His claim to have surpassed the Nietzschean Superman rings ambiguously in the light of his original ambition to become the complete "creative man," the self-created artist.

Even if Tarr's shift from artistic to "Life" values could be allowed as legitimate, his lack of "the go to initiate anything of his own accord" could hardly bring about the triumphant, super-Nietzschean results he claims, since such a force of iniative is, in the form of "will to power," the prime faculty of the Superman as the completed human being: "Will to power is the ultimate *factum* to which we come," Nietzsche asserts.[22]

In fact, the invocation of Nietzsche in *Tarr* is itself ambiguous. Other than the instance cited toward the end of the novel, there is only one other, during Tarr's collaboration with Kreisler in the downfall of Bertha:

'All Germans *lie*?' Kreisler exclaimed shrilly.
"'*Deutsches Volk* – the folk that deceives!" is your philosopher Nietzsche's account of the origin of the word Deutsch.'
…'Nietzsche was *paradoxal*: he would say anything to amuse himself. You English are the greatest liars and hypocrites on this earth!'
"'See the Continental Press"! I only dispute your statement because I know it is not first-hand. Hypocrisy is usually a selfish stupidity." (228)

While Kreisler is openly offended at the implication that he is a liar, Tarr is involved in a subtle self-justification here. Yes, the English are hypocrites, but hypocrisy is only "selfish stupidity," a kind of thickheaded egoism, more of an innocent foible than an open deception of others. There is a kind of frankness in Kreisler's machinations, a lack of pretence and subtlety. When he has made the world pay for treating him so badly, he kills himself with the same mixture of frustration and revenge. Tarr's manoeuvrings, however, are an artifice by which he can avoid confronting his fundamental passivity and lack of initiative. He allows himself to be passively determined by his sensuous desire for Anastasya without having to acknowledge it consciously and take responsibility for its implications. "'Life' would be given a chance" (213), as if "life" had to impose on and prove itself to Tarr, not Tarr to "life." Nietzsche is first invoked negatively and defensively by Tarr, only later to appear, again negatively, as a witness to Tarr's transcendence of the Superman. Yet it is the most central tenet and *factum* of Nietzsche's philosophical position that is most strenuously avoided by Tarr's artifice, namely, the will to power. The arch and humorous quality of Tarr's references to Nietzsche do not achieve the self-irony that would qualify them, in Davies's term, as "metaphysical gaiety," but are perhaps rather farcical manoeuvrings to avoid the courage and self-reliance of the will to power. The farcical quality of Tarr's Superman pretensions are nowhere more evident than in the seduction sequence to which his claim is the culmination. As our earlier discussion amply illustrated, it is Anastasya who leads, distracts, disarms, and seduces, and Tarr who surrenders. In the event, Tarr cannot sustain the relationship with her on an equal basis and proceeds to a succession of lesser affairs, on the same pattern as those with Bertha and Anastasya, with Rose Fawcett and Prism Dirkes.

The ending of *Tarr*, then, in keeping with the dualistic formulation of his character, is clearly satirical, with Tarr pretending to an attainment and a liberation which he very clearly has not achieved. Just as Tarr has not exerted the self-control, the power over his own will, that constitutes Nietzschean will to power, neither apparently has Lewis controlled the reflexive dimension of his novel such that the "object chosen for subjugation," namely the dualism that brought *Enemy of the Stars* to its nihilistic conclusion, could be said to have been "harmonized" and rendered "sane." These questions need to be clarified in the light of the element invoked in *Tarr* only to be denied: Nietzschean will to power.

Nietzsche's Superman (or "Overman," as current translators prefer it)[23] is the realization of the essence of man as the will to power.[24] This realization is consequent upon a recognition of what Nietzsche considers the most characteristic fact about the modern world: "God is dead. He remains dead. And we have killed him."[25] By God, Nietzsche means not only the object of theistic religious belief, but also the whole of the supersensory world as defined by Western philosophy. Platonic thought is definitive in this sense for the Western tradition, since it grounds the true in the supersensory realm of Ideas and ideals in opposition to the sensory and concrete:

This realm of the supersensory has been considered since Plato, or more strictly speaking, since the late Greek and Christian interpretation of Platonic philosophy, to be the true and genuinely real world. In contrast to it the sensory world is only the world down here, the changeable, and therefore the merely apparent, unreal world. The world down here is the vale of tears in contrast to the mountain of everlasting bliss in the beyond. If, as still happens in Kant, we name the sensory world the physical in the broader sense, the supersensory world is the metaphysical world.

The pronouncement "God is dead" means: The supersensory world is without effective power. It bestows no life. Metaphysics, i.e. for Nietzsche Western philosophy as understood as Platonism, is at an end. Nietzsche understands his own philosophy as the countermovement to metaphysics, and that means for him a movement in opposition to Platonism.[26]

The "death of God," then, is this loss of the "effective power" of the supersensory world. Nietzsche identifies this loss of power of metaphysics with the term "nihilism." Nihilism, as the product of metaphysics, is "the fundamental movement of the history of the West,"[27] because "metaphysics is history's open space wherein it becomes a destining that the supersensory world, the Ideas, God, the moral law, the authority of reason, progress, the happiness of the greatest number, culture, civilization, suffer the loss of their constructive force and become void."[28]

The loss of the constructive power of the highest values happens with "the insight that the ideal world is not and is never to be realized within the real world."[29] Values do not provide for their own re-alization and fulfilment but hold themselves beyond man's actual condition, and so undermine their own authority by their ineffec-tuality. Thus, nihilism for Nietzsche is the "inner logic" of meta-physics and of the Western tradition: "What does nihilism mean? ... *That the highest values are devaluing themselves.*"[30] The de-valuation of values in nihilism, however, is not in Nietzsche's view the end of values as such, but only of metaphysical or transcendental values. He counters nihilism with a "revaluation of all values" based not on the inherent dualism of metaphysics but on the affirmation of Life as a unitive spiritual/physical, mind/body existence, "the idea of superabundant life."[31]

It is as the principle of the affirmation of values and of the superabundance of life that the will to power emerges in Nietzsche's thought. For Nietzsche, will is neither a "faculty of the soul" nor a "striving in general": "For the will, as an affect of command, is the decisive distinguishing mark of self-mastery and force":[32] "In con-trast, striving can be indeterminate ... For that reason it is not pos-sible for us to strive beyond ourselves; rather, we merely strive, and get wholly absorbed in such striving. By way of contrast, will, as resolute openness to oneself, is always willing out beyond one-self."[33] Thus, "Willing itself is mastery over ... which reaches out beyond itself; will is intrinsically power."[34] That is, will to power is a "self-mastery" for the purposes of "willing out beyond oneself" to the "superabundance of life." Contrary to their apparent negative connotations, both nihilism and the will to power are constructive concepts for Nietzsche. Their negativity is a "no" to the metaphysical "devaluation of the highest values" and a "yes" to the "revaluation of all values" grounded in the affirmation of life.

Nietzsche's Overman, then, is the man who has faced nihilism – the death of God and of the higher values – and affirmed life through self-mastery and openness to the will to power: "The name 'over-man' designates the essence of humanity, which, as modern humanity, is beginning to enter into the consummation of belonging to the essence of its age."[35] The Overman is man passing from under the rule of "God" and of the supersensory realm of values into the realm of mastery over self and the affirmation of complete physical/spiritual life.

The "revaluation of all values" for Nietzsche is grounded in the priority of this complete, unitive, superabundant life over traditional values. Life defines values; values do not define life: "The point-of-view of 'value' is the point-of-view constituting the *preservation-enhancement condition* with respect to complex forms of relative duration of life within becoming."[36] The preservation and enhancement of life as a becoming, an openness and abundance of life are "constituted" by the will to power. The revaluation inherent in these values is the shift from the static emphasis on an unreachable transcendent Being characteristic of metaphysics, in which the *preservation* of life is the highest value, to the opening, expanding "life within becoming," which in its wholeness wills its own *enhancement* and increase. For Nietzsche, becoming is more valuable than Being.

This overturning of the priority of Being has a foundational impact on the role of art and truth in Nietzsche's revaluation: "With respect to the making secure of the level of power that has been reached at any given time, truth is the necessary value. But it does not suffice for the reaching of a level of power ... These possibilities are given only through a penetrating forward look that belongs to the essence of the will to power; for, as the will to more power, it is, in itself, perspectively directed toward possibilities ... The creating of possibilities for the will on the basis of which the will to power first frees itself to itself is for Nietzsche the essence of art."[37] Art is the basic expression of the will to power, such that the world is "a work of art that gives birth to itself."[38] As such, "Art is *worth more* than truth" because it is "the great stimulant to life."[39] Truth is a preservative that focuses on life as a static, transcendent Being, while art is a creating which expands from "within becoming" to the enhancement of life: "We have *art* in order, *not to perish from the truth* ."[40] In Heidegger's words, "Art is the distinctive countermovement to nihilism": "The artistic creates and gives form. If the artistic constitutes metaphysical activity pure and simple, then every deed, especially the highest deed and thus the thinking of philosophy too, must be determined by it. The concept of philosophy may no longer be defined according to the pattern of the teacher of morality who posits another higher world in opposition to this presumably worthless one. Against the nihilistic philosophy of morality ... must be deployed the philosopher who goes counter ... the 'artist philosopher.'"[41] Nietzsche's artist-philosopher Overman is concerned with the sensuous, not as distinct from the supersensuous (i.e., the *sensual*), but in the sense of the wholeness of life as becoming: "The will to the sensuous world and to its richness is for Nietzsche ... the will to what 'metaphysics' seeks. Hence the will to the sensuous is metaphysical. That metaphysical will is actual in art."[42] In Nietzsche's words, "The will to *semblance*, to illusion, to deception, to Becoming and change is deeper, more 'meta-physical,' than the will to *truth*, to reality, to Being."[43] Again, as Heidegger puts it: "Art, particularly in the narrow sense, is yes-saying to the sensuous, to semblance, to what is not 'the true world,' or as Nietzsche says succinctly, to what is not 'the truth.'"[44]

Nietzsche's revaluation of values is a "philosophy that goes counter" to the two-and-a-half millennia of Western thought that precedes it. It attempts to turn the metaphysical and theological tradition (what Heidegger calls the "onto-theo-logical" tradition)[45] on its head by a redefinition of the criteria of value and of the new means by which these new values can be affirmed. The transvaluation consists of a redefinition of "life" as a unitive, physical/spiritual continuum, such that the *actuality* of lived experience – rather than the *idea* of life – defines values. This responsiveness to actuality rather than idea produces a new emphasis. The fundamental faculty for the apprehension and affirmation of value is no longer intellect, in its supersensory distinctness from mere sensuous, visceral experience and its attendant emotions and passions, but is now the integration of thought and feeling in the *will*. The will as unified expression of intellectual and somatic life is given by Nietzsche the formulation *will to power*, not because, "in accord with the usual view, will is a kind of desiring that has power as its goal rather than happiness or pleasure."[46] Will to power as "the innermost essence of being"[47] affirms that will is essentially self-determining and self-constituting. It does not need to appeal to objective idea or sensation for its identity: "Willing wills the one who wills as such a one; and willing posits the willed as such."[48] That is, it defines itself as self-will and knows itself not as an idea but as a creative act, as art rather than as truth:

> Art, thought in the broadest sense as the creative, constitutes the basic character of beings. Accordingly, art in the narrower sense is that activity in which creation emerges for itself and becomes most perspicuous; it is not merely one configuration of will to power among others but the *supreme* configuration ... It is the principle of the new valuation, as opposed to the prior one which was dominated by religion, morality, and philosophy. If will to power therefore finds its supreme configuration in art, the positing of the new relation of will to power must proceed from art.[49]

Art, in the broadest and in the narrowest sense, converges in Tarr's evocation of an "emotionality" whose "first creation is *the Artist* himself" as "a new sort of person; the creative man" (20). The artist is no longer the individual subjectivity or ego but self-affirming and manifesting reality: "The world [is] a work of art that gives birth to itself."[50] Lewis has Tarr reaching out beyond religious, moral, and philosophical values, beyond in fact his own subjectivity in its isolation and distinctness from an objective world, toward art as "the *supreme* configuration" of the will to power. Since Tarr is Lewis's own artistic creation, and "the positing of the new relation of will to power must proceed from art," *Tarr* is the vehicle of Lewis's own reaching after and attempt to posit this new relation to the religious, moral, philosophical, and artistic tradition. Tarr, and the novel of which he is the focus, are Lewis's reaching after the will to power, after his own self-creation as "the artist himself." That is, they are Lewis's search for a "*supreme* configuration" beyond the duality of subject and object, ego and world, self and not-self.

The claim that Lewis is himself pursuing Nietzschean will to power in *Tarr* needs more precise delineation. Recall that Lewis's project, formulated in "VORTEX: BE THYSELF" at the time *Tarr* was being written, was the transformation of an abstract, dialectical dualism into a "harmonious and sane duality," and that this took the form of an attempted parallel or differential characterization in *Tarr*. Gilles Deleuze observes the following about the Nietzschean Overman: "The Overman is directed against the dialectical conception of man, and transvaluation is directed against the dialectic of appropriation or the suppression of alienation. Anti-Hegelianism runs through Nietzsche's work as its cutting edge ... For the speculative element of negation, opposition or contradiction Nietzsche substitutes the practical element of *difference*, the object of affirmation and enjoyment."[51] This substitution attempts a "suppression of alienation" through the positing of supersensory ideas and ideals. As outlined already, these are precisely Lewis's concerns in the transition from the abstract exploration of dialectical alienation in *Enemy of the Stars* to the more concrete differential characterizations of *Tarr*, from Arghol's attempted suppression of alienation to Tarr's attempted "affirmation and enjoyment" of "the creative man."

Paralleling the definitive role of anti-Hegelianism in Nietzsche is the philosophic collapse at the core of *Enemy* brought on by the anti-Hegelianism of Max Stirner. Arghol's "enlightenment" is his realization that there is no escape from Hegel, from the dialectic of mind and body and therefore from Stirnerian solipsism. Lewis's own discovery is that the inescapable result of solipsism is nihilism. He traces to its logical conclusion in *Enemy* the "self-devaluation of the highest values" that Nietzsche sees as inherent to the Western philosophical, moral, and religious tradition. His decision in "VORTEX: BE THYSELF" to adopt the differential "four eyes vacillating concentrically at different angles upon the object chosen for subjugation" finds in *Tarr* exactly the concrete, practical strategy attributed above to Nietzsche. *Tarr* is Lewis's attempt at a "revaluation of all values" on the only ground conceivable to both himself and Nietzsche, that of the work of art: "Art is the most perspicuous and familiar configuration of the will to power."[52]

As we have already seen, Lewis confessed that Nietzsche was the major influence on his early career, though he discriminated between the "titanism and supernatural afflatus" of *Thus Spoke Zarathustra* and the "genius which expressed itself in 'La Gaya Scienza', or those admirable maxims."[53] His turn from the abstraction of *Enemy* to the comparative realism of *Tarr* was continuous with his critique of romantic egoism and search for an objectivist avant-garde aesthetic in touch with the "praxis of life." While the omniscient narration of *Tarr* constitutes an apparently objective relation to character and action, it does not overcome the autonomy of the traditional narrator from the "life" which he is retailing. Lewis has subjugated himself to the form of the realist novel, rather than having inscribed the dualist strategy of "VORTEX: BE THYSELF."

Lewis's attempted escape from the "abstractist cul-de-sac" through the concreteness of "character in action" is just such a search for an art that would transcend the egoism, solipsism, and ultimate nihilism of the Western tradition. But Lewis's characterization of Tarr is deeply contradictory. He is that "notable *ambitieux*" (18) who, on the one hand, aspires to be a "new sort of person; the creative man" (20), and, on the other, is in search of "a *substitute* for his defective self" (22) in the form of a woman. Tarr's attempt to transcend the narrower function of ascetic artist to become "the Artist himself" is thwarted by his flight from himself, his search for a substitute for a self that will not submit to the demands of a deeper will to power as art, the need *to create himself* as his first and primary work of art. This would entail a relinquishing of his identity as ascetic artist and an embracing of his senses, that is, a submission of his intellect to his will *through his senses*. It is this subordination that Lewis will not permit Tarr: his "intellect conspired that his senses never should be awakened" (213). Tarr's "attachment to stupidity" is such that "his artist's asceticism could not support anything more serious than such an elementary rival" as sexual passion, since "when he was on heat, it turned his eyes away from the highest beauty" (213). Tarr clings, then, to this higher ascetic and abstract beauty, to a fundamentally *dialectical* image of beauty in the form of a supersensuous Platonic ideal. His pursuit of Anastasya partakes of this "stupidity" since her "highly artistic beauty" requires the "betrayal of the artist in him." Tarr's intellect and intellectualized aesthetic enter into a hypocritical "selfish stupidity" rather than subordinate themselves to a reshaping and transformation by the will. Thus the hypocrisy of Tarr's invocations of Nietzsche first as selfjustification and then as self-aggrandizement.

Nietzsche is Tarr's bad conscience, one that he manages to quiet through the beneficence of the sought-for substitute for his defective self, Anastasya. Not only does she effect the seduction that Tarr's commitment to "the role marked out by reason" would prevent, but she very skilfully disarms his intellect and flatters his masculinity. Anastasya is a more admirable and masterful character than Tarr, her sole weakness being her attraction to him, one which he soon exploits by marrying Bertha and reverting to his earlier misogyny: "God was man; the woman was a lower form of life" (327). Tarr in fact repudiates Anastasya because she is "too big" for him: "He saw this quite clearly: he and Anastasya could not combine otherwise than at present: it was like a mother being given a child to bear the same size already as herself. Anastasya was in every way too big; she was too big physically, she was mentally outsize: in the sex department she was a juggernaut" (327). Tarr could "sacrifice" Anastasya "with a comparatively light heart" because in combining with her he would be eclipsed, a "*nothing*" (327).

Anastasya, the artistic, intellectual, and sensuous woman, stands for "Life," as opposed to Bertha, the merely sensual bourgeoisbohemian. But since Tarr's opening himself up to "life" involves intellectual hypocrisy and artistic self-betrayal, such an expansion is essentially emptied of content and the power to transform him into the "creative man." Tarr's desire to become "a new sort of person" is in fact devalued into a claim at the end to be "the new *animal* ... the thing that will succeed the Superman" (321). What had at the beginning been a crippling intellectual dualism becomes at the end a sensuous dualism: Bertha gives way to Anastasya, Anastasya to Rose Fawcett, bearer of three of his children: "But yet beyond the dim though solid figure of Rose Fawcett another arises. This one represents the swing back of the pendulum to the swagger side. The cheerless and stodgy absurdity of Rose Fawcett required as compensation the painted, fine and enquiring face of Prism Dirkes" (333). Tarr is now ensnared in a sexual dialectic, of sensual and sensuous "compensation," in which his "lonely phallus" is a "pendulum" never coming to rest or fulfillment.

Since "life" involves Tarr in a repression rather than a sublimation of art, it cannot open out into the broader creativity exercised by the will to power of "the Artist." As a characterization, Tarr is an example of what Nietzsche would term "incomplete nihilism," which "does indeed replace the former values by others, but ... still posits the latter always in the old position of authority that is, as it were, gratuitously maintained as the ideal realm of the supersensory."[54] "Life" is for Tarr an "object" outside of him in which sexual and artistic values are in uneasy alliance, since the former are dominant. He passively decides that "life" will be "given a chance" rather than actively shaping it in relation to himself through a creative exercise of will, a decision that would unite him (the subject) with Anastasya (his object). As an "object," "Life" is in "the old position of authority" as an ideal which Tarr can never realize, and can never give form as an expression of *"the Artist* himself."

The same "incomplete nihilism" is detectable in Lewis's artistic goal, described as the choosing for subjugation of an "object." It was a strategy in reaction to the goal of the traditional literary practice of unified literary identity, a goal he found inherently contradictory in the light of the dualistic nature of the tradition itself. His aim was to reach a "harmonious and sane duality," achievable by the "different angles" of the "concentric vacillations" of Tarr and Kreisler. Because they share a parallel "immense collapse of chronic *volition*," their respective "objects" (survival and creative fulfilment, preservation and enhancement of life) are not permitted by Lewis to come under the integrating influence of subjectivity as will to power: "The subjectivity of the subject is, as such a gathering together, *co-agitatio* (cogitatio) ... a gathering of knowing, consciousness ... But the *co-*

agitatio is already, *in itself*, *vell*, willing. In the subjectness of the subject, will comes to appearance as the essence of subjectness."[55] Lewis himself does not achieve an integration of his differential characterization in *Tarr*, because for him the novel remains an "object chosen for subjugation" rather than a vehicle of the necessary self-transformation. He does not control and shape the inherently subjective and autobiographical dimension of the novel, but gives sensuous "life" a chance in the novel to shape him. It did so. It "dragged" him out of the cul-de-sac of abstract painting and "imposed itself on [him] as a complementary creation."[56] Lewis has much the same attitude to the novel as does Tarr to Anastasya. He passively adheres to the "rôle marked out by reason," relying on the inherent seductive power of language and literature to work its sensuous will. Tarr opened up to "life," Lewis to a more concrete artistic medium, but a mere transposition of values rather than a transvaluation has taken place. The same abstract dualistic principle as that in *Enemy of the Stars* dominates the characterization and the narratorial stance.

Admittedly, Lewis never espouses the romantic creativity to which his character aspires, but in this, in fact, the devaluation of values in *Tarr* appears. He allows Tarr this ambition only on the condition of an adherence to dualism, an "attachment to stupidity" and a passivity that totally undermines and negates him as artist in either the narrower or the broader sense. The effect is a devastating satire of Tarr in which Lewis betrays his own defensive attachment to the "truth" of dualism. He does not allow himself to imagine a character with the force to create himself. Lewis stands back in his role as narrator and gives a destructive inside commentary on Tarr. This is especially glaring at crucial points: we are given the all-important diary passage in the first chapter, but the diary is never heard from again; at the very inception of Tarr's encounter with Anastasya we are told Tarr must betray himself as artist. The narrator explains the what and why of Tarr's behaviour before the fact, rather than allowing the character to be represented "in action." The narrator stands outside the action in the capacity of a God, in his omniscience exempt from precisely the limitations that are not merely the characters' downfall, but are heavily satirized in the narratorial commentaries. The narrator disclaims all sympathy with the characters, as if they were not his creation and therefore a commentary in their own right on the force of his imagination. As Flory puts it, "He would describe the repulsiveness of his characters as though the cause of his revulsion lay entirely in their shortcomings rather than largely in his own nihilistic and claustrophobic view of the human condition."[57]

I have stated the full force of the harsh view of Lewis's satirical stance in *Tarr* because this view is consistent and persuasive and perhaps best characterizes the feeling about Lewis's work on the part of a literary establishment that expects an ethical positivity and a moral responsibility in its artists.[58] On the one hand, we have seen Lewis struggling to free himself in *Enemy of the Stars* and "Physics of the Not-Self," from a pragmatic, anti-intellectual moralism, in place of which he advocates the *apatheia* of the artist as "indifferent god" according to the ethic of arete. On the other hand, Lewis also sees the inherent dangers of the Nietzchean reach beyond good and evil toward a transvaluation of values as will to power. The Nietzschean "impulse to titanism and supernatural afflatus,"[59] to an overweening egoism, leads, in Lewis's view, not beyond but more deeply into the nihilism that it purports to transcend. Such is the condition of both Arghol and Tarr. Arghol's embracing of a "not-self" and Tarr's of an ascetic artistic self-creation negate the dialectic of mind and body in an attempted non-ethical synthesis, or, rather, an intellectual/artistic ethics. The "wild body"[60] reasserts itself in a "return of the repressed," which results in Arghol's murder and in Tarr's self-aggrandizing affair with Anastasya. The added subtlety of *Tarr* is that Lewis allows us to feel the horror of Tarr's ongoing inauthenticity, his self-deluded belief that he has transcended the Nietzschean Superman.

The lineaments of Lewis's satiric stance in *Tarr* are clearly visible in the advocacy of artistic *apatheia* in "Physics of the Not-Self": "There is ... no emotional value attached to goodness whatever ... You cannot, logically, 'love' or admire ... if you truly understand."[61] Lewis adopts the stance of an "indifferent god" with *Tarr*, as with *Enemy of the Stars*, but with the additional subtlety of the dualist strategy of "VORTEX: BE THYSELF." Rather than the mutual cancellation of Arghol and Hanp, Lewis gives us the more frightening vision of Tarr's self-delusion. The utter detachment of Lewis's narratorial stance in *Tarr* entails no element of self-reflection or criticism. Nor is there the communal gesture, as in *Enemy*, in which narrator and reader are seen to share the spiritual crisis of the main character. Lewis has gone resolutely beyond traditional moral positivity in his representation of nihilism, and beyond nihilism itself in its Nietzschean, romantic form as an egoistic self-apotheosis through the will to power. His artistic persona has become a non-persona, in fact a merely impersonal registering consciousness, the objective "eye" that renders the world as external appearance.

Except that, of course, Lewis's objective narratorial stance, as informed by his ideals of arete and *apatheia* as it may be, is impersonal only in the traditional, humanistic sense, which affirms unified subjectivity and ego identity. Lewis's dualist strategy and his narratorial perspective in *Tarr*, despite certain weaknesses of technique, is more consistent than it was in *Enemy of the Stars*. Lewis has Tarr voice the aesthetic principles at work in the novel: "'Death differentiates art and life. Art is identical with the idea of permanence. Art is continuity and not an individual spasm: but life is the idea of the person'" (312). Further, death is the "*motif* of all reality: the purest thought is ignorant of the motif" (311). The tension, then, is between art as permanence and death, and life as thought and personhood ("the *idea* of the person"). Tarr's "betrayal of the artist in him" for Anastasya as "life" is a symptom of Tarr's abstract and dialectical conception of the art/life relation. Lewis satirizes Tarr's inability to live both sides of the art/life dialectic at once. In "VORTEX: BE THYSELF," Lewis conceived the strategy of a non-dialectical dualism. His practical execution of this strategy in *Tarr* employs satire, we could say, precisely because it is the unary *identity* of person as an *idea* that is criticized. What we get in Tarr as a character is a *caricature* of the artist caught in a dialectic of Apollonian and Dionysian impulses (ascetic art/sexual life), unable to make the leap to a concrete and synthetic will to power. By satirizing the will to power in Tarr, Lewis himself makes the leap beyond Nietzsche that Tarr delusively claims, since his character is the concrete *image* for that of which the character himself has only the necessarily dualistic idea. Art is concrete image and representation, whereas "life is the idea of the person."

Emmanuel Levinas addresses such an art/thought dichotomy in his *essay* "Reality and Its Shadow": "Does not the function of art lie in not understanding? Does not obscurity provide it with its very element and a completion sui generis, foreign to dialectics and the life of ideas? Will we then say that the artist knows and expresses the very obscurity of the real?"[62] The basic procedure of art, Levinas says, is its "substituting for the object its image." Further, an "image does not engender a *conception*, as do scientific cognition and truth … An image marks a hold over us rather than our initiative, a fundamental passivity" (3). The image as resemblance to its object is a "not understanding," a passive response which doubles the object, and makes of it not the timeless *concept*, but a sensuous impression in the midst of duration: "The petrification of the instant in the heart of duration … the insecurity of a being which has a presentiment of fate, is the great obsession of the artist's world" (11). The image, then, is the imaginative *response* (rather than the "initiative" of the concept) to death in the midst of concrete life. As Lewis puts it, death is the "*motif* of all reality: the purest thought is ignorant of that motif." The image as motif is a caricature of life,

Levinas says: "The artist has given the statue a lifeless life, a derisory life which is not master of itself, a caricature of life ... *Every image is already a caricature*" (9). Nor is Tarr master of the conflict between art and life into which Lewis writes him.

Classical art, Levinas says, "corrects the caricature of being – the snub nose, the stiff gesture. Beauty is being dissimulating its caricature" (8). Modern art, on the other hand, dwells on sadness rather than the happiness of classical beauty, concentrating on the tragedy of art's "petrification of the instant," its "presentiment of fate": "The value of this instant is thus made of its misfortune" (12). But the passivity of imagination is an escape from the initiative and responsibility of thought and understanding. It dwells on the world's self-caricature "as though ridicule killed, as though everything really can end in songs. We find appeasement when ... we throw ourselves into the rhythm of a reality which solicits only its admission into a book or a painting" (12). That is, by holding up to the world its image, we allow it to criticize itself, just as Lewis allows Tarr to reflect the inherent inauthenticity of holding art opposed to life. But, Levinas says, because art plays with and revels in the world in its capacity to be imaged, "the value of the beautiful is relative. There is something wicked and egoist and cowardly in artistic enjoyment. There are times when we can be ashamed of it, as of feasting at a plague" (12). It is this irresponsibility of Lewis's satire that makes us uneasy with the objectivity and detachment he discovers in it. It is here that criticism finds its role for Levinas: "Criticism already detaches [art] from its irresponsibility by envisaging its technique" (12). Lewis's satiric stance in *Enemy of the Stars* and *Tarr* is answered by *The Caliph's Design* and "Physics of the Not-Self." In the former, art and life, satirized in their abstract polarization in *Tarr*, are conceived in a dynamic avant-garde interdependence. In the latter, the technique of satiric self-caricaturing is given an attempted conceptual foundation. As Levinas explains, "Modern literature, disparaged for its intellectualism ... certainly manifests more and more clear awareness of this fundamental insufficiency of artistic idolatry. In this intellectualism the artist refuses to be only an artist, not because he wants to defend a thesis or cause, but because he needs to interpret his myths himself" (134). Lewis's drive to critically and conceptually defend his aesthetic efforts is a sign of his sensitivity to the inherent irresponsibility of artistic expression. He does not fall back from the rigour of his nihilistic satire to a traditional moral or humanist defence of art, but pushes on, as we see in his critical and creative work of the twenties and thirties, to radically impersonal and amoral satire that affirms the absurdity of the human condition without escaping into a Nietzschean or Stirnerian egoism. One of the most challenging and intriguing characteristics of Lewis's profile as an artist is precisely his attempt to intellectually mediate his own artistic effort. He successfully pre-empts his critics to the point that he remains the least studied and understood of significant modern English writers, and this, I suggest, is largely because he radically anticipates an objectivism and anti-humanism that has been theoretically articulated only with the advent of structuralist and post-structuralist criticism.[63]

The radicality of Lewis's vision penetrates more deeply into the problematic of concrete image and abstract concept than is provided for in the simple opposition of play and serious work, escape and social responsibility offered by Levinas in "Reality and Its Shadow." The force of Levinas's overall philosophical project is, indeed, in essential agreement with Lewis, a critique of the inherent egoism and imperialism of Western metaphysics. He argues for the primacy of ethics over ontology, of attitude over category, a perspective which is capable of a more nuanced exploration of the critical (and therefore, in Levinas's terms, morally serious and responsible) role of art than is provided in "Reality and Its Shadow."[64] Levinas has had a seminal influence on the deconstructive critique of Western metaphysics launched by Jacques Derrida, who assigns an important place to literature in deconstructivist strategy.[65]

I have argued that, in its impersonalism and amoralism, Lewis's dualist satiric strategy is a critique, in the tradition of Stirner and Nietzsche, in which, in Levinas's words, satire functions on the principle that "ridicule kills." But Lewis's satire ridicules not only rationalism and moralism, in a Nietzschean fashion, for their inherent devaluation of values, but also the critical responses to them of Stirner and Nietzsche themselves as failing to provide an adequate answer in the context of conceptual discourse. His satiric technique is indeed a literary critique of philosophical reason, a Blakean "diabolical reading" of the scripture of Western humanism, of the "onto-theo-logical tradition" and of "logocentrism."[66] Arghol is a demonstration of how impossible it is for reason to escape itself, while Tarr displays the penetration of an abstract philosophical dualism into the aesthetics and art practice of a modernity influenced by Nietzsche and anti-metaphysical thinking.

In a revealing interview with Richard Kearney, Derrida has spoken of the difficulty of escaping metaphysical language sufficiently to meaningfully question it. In response to the question of whether or not he considers himself a philosopher, Derrida responds, "I have attempted more and more systematically to find a non-site, or a nonphilosophical site, from which to question philosophy ... My central question is: from what site or non-site (*non-lieu*) can philosophy as such appear to itself as other than itself, so that it can interrogate and reflect upon itself in an original manner ... But the problem is that such a non-site cannot be defined or situated by means of philosophical language."[67] Derrida goes on to acknowledge the role of literature in his attempt to formulate an extra-philosphical position: "In literature, for example, philosophical language is still present in some sense; but it produces and presents itself as alienated from itself, at a remove, at a distance. This distance provides the necessary free space from which to interrogate philosophy anew; and it was my preoccupation with literary texts which enabled me to discern the problematic of *writing* as one of the key factors in the deconstruction of metaphysics."[68] In other words, the inner tension and alterity that Derrida seeks to achieve in deconstruction is, in his view, a property of the "alienation" inherent to literary language. Deconstruction involves the need, he says, to "maintain two contradictory affirmations at the same time."[69]

In "VORTEX: BE THYSELF," Lewis is calling for just such a position, or non-position, outside of the system of logocentric discourse, free of the metaphysical opposition of individual and collective, self and other that led him to such inexorable conclusions in *Enemy of the Stars*. As a student of both Stirner and Nietzsche, but one who sees precisely philosophical limitations in their positions, Lewis is in search of what Derrida has described as the implicit alterity and alienation in literary language, its inherently deconstructive potential. A point to be emphasized is that Lewis is not a merely instinctual proto-deconstructionist. He recognizes the need to escape metaphysical oppositions because of what he has proven to himself are their inevitably nihilistic property. By the same token, no more is he a modernist in the received sense of the term, trying to achieve transformations in consciousness primarily through the exploitation of literary style. Lewis is consciously in search of what Derrida calls "an alternative dimension beyond philosophy and literature," but Lewis searches for this critical dimension within literary discourse, finding it in a satire that displays the inherent self-caricaturing quality of the image: "Every image is already a caricature," as Levinas says. That Lewis is being drawn increasingly into the orbit of language away from his commitment to painting is indigenous to the problematic he confronts. As Derrida implies, the inherent alienation in literature derives from its greater materiality than philosophy as writing, a discursive practice which escapes the immediacy and self-presence characteristic of spoken discourse, and which is also shared by the objective presence of the visual work of art.[70] Lewis is looking for a position of control in the relation of self and other ("the object chosen for subjugation" in "VORTEX: BE THYSELF,"), such that he is rendered free of the infinite regress of polar oppositions.

But it is here that we locate what is the primary conflict and irresolution in Lewis's proto-deconstruction. As we see in "VORTEX: BE THYSELF" Lewis at once calls for control and mastery of the self's multiplicity and also for the abandonment of the rational dream of such control: "Why try and give the impression of a consistent and indivisible personality?" Here we see the basis for Lewis's vacillation between representation and analysis, between literary and critical discourse, which appears at its most contradictory in the tension between *Enemy of the Stars* and "Physics of the Not-Self." So that we could say, modifying Levinas, that Lewis is the artist in his desire to allow the play of the inherent contradiction and absurdity of the human condition, and he is the *modern* in being unable to control that play and unwilling to render it as simply beautiful.[71] Lewis becomes, after his character Tarr, the artist himself in embodying the sadness of the undecidable relation in modernity between image and concept, art and criticism. Underneath the comic bathos of Tarr's and Arghol's absurdity is a tragic pathos of inner contradiction which Lewis himself is seeking strategically to circumvent in his art practice. His amoral and impersonal satiric perspective, open to the criticism of irresponsibility and lack of self-reflection, is rooted in his largely Nietzschean perception of man: "It is comparatively easy to see that another man, as an animal, is absurd; but it is far more difficult to observe oneself in that hard and exquisite light. But no man has ever continued to live who has observed himself in that manner for longer than a flash. Such consciousness must be of the nature of a thunderbolt. Laughter is only summer-lightning. But it occasionally takes on the dangerous form of absolute revelation."[72] As, then, a strategy of avoidance of self-reflection, of the spiritual and personal roots of the modern crisis, Lewis's satiric stance is a revelation of the vagaries of the human beyond the protective boundaries of humanism.[73]

4 The Will to Satire: *The Revenge for Love*

The present chapter proceeds somewhat more circuitously than previous ones. It attempts to chart the development and interrelation of Lewis's critical and creative writing from 1918 to 1937, his most productive period in both genres. The focus of the chapter is his best novel, *The Revenge for Love* (1937), in which he achieves the clearest and most advanced expression of his concerns during these years. In order to approach *Revenge*, however, we pass first by way of the satiric novel *The Apes of God* (1930). The problems addressed and only partially overcome in *Apes* are then traced in Lewis's critical writings, from *The Art of Being Ruled* (1926), through *Time and Western Man* (1927), to *Men Without Art* (1934). The crucial role of Nietzsche as the silent protagonist of Lewis's thought is given careful attention. Nietzscheanism emerges clearly as the dynamic source of his thinking during these years, maturing and gaining a unique Lewisian twist in *The Revenge for Love*.

Blasting and Bombardiering, Lewis's first autobiography, deals with the years 1914 to 1926. The title refers to his pre-war career as art-militant and editor of *Blast* and to his involvement in the Great War as a bombardier, an artilleryman. In the introduction to the book, he addresses the reader:

You will be astonished to find how like art is to war. They talk a lot about how a war just-finished affects art. But you will learn here how a war *about to start* can do the same thing ... It is somewhat depressing to consider how an artist is always holding the mirror up to politics without knowing it. My picture called 'The Plan of War' painted six months before the Great War 'broke out', as we say, depresses me. A prophet is a most unoriginal person: all he is doing is imitating something that is not there, but soon will be. With me war and art have been mixed up from the start ... I wish I could get away from war. This book is perhaps an attempt to do so.[1]

Lewis continues, "I have set out to show how war, art, civil war, strikes and coup d'états dovetail into each other."[2] In effect, Lewis is acknowledging in *Blasting and Bombardiering* the overwhelming and decisive impact of the war on his art and personality. In 1937, he is still trying to "get away from war": "Writing about war may be the best way to shake the accursed thing off by putting it in its place, as an unseemly joke."[3]

The war represents a challenge to Lewis. Two decades later, it needs to be contested and "put in its place." It has come to define art itself ("how like art is to war"), so much so that even the art done before the war began is shaped by it. It has made of Lewis a mere "imitator" of what is "not there, but soon will be." His very identity as an artist is put into question in his own mind, then, by his war experience and its impact on his career. As Lewis describes it, "I started as a novelist and set a small section of the Thames on fire. My first book *Tarr* was a novel (1918). Then I buried myself. I disinterred myself in 1926, the year of the General Strike – but as a philosopher and critic."[4] He is being deliberately bumptious here, but the clear implication is that his war experience caused him to "bury himself," and that as a result he emerged in a different role from the one he had chosen prior to the war. Later in *Blasting and Bombardiering,* he describes his war experience as an "education": "I started the war a different man to what I ended it. More than anything, it was a *political* education. I am slow to learn but quick to understand. As day by day I sidestepped and dodged missiles that were hurled at me, and watched other people doing so, I became a politician."[5]

If, then, war was for Lewis a political education, when he asserts "how like art is to war" he is confronting the primarily political implications of art, and he is in *Blasting and Bombardiering* attempting to come to terms with an understanding of art which places it in a far larger context than his youthful art-militancy could have allowed. The battleground of art, as he observed in *The Caliph's Design* in 1919, is not the studio, the gallery, and the press, but the larger stage of society as a whole, functioning as a struggle of conflicting interests

– that is, as politics. In 1937, Lewis is still attempting to come to terms with the implication of his political education – that the artist is nothing like Shelley's "unacknowledged legislator of the world," but is rather an unwitting mouthpiece, an unoriginal imitator of the social and political conditions in which he finds himself.

The similarity between modern art and war observed by Lewis in 1937 is clear: they are both founded upon conflict. But the position of Lewis as artist in these contexts is not the same. When he is "blasting," he is the avant-garde artist who actively attacks the bourgeois art establishment, and has it in his power to renounce "consistent and indivisible personality"[6] in the face of irreconcilable contradictions of mind and body, self and other. When he is "bombardiering," he is the passive servant of the war machine and of historical and political conflicts beyond his control. His individuality, especially his identity as an artist, is a matter of utter irrelevance to his role as an artillery officer. This absorption by and subordination to a reality in which art is of no importance is a shattering experience, which uncovers a weakness and contradiction inherent in Lewis's prewar art theory: the persona that renounces "consistent and indivisible personality" as a persistent strategy is itself a consistent and indivisible personality, one to which he shows himself to be deeply attached when it is threatened by the impersonal forces behind war. The years 1918 to 1937, culminating in *Blasting and Bombardiering* and *The Revenge for Love*, are motivated by this external challenge to Lewis's identity as an artist. The political education undergone in the Great War initiated two decades of intense struggle to establish a position of power and influence for art within an indifferent cultural arena. Given the impersonal and "indifferent" notion of the artistic persona imposed on him by his Vorticist vision, this was to prove a complex task.

The Apes of God, privately published by Lewis in 1930, was a book of 625 pages and "weighed five pounds, was three inches thick and illustrated with Lewis's own drawings and designs."[7] The novel embodies, in its caricatural proportions and marginal origins, Lewis's critique as "The Enemy" of the drift of modern art into social élitism and its subservience to economic conditions – in short, its capitulation to a politics inimical to art. *The Apes of God* is a savage satire of Bloomsbury art culture, the adoption of art as an avocation by a moneyed class whose leisure allowed it to dabble, without commitment or risk, in matters which Lewis saw as vital to the survival of culture. As Lewis observed of *The Apes of God* in *Rude*

Assignment, "All social Satire is political Satire. And in the case of my solitary book of Satire, that is the answer too. If anyone smarted because of it ... they smarted for a political reason. As a class, they had outstayed their usefulness and grown to be preposterous parasites ... It was incumbent upon all good citizens to turn satirists on the spot, at the sight of such as those exhibited in 'The Apes of God' – if they had any Satire in them, of which I happened to have an adequate supply."[8]

Lewis speaks of *The Apes of God* here as "my solitary book of Satire" and "the only one of my books which can be classed as pure Satire."[9] He viewed it as a pure exercise in what he called objective or externalist art. As he explains in *Satire and Fiction,* the polemical pamphlet also produced under his imprint, The Arthur Press, in which he defends his novel, "For *The Apes of God* it could, I think, quite safely be claimed, that no book had ever been written that has paid more attention to *the outside* of people."[10] He quotes with approval a critic's personal letter of response: "Everything is told from the outside. To this extent it is the opposite of, say, James who sought to narrate from *inside* the character's mind. James in short, was a Bergsonian where you are a Berkeleyan!"[11] Lewis further emphasizes his objectivist stance by claiming, "But Satire is in reality often nothing else but *the truth,* in fact that of Natural Science. That objective, non-emotional truth of the scientific intelligence sometimes takes on the exuberant sensuous quality of creative art: then it is very apt to be called 'satire' for it has been bent not so much upon pleasing as upon being true."[12]

But we have seen that Lewis's satiric detachment was already fully intact in *Tarr.* The difference, of course, between *Tarr* and *The Apes of God* is that Lewis has shifted by the latter to his stance as *political* artist, as "philosopher and critic"[13] employing the novel for polemical purposes, rather than as "indifferent god." His critical defence of a scientific satire is a masking of a specifically *interested* politics, in which art, in its amoral and intellectual value (arete), is opposed to a politics that uses traditional moral, social, and aesthetic values to shore up power and privilege.

The complex inner dualism of *Enemy of the Stars* and *Tarr,* then, is abandoned for the most part after the war in favour of an external social and political dualism: art and politics. *The Apes of God* is, in fact, Lewis's sole experiment in political satire, in a stance critical of conditions which he saw as completely external to himself as artist and intellectual. Even so, he directs his critique toward the reigning politics, economics, and social values of the art community. But the point to be emphasized is that the complex issues of consciousness and identity, of the interior duality of mind and body, which dominate *Enemy of the Stars* and *Tarr* (and the theoretical statements associated with them) are subordinated to the opposition external to Lewis, between himself and historical and cultural forces that had overwhelmed him in the war.

The plot of *Apes* is relatively simple in structure. The social education of Dan Boleyn, a naïve young Irishman in London, is undertaken by Horace Zagreus, a seasoned bachelor with a devotion to young men of "genius." Horace gives to Dan an "Encyclical" from a certain mysterious Pierpoint. Horace explains, "As to the document that accompanies this [letter], show it to no one. Several years ago I received it, it is written by a man who is in everything my master – I am nothing, he is everything. It speaks for itself. In it he describes what he then undertook to do. He was successful I rejoice to say: I will (not as he could but to the best of my power) perform in your case a similar service."[14] Zagreus professes to "believe absolutely" in Dan's "genius," so that the society Dan is entering he must "understand or perish" (117). Horace must pass on to him the "system of enlightenment" (117) that he received from Pierpoint, spelled out in the Encyclical.

The Encyclical, an "extract" of which is given in the novel, professes to expose the decadent condition of contemporary culture, in which moneyed dilettantes claim to be true artists: "The whole of this immense and costly *aping*, by the idlest of the rich, of the artist's life has affected, and is likely to affect, the occasional apparition of genius" (120). Pierpoint analyzes how these artistic "apes" came into such a damaging role. He gives two main reasons. They are unlike a "genuine 'amateur,' or collector of pictures" (121) who has, at the least, a pride of ownership and to that extent a legitimate participation in the art object: "The legions of contemporary 'amateurs,' with rare exceptions, have no such interests. For they are careful not to involve themselves economically in a thing they can get as much out of as they require without spending a pennypiece" (122). But it is the second reason that chiefly concerns Pierpoint:

Some (born with a happy or unhappy knack not possessed by their less talented fellows) produce a little art themselves – more than the inconsequent daubing and dabbing we have noticed, but less than the "real thing." And with this class you come to the Ape of God proper. For with these unwanted and unnecessary labours, and the *amour-propre* associated with their results, envy steps in. The complication of their malevolence that ensues is curious to watch. But it redoubles, in the natural course of things, the fervour of their caprice or ill-will to the "professional" activities of the effective artist – that rare man born for an exacting intellectual task, and devoting his life unsparingly to it. (122)

Pierpoint's design is to "make them parade before you in their borrowed plumes like mannequins, spouting their trite tags, and you shall judge if my account is true" (123).

The bulk of the novel is constructed of the encounters of Dan Boleyn with various herds of art apes, whose "mannequin"-like quality, coupled with Dan's *naïf-précieux* responses, produces a double-edged caricatural satire described by Lewis as the "absurd" effect of "things behaving as if they were persons."[15] The guiding or controlling consciousness within the novel would, at first, appear to be Zagreus in that it is he who undertakes Dan's initiation. But Horace is himself the disciple of Pierpoint. Pierpoint never appears from behind the backdrop, but is an invisible presence throughout; or, rather, he appears in his Encyclical.

Horace directs Dan, in the first half of the novel, to visit on his own various groups of apes. But the novel's second half is taken up with a single prolonged episode, "Lord Osmund's Lenten Party," in which Zagreus gathers several of his satellites and appears to direct them in a complex masque within a masque. They attend an elaborate costume party in which they are to perform a mysterious play, the roles being quite undefined, in both the party and the play, though closely choreographed by Horace. The bizarre intricacy of this 250-page sequence is impossible to summarize, but we learn during the course of it that Zagreus's apparent leadership is really Pierpoint's:

"Was it all Pierpoint this time Horace?"

"Every word!... What do you think I paid him for it?... Of course I pay Pierpoint for *everything* I get! The labourer's worthy of his hire." (453)

With this intrusion of the question of money, Horace's lack of originality is revealed, and he is denounced in front of Dan by Starr-Smith, "Pierpoint's political secretary" (477): "'All this taking you about to show you *the Apes*! Well of course they *are* Apes. What however in Jesus' name are you but an Ape and Horace Zagreus himself is the worst Ape of the lot! Does he not take all his ideas from Pierpoint? Is he not essentially a rich dilettante? Is it not owing to his *money* – not that he pays! It is absurd!'" (481).

The clash between Zagreus and Starr-Smith, the "Fascist" political secretary, and the only man Horace likes among his own and Pierpoint's followers (595), uncovers the structure of absurdity that moves the action forward and functions, at the same time, as an alternative to a logical destination and conclusion to the novel. Neither characters nor action provide a centre or a teleology. All revolves around the invisible Pierpoint, who, we learn, is literally selling his enlightened services on the one hand (to Zagreus) and inspiring maniacal authoritarian devotion on the other (from Starr-Smith). Pierpoint "does" nothing but issue his Encyclical, his analysis of bourgeois bohemia, which "speaks for itself," and in which he is very careful to disavow personal authority:

In my review of this society, especially with regard to its reaction upon art, I rather insist upon than seek to slur over the fact that I am a party. But it is from the parties that the acting judge is ultimately chosen. Where else should you get him from? The supreme judge is constantly absent. What we call a judge is a successful partizan [sic]. It is on account of the superior percentage of truth in the composition of your glosses that your statement is erected into a standard. And 'Of an opinion which is no longer doubted, the evidence ceases to be examined.' The finding of the supreme judge would automatically dissolve us into limbo. (118)

Pierpoint does not claim a position outside and above the "action," but participates in it as one who judges it from a necessarily interested point of view. There is no absolute judge – or, rather, he is "absent." If he were present, we, in our relativity, would be rendered superfluous, void. In the absence of absolute truth, the only recourse is to "examine the evidence" of competing viewpoints until doubt is, for practical purposes, dispelled.

Pierpoint claims not to elevate himself to the level of supreme judge, disinterested sage, or absolute dictator. He refuses to "ape" God, but rather is aped as such by Zagreus and Starr-Smith. For his part, "I am not in agreement with the current belief in a strained 'impersonality' as the secret of *artistic* success. Nor can I see the sense of pretending ... that in my account to you of what I have seen I can be impartial and omniscient. That would be in the nature of a bluff or a blasphemy. There can only be one judge, and I am not he" (125). Pierpoint adopts a posture of *relative* detachment, rather than an absolute, philosophical, or religiously transcendent relation, to the phenomena he is describing. Yet, the effect is the same. The Pierpointian theory, which they are supposed to weigh carefully and objectively against the evidence, and so prove its greater explanatory power, is treated by them as religious directive, an encyclical from a pontiff. The reader does not know what to make of Pierpoint's acceptance of Zagreus's money or of Starr-Smith's

Fascist allegiance. Is Pierpoint a charlatan and exploiter of "apes," or is he a misunderstood "genius"?

The narrative structure of *The Apes of God* is built upon this ambiguity. As a character, Pierpoint is clearly a type of narrator. He is the unifying intelligence that directs the action from behind the scenes, never emerging fully or interfering directly in the action. He claims for himself an objectivity toward (which is at the same time a particular interpretation of) the state of affairs at issue. He insists that this objectivity will be validated when tested against the facts. Of course, here is where the fallacy in an absolute narratorial objectivity appears. The danger that the natural scientist, by making certain assumptions, merely confirms his own expectations in designing an experiment is doubled in the case of an author/narrator who not only theorizes but designs the very world of which he presents the interpretation.

Laughter, as the power of satire, Lewis says, is "the emotion of tragic delight," "the climax in the tragedy of seeing, hearing, and smelling self-consciously."[16] But, while this "sense of absurdity, or, if you like, the madness of our life, is at the root of true philosophy," it is also "the chasm lying between being and non-being, over which it is impossible for logic to throw any bridge, that, in certain forms of laughter, we leap. We land plumb in the centre of Nothing."[17]

The satiric laugh at the absurdity of the human condition reveals its tragic proportions in a passage quoted in the previous chapter, the recitation of which gathers together several strands of the argument: "It is comparatively easy to see that another man, as an animal, is absurd; but it is far more difficult to observe oneself in that hard and exquisite light ... Such consciousness must be in the nature of a thunderbolt. Laughter is only summer lightning. But it occasionally takes on the dangerous form of self-revelation."[18] The "Nothing" into which the laughter of reflexive satire plunges us is indeed a "hard and exquisite light," which Lewis himself finds difficult to withstand.

This becomes apparent even in the character of Pierpoint through the closing paragraph of his Encyclical, which follows directly on the one quoted above criticizing artistic and critical "impersonality": "I am not a judge but a party. All I can claim is that my cause is not an idle one – that I appeal less to passion than to reason. The flourishing and bombastic role that you may sometimes see me in, that is an effect of chance. Or it is a caricature of some constant figure in the audience, rather than what I am (in any sense) myself. Or, to make myself clearer, it is my opposite" (125). In this passage, Pierpoint appears to completely reverse himself. Having denounced the "bluff" and even "blasphemy" of pretensions to impersonality and god-like objectivity and proclaimed his own "partizan" and fallible stance, with its appeal to the reader as his rational equal, Pierpoint proceeds to refuse any participation in the implications of his role as critic and satirist. He is not the "flourishing bombastic" that he may seem. No, that is a "role" that is determined from the *outside*, by what he caricatures, "some constant figure in the audience" (i.e., by analogy, one of *us*, his readers) rather than anything he really *is* in himself. But Pierpoint does not embrace the Nothing of satiric absurdity as he could do. He is not only *not* identifiable by what he satirizes, he is the *opposite*, and by saying so he undoes every word he has uttered against impartiality and the absence of the supreme judge. What is it to be the opposite of the absurd, but to be a fully rational, god-like knower or artist?

Pierpoint protests too much. It is difficult not to see the fictional persona slipping here and the polemical persona of Lewis the Enemy, a truly "flourishing and bombastic role," emerging.[19] The absurdist Nothing into which tragic laughter propels us is indeed uninhabitable except by "things behaving as if they were persons." Genuine knowledge, volition, or creativity cannot live there, as Lewis observed, in the light of the thunderbolt of tragic or absolute self-revelation: "This fundamental self-observation, then, can never be in the whole absolute. We are not constructed to be *absolute observers*. Where it does not exist at all, men sink to the level of insects. That does not matter: the 'lord of the past and the future, he who is the same to-day and to-morrow' – that 'person of the size of a thumb that stands in the middle of the Self' – departs. So the 'Self' ceases, necessarily. The conditions of an insect communism are achieved."[20] On the one hand, Lewis says, absolute self-observation is a destructive thunderbolt, but where no insight into self exists at all "men sink to the level of insects." What he argues for is, rather, *laughter*, which is only "summer-lightning." At the same time, however, Lewis is holding to a Hindu notion of Self, in which there is no absolute distinction between Atman and Brahman, between Self and God, and therefore no middle ground between the natural and the supernatural, such as man constitutes in the Judeo-Christian tradition.[21] There is no relative observation of self; there is either absolute knowledge or no knowledge at all, the condition of insect life. In pursuing Pierpoint's character to the limit in *The Apes of God*, Lewis uncovers the *interior* dualism that preoccupied him in his earlier work, and that had necessitated the detached and indifferent stance of artistic *apatheia*. His attempt to turn his interior objectivism to social and political purposes in *The Apes of God* founders on a lack of secure basis for observing and criticizing the external world, since *the observer* is himself no more "a consistent and indivisible personality" than is the observed. That is, Pierpoint and the narrator which he figures are as susceptible to being seen as "apes," dependent on the imitation of others even as critics, as are any Bloomsbury so-called dilettantes. Lewis's "political" satirical drive in *The Apes of God* reveals attachment to an identity from which he had earlier seen it necessary to remain free. His theoretical defence of satire as objective art, then, is specifically polemical, interested, and committed – a significant distance from the detached caricature he had achieved in *Tarr*.

"Inferior Religions," written in 1917 as an introduction to the stories eventually published in 1927 as *The Wild Body*, is an attempt by Lewis to move beyond the dualistic strategy of "VORTEX: BE THYSELF" and *Tarr*. Laughter, as a tragi-comic vision of the absurd, is defined as a mid-point between the unconsciousness of mere animal or insect life and the naked, tragic vision of the human condition. Laughter is an attempt to halt the endless oscillation between the poles of mind and body, subject and object:

Laughter is the one obvious commotion that is not complex, or in expression dynamic.
    Laughter does not progress. It is primitive, hard and unchangeable.[22]

Laughter is claimed as a point of transcendence of dualism within or immanent to the world, another attempt by Lewis to circumvent the Hegelian dialectic and its synthetic *Aufhebung* of thesis and antithesis, in which the particular and individual are ultimately subsumed in the Absolute. Lewis, as a student of Stirner and especially of Nietzsche, sticks to his neo-Hegelian, anti-Romantic guns in this attempt to affirm the *particular* originality of the self (as opposed to the Romantic artist as incarnation of the ideal), its uniqueness and individuality, so essential to the modern (anti-)heroic notion of the creative artist.[23]

    Laughter is "not complex" – that is, is not made up of polarities and their "dynamic" struggle – but is simple and "primitive," not having a discernible origin in time. It does not "progress," but is "hard and unchangeable," a point within time which is somehow beyond time, an access to a stability and a permanence within the otherwise transitory condition of mind-body dualism.[24] This is the theory that Lewis is working with in *The Apes of God* and that informs the satiric structure of the novel, but its application in *Apes* brings Lewis up against some implications of the theory which he clearly finds unacceptable. Laughter vaults "the chasm lying between being and non-being, over which it is impossible for logic to throw any bridge ..."[25] But in doing so, it also dissolves the chasm: "We land plumb in the centre of Nothing."[26] The result is that, as Lewis suddenly sees in Pierpoint, there is no distinction between satirist and satirized, between self and other, between subject and object. Lewis has Pierpoint anxiously scrambling back to solid ground by disclaiming that his bombastic satirical mask identifies him. No, it is his "opposite."

Strictly speaking, Pierpoint's anxiety is unfounded. The nothing of the absurd, in dissolving the logical chasm between being and non-being, dissolves the substantiality of both the laughter and that which is laughed at, the satirist and the satirized. There is nothing substantial in Pierpoint's critical stance to which he need, or can, assert a contradictory identity. The laugh, that "sudden handshake of mystic violence and the anarchist,"[27] rings in a void where no one hears it.

Pierpoint's anxiety contradicts everything he has asserted; it undermines, rather than satirizes, his characterization. We are compelled to see it as an authorial problem, and, as such, it calls for a further exploration of the tensions informing Lewis's work during this period. This prepares the ground for the consideration of a more complex novel than *The Apes of God*, *The Revenge for Love*.

As *Blasting and Bombardiering* reveals, the Great War constituted an important initiation for Lewis into a wider perspective, functioning, he says, as a political education of such power that he afterward went "underground" to deepen what he now felt to be an incomplete artistic education: "The War, of course, had robbed me of four years, at the moment when, almost overnight, I had achieved the necessary notoriety to establish myself in London as a painter. It also caught me before I was quite through with my training. And although in the 'post-war' I was not starting from nothing, I had to some extent to begin all over again" (213). There is a tension in Lewis's attitude, writing here in 1937, in sorting out the significance of these events. On the one hand, the war "robbed" him of four crucial years, but then again, "The War, as it turned out, was not for me either bad or good, because ... the obligation to make a new start – and the decision I took to make a *really* new start while I was about it – was in the long run beneficial" (213). There is a tension between "blasting" and "bombardiering," between Lewis, the avant-garde artist, and Lewis, the "politically educated" artist. On the other hand, he "buried himself" (5) with the objective, as a painter, of "creating a system of signs whereby I could more adequately express myself," (215) while, as a writer, he emerged "in 1926, the year of the General Strike – but as a philosopher and critic" (5) rather than as a novelist.

The tension between his roles of artist and philosopher-critic can be seen in terms of painting and writing. Although painting was his most uncompromising artistic role, Lewis could not make a living as a painter as easily as he could as a writer. This is the case, it might be argued, because his newly awakened political consciousness could not find adequate expression by "creating a system of signs." Writing, which had earlier "dragged [him] out of the abstractist cul-de-sac,"[28] was a better vehicle for the more objective concerns of political criticism, with which Lewis explodes from his postwar seclusion in *The Art of Being Ruled* (1926), *Time and Western Man* (1927), *The Lion and the Fox* (1927), and *Paleface* (1929). Even as an artist Lewis had begun to move out of the self-contained realm of abstract signs into a greater involvement with the concrete world, with "life" as he termed it in *Tarr* and *The Caliph's Design*. The war separated him completely from "art" and immersed him in "life."

Lewis describes his arrival at the front as an artillery officer, in the midst of a battle, as being "plunged into the romance of battle." It "matched the first glimpses of the Pacific, as seen by the earliest circumnavigators" (114). "But [that] all was henceforth romance" was not a fine sentiment for Lewis, since "romance is the enemy of beauty": "Romance is partly what you see but it is much more what you feel. I mean that *you* are the romance, far more than the romantic object. By definition, romance is always inside and not outside. It is, as we say, subjective. It is the material of magic. It partakes of the action of a drug" (115). The experience of the war completely invaded Lewis at the core of his person. In stressing its "romantic" impact, he separates it from everything he identifies with as an artist: "Give me the *outside* of all things, I am a fanatic for the externality of things" (9). In the war, Lewis had to *become* romance, immersed in sensation, in the unseen, "the dark night, with the fearful flashing of a monstrous cannonade – all things which do not come into the picture, which *are not seen*, in other words, but are suggested in its darkest shadows" (115). As an art revolutionary, Lewis had fought to discover a principle of order in the midst of the inner chaos of European thought. In the war, he was overwhelmed by the external chaos of European society, such that, henceforth, he was conducting a complex war on two fronts, artistic and political.

If painting was Lewis's purest artistic practice, and the writing of philosophical criticism his adopted political platform, then imaginative literature was the point of confrontation between his postwar artistic and political concerns. As we know, Lewis saw *The Apes of God* as a political book, since "All social Satire is political Satire."[29] He had developed his theory of laughter in response to his personal, artistic battle with philosophical dualism. As a theory, it was easily recruited in waging the public, political war. Directed outward, absurdist laughter offered devastating energy for satire. But Lewis's stance in these respective battles is not constant, and, though he may use the same artillery on both fronts, their significance is different. In the art revolution, Lewis is in the position of the aggressor. He chooses the stance of a rebel[30] and vorticist "blaster" of the cultural establishment. Not so the bombardier: "I, along with millions of others, was standing up to be killed. Very well: but *who* in fact was it, who was proposing to kill or maim me? I developed a certain inquisitiveness upon that point. I saw clearly that it was not the German opposite number. He, like myself, was an instrument. That we were all on a fool's errand had become plain to many of us, for, beyond a certain point, victory becomes at best a Pyrrhic victory, and that point had been reached before Passchendaele started" (187). He had become the mere instrument of anonymous powers apparently bent on senseless destruction. The absence of a controlling identity at the heart of modern subjectivity had been a battle cry for Lewis, the vorticist. The absence of identifiable and responsible authority behind the massive destruction of the Great War was experienced by Lewis as a direct threat to European culture, the very possibility of art, and most of all to his personal survival as an artist. The experience of this anonymous political aggression sent Lewis "underground" from 1918 to 1926, whence he emerged the "philosopher and critic" of *The Art of Being Ruled*. Since he now experienced the cultural crisis as political and social as well as artistic, his personal and public outrage took the "responsible" and "aggressive" form, Levinas's terms,[31] of a rational and conceptual attack on the established power structure.

The experience of powerlessness, of being the instrument of an impersonal engine of destruction, is reflected in the title of *The Art of Being Ruled*. It was intended as a manual of survival in what he saw as an apocalyptic situation: "In such a fluid world we should by all rights be building boats not houses. But this essay is a sort of ark, or dwelling for the mind, designed to float and navigate; and

we should all be wise, with or without covenants, to provide ourselves with some such shell in everything, rather than to rely on
conservative structures. For a very complete inundation is at hand.
After *us* comes the Deluge" (16).

The disturbing fluidity of the modern world is – according to Lewis
– the dominant characteristic of current political consciousness. The
desire for revolution has become a hunger for continuous change:
"The revolutionary state of mind is then, to-day, instinctive: the *all
that is is bad, and to be superseded by a better* attitude" (3). He traces
this instinctual dissatisfaction to the impact of science on the modern
mind: "All serious politics to-day are revolutionary, as all science is
revolutionary" (3). In enabling us to liberate ourselves, through technology, from subservience to nature, science has given us a me-
chanistic model of ourselves: "Science, in making us regard our life
as a machine, has also forced us to be dissatisfied at its sloth, un-
tidiness, and lack of definition, and given us in our capacity of
mechanics or scientists the itch to improve it" (12).

In tracing modern political consciousness to the impact of science
on our world-view, Lewis is careful to distinguish the "pure" activity
of science from the forces that have co-opted it: "When we say
'science' we can either mean any manipulation of the inventive and
organizing power of the human intellect: or we can mean such an
extremely different thing as the *religion of science*, the vulgarized
derivative from the pure activity manipulated by a sort of priestcraft
into a great religious and political weapon" (3–4). Science has become
what he calls (after Fouillée) an *idée force*, an idea which is forceful
enough to appeal to our feelings and impulses, and therefore to gain
a hold on our thinking at an instinctual level. Lewis uses as an
example Marx's notion of "class" as the means to promote the consciousness to overthrow class as a system of oppression. His example
is deliberately chosen in that he uses it to illustrate how the sub-
intellectual, instinctual functioning of *idées forces* are inherently violent and materialistic, as heading to "an undesirable confusion of
mind and body" (8): "But this 'catastrophic' conclusion to the 'revolutionary' process is not only inessential; it distorts, and I think
degrades as well, the notion of revolution. To say that people cannot
change their souls (or a good part of them) without destroying their
bodies, is a very material doctrine indeed" (7–8).

This confusion of the dualism of mind and body is at the root, for
Lewis, of the vulgarizing of science. Insofar as science, as a me-
chanistic model, achieves its transformation of the human condition
through technology, its impact as an *idée force* is largely materialistic,
breeding a utopian political consciousness which sees itself as op-

pressed by classical spiritual, intellectual, and artistic values. As a utopian ideology, the "religion of science" is future-oriented, committed to the present only in the form of change: "It is because our lives are so attached to and involved with the evolution of our machines that we have grown to see and feel everything in revolutionary terms, just as once the natural mood was conservative. We instinctively repose on the future rather than the past" (11).

Lewis offers an explanation for why the materialistic rather than the "pure" or disinterested aspects of science have been so influential and why that influence has been not intellectual but religious:

The modern 'soul' began, of course, in the Reformation. When Luther appealed for the individual soul direct to God, and the power of all mediating authority was definitely broken, God must have seen that he would soon follow his viceregents. The individual soul would later on, had he been God, have known very well that when he abandoned God, he would before long himself be abandoned. The mediator would have known that too. In any case this necessary triad has vanished. The trinity of God, Subject, and Object is at an end. The collapse of this trinity is the history also of the evolution of the subject into the object. (17)

With this rather wayward Trinitarian hypothesis, Lewis nonetheless makes a cogent point about the origins of modern attitudes toward science. With the breakdown, first, of the authority of the church, then of the stable adherence to a transcendent God, the modern subject has lost its interior stability and is focused solely on its relation to the material world. Science provides the only reliable method by which modern man can orient himself in a world lacking transcendence. Scientific technique reflects man's image back to him as object, as machine, but also, according to the experimental method, as being in continual change and revision. Old attitudes and ideas are always wrong for a scientist. There is a "disposition to regard his personality as discontinuous" (16), which, when held unscientifically, uncritically, Lewis claims, is a forfeiture of intelligence, responsibility, and, in short, humanity itself.

The Art of Being Ruled is an ambitious attempt by Lewis to explore the roots of modern political consciousness and to distinguish between "Creative and Destructive Revolution." Religious and apocalyptic analyses and analogies are much in evidence, for instance: "In our society two virtues are baldly contrasted, that of the *fighter* and *killer* (given such immense prestige by nineteenth-century darwinian science and philosophy) and that of *civilizer* and *maker*. But the ancient and valuable iranian principle of duality is threatened.

We confuse these two characters that we violently contrast. The effort in this essay is to separate them a little. It is hoped that certain things that have flown a grey and neutral flag will be forced to declare themselves as Ozman or Ahriman, the dark or the light" (15). This reference to the gods of Zoroastrianism is an invocation of Nietzsche's *Thus Spoke Zarathustra*.[32] By referring to this great rhetorical and prophetic work without explicitly naming it, Lewis would seem to be both comparing himself to Nietzsche and claiming independence from him. If the religious strain of Lewis's analysis is further pursued, however, the influence of Nietzsche's thought becomes more and more evident:

The moralist does not necessarily love men at all ... The early christian insisted on *the destruction of the world*. Nothing short of that would satisfy him. He wanted *to wipe out entirely* everything that existed, in order to install his Kingdom of Heaven. Absolute denial of life is the logical solution of the thought of the religious fanatic: and whenever you follow him for long, you find him leading you to destruction, so far as this life is concerned. Péguy, Proudhon, Sorel, Bakunin, Herzel, etc., all desired the End of the World as thoroughly as any primitive Christian awaiting with pious satisfaction that much-canvassed event ... *Hatred of the oppressor is a more chronic and lasting sentiment than love of the oppressed.* (321)

Lewis characterizes modern revolutionary consciousness as religious, moralistic, and founded on destructive hatred of the strong rather than compassion for the weak. This analysis is a very clear application of Nietzsche's view of conventional Christian morality as rooted not in love, but in resentment and envy by the weak of the strong. His notion of *ressentiment* is considered by Kaufmann "one of the key conceptions of Nietzsche's psychology and the clue to many of his philosophical contentions ..."[33] As the principle by which Lewis distinguishes creative and destructive revolution, it is the pivotal concept of *The Art of Being Ruled*.

As observed in the previous chapter, morality for Nietzsche is a condition of the freedom and power of choice (the will to power). He calls for a "revaluation of all values," because those values are modelled on a notion of transcendental good which is, by definition, beyond the reach of free human beings. These values therefore "devalue themselves," acting as an excuse for present human imperfection and a forfeiture of self-determination, requiring the acceptance of suffering and the expectation of reward from outside, in an after-life. Nietzsche sees this appeal to a good beyond or independent of man as a subservience to moral authority, hence his characterization of Christianity, in particular, as a "slave morality":

To be kindly when one is too weak and timid to act otherwise, to be humble when any other course would have unpleasant repercussions, and to be obliging when a less amiable gesture would provoke the master's kick or switch – that is the slave's morality, making a virtue of necessity. And such "morality" may well go together with impotent hatred and immeasurable envy, with *ressentiment* which would like nothing better than revenge ... The graciousness of slaves who crave a heaven from which they will behold their masters frying in the flames of hell – that is to Nietzsche's mind no virtue. In the strong, however, and "in them alone, graciousness is not a weakness."[34]

Of course, Christianity is for Nietzsche a powerful historical example because of the circumstances of its growth into dominance in Europe from roots in the slave population of the Roman Empire.

Nietzsche's "revaluation of *all* values" is extended not only to spiritual and ethical values but to aesthetic and political ones as well. Christian morality has permeated and shaped all levels of European culture, even in his own time, which is characterized by the "death of God." Speaking of nineteenth-century romanticism, he traces its roots to Christian morality:

Thus I gradually learned to understand ... the 'Christian' who is essentially a romantic – and my eye became ever sharper for that most difficult *backward inference* ... from every way of thinking and valuing to the *craving* behind it that prompts it. Regarding all aesthetic values I now avail myself of this main distinction: I ask in every single case, "Is it hunger or overflow that has here become creative?"... The desire for *destruction*, change, and becoming can be an expression of overfull, future-pregnant strength (my term for this is, as one knows, the word "Dionysian"); but it can also be the hatred [i.e., *ressentiment*] of the misdeveloped, needy, underprivileged who destroys, who *must* destroy, because the existing, and even all existence, all being, outrages and provokes him. To understand this feeling one should closely examine our anarchists.[35]

Thus, what Nietzsche sees as the trend toward aesthetic and political decadence in his own time is rooted in Christianity, in its fostering of a defensive morality of hatred and seething *ressentiment*.

That this is a central concern of Nietzsche's philosophy is apparent in a passage in *Thus Spoke Zarathustra*:

For *that man be delivered from revenge*, that is for me the bridge to the highest hope, and a rainbow after long storms. The tarantulas, of course, would have it otherwise. "What justice means to us is precisely that the world be filled with the storms of our revenge" – thus they speak to each other. "We shall wreak vengeance and abuse on all whose equals we are not ... against all that has power we want to raise our clamor?" You preachers of equality ... Aggrieved conceit, repressed envy ... erupt from you as a flame and as the frenzy of revenge ... But thus I counsel you, my friends: Mistrust all in whom the impulse to punish is powerful ... do not forget that they would be pharisees, if only they had [worldly] power. My friends, I do not want to be mixed up and confused with others.[36]

Speaking in his Zarathustra persona, Nietzsche's hope is that man will be freed from the bonds of revenge, from the spirit of *ressentiment* directed against those who have power and authority. But the "power" to which Nietzsche refers here is not primarily power over others, since, in the hands of "tarantulas," or believers in equality among men, it remains phariseeism, the desire to judge and punish the weak. Power, for Nietzsche, is the will to power, a Dionysian strength flowing from abundance of life, rather than the privation of the will to live which breeds *ressentiment*. Both Kaufmann and Heidegger agree that for Nietzsche the will to power is a will to power over oneself, to self-mastery, rather than to the rule of others: "In the strict sense of the Nietzschean conception of the will, power can never be pre-established as will's goal, as though power were something that could first be posited outside the will. Because will is resolute openness toward itself, as mastery out beyond itself, because will is willing out beyond itself, it is the strength that is able to bring itself to power."[37] Will to power is a Dionysian "enhancement of life," rather than its merely defensive "preservation."[38]

It is significant that, far from receiving an open acknowledgement in *The Art of Being Ruled* as a source or corroborator, Nietzsche is openly attacked by Lewis, and specifically with regard to the doctrine of the will to power. First, in a chapter on Shaw and Russell, Lewis attacks the idea of will to power as self-mastery: "[Shaw] misrepresents his hero Nietzsche, whom he interprets as follows: 'Nietzsche, for example ... concluding that the final objective of this Will was power over self, and that seekers after power over others and material possessions were on a false scent.' This sense is certainly not obtained from a reading of Nietzsche's works. 'Power over others' came very vividly into the programme of that philoso-pher" (54). Lewis does not make any attempt to prove this assertion; but devotes a later chapter to Nietzsche as a "Vulgarizer." By "vul-garization" Lewis means the directing of modern energies toward revolutionary destruction, of which Nietzsche's was "the most fla-grant of all, and certainly the strangest" (120). He claims that the doctrine of will to power is an "aristocratism," which became "the greatest popular success of any philosopher of modern times" (122). He accuses him of consciously appealing to the most superficial bourgeois aspirations to power, pleasure, and status, particularly of the "bourgeois-bohemian" type (124). Lewis acknowledges that Nietzsche was a "very great" writer (123), only to make seem, how-ever, his manipulation of a popular audience the less justifiable. In the end, however, Lewis makes an interesting point about the will to power as manifested in Nietzsche himself: "In this idea of the superfluity of energy, enabling the warring organism to aim beyond mere destruction – higher than equilibrium or balance of power – there was a beneficent effectiveness which was spoilt by one thing, but that a very fundamental one ... Any criticism of Nietzsche must rest on that point: that of his suggested employment and utilization of this superfluous energy *to go on doing the same things that we should be doing without it*" (126).

Lewis is, no doubt, referring here to Nietzsche's doctrine of the "eternal recurrence of the same" as a manifestation of the self-overcoming of the will to power. This is a subtle notion which cannot be gone into here,[39] but Lewis's criticism suggests the question with which Heidegger concluded his fifteen-year study of Nietzsche. Hei-degger acknowledges that Zarathustra's "highest hope," the *deliv-erance from revenge*, is the "sole step, of the entire thinking in which Nietzsche's metaphysics is developed."[40] If that is the *goal* of his thought, then "the thought of the eternal recurrence of the same is Nietzsche's weightiest thought ... It is the heaviest thought to bear. And while we must guard in every respect against taking the weightiest thought of Nietzsche too lightly, we still will ask: does the thought of the eternal recurrence of the same, does the recurr-ence itself bring with it deliverance from revenge?"[41]

The weight of Nietzsche's own thought bore him into a final in-sanity.[42] Lewis may very well have had this fact to some extent in mind in criticizing the will to power as an on-going, endless agon. However, to have accused Nietzsche of a deliberate exploitation of a popular audience, who, far from understanding his thought, he very well knew would misconstrue and misapply it in a destructive way – in short, to have accused him of conspiring in the corruption of his own thought – is surely to take his thought too lightly. But, quite apart from his unfortunate judgement of Nietzsche, for Lewis to accuse him of "intellectual opportunism" (120) is doubly unfortunate in that he had to such an extent absorbed Nietzsche's philosophical perspective that to dismiss him was also to close off the possibility of self-reflection and self-criticism.

If the pivotal concept of *The Art of Being Ruled* is indeed Nietzsche's notion of *ressentiment*, and yet Lewis deliberately attacks Nietzsche in the work as a corrupt thinker (without bothering in any way to demonstrate or substantiate his accusations), then Lewis can himself be seen to be labouring under an acute animus of *ressentiment* in relation to the foundations of his argument. He is reacting in envy to the popular success of his master, and taking revenge on that master for minimizing his own claim to originality. From the point of view of his Marxist critique of Lewis as fascist, Fredric Jameson makes an acute observation about the cultural dynamics of such a theory as *ressentiment*: "Yet in a world dominated by the weak and their various slave-ethics, Nietzsche's own position must necessarily be reactive; indeed, the bitterness with which the 'phenomenon' of *ressentiment* is inevitably evoked – and it is the fundamental conceptual category of all late-nineteenth and early twentieth-century counter-revolutionary literature – suggests that, as an explanatory category, *ressentiment* is always itself the product of *ressentiment*."[43] Jameson's analysis reminds us of Zarathustra's attack on the "tarantulas," the preachers of equality, and of his fear of being "mixed up and confused with others,"[44] and also of Lewis's characterization of destructive revolution as leading to "an undesirable confusion of mind and body" (8).

Lewis's "reaction" to what he himself terms a corrupt "religion of science" in the modern world does indeed lead him to openly recommend fascism in *The Art of Being Ruled*:

All Marxian doctrine, all etatisme or collectivism, conforms very nearly in practice to the fascist ideal. *Fascismo* is merely a spectacular marinettian flourish put on to the tail, or, if you like, the head, of marxism: that is, of course, fascism as interpreted by its founder, Mussolini. And that is the sort of socialism that this essay would indicate as the most suitable for anglo-saxon countries or colonies, with ... as little coercion as is compatible with good sense. In short, to get some sort of peace to enable us to work, we should naturally see the most powerful and stable authority that can be devised. (369–70)

Lewis's interest in politics is fundamentally reactive. He is concerned to gain the "sort of peace to enable us to work," and, for him, "work" means *art*, and art means the work of the mind rather than the body. In the final chapter of *Being Ruled*, entitled "The Politics of the Intellect," he defends intellectuals as "this splendid and oppressed class" to whom men "owe everything they can ever hope to have" (431). The "passing of democracy" and vulgar market competition "should have as its brilliant and beneficent corollary the freeing for its great and difficult tasks of intelligence of the first order" (433). It is such a hapless idealism and culpable naïveté that enabled Lewis to welcome German National Socialism in *Hitler* (1931),[45] the book that more than any other undermined his credibility. But what is palpable in Lewis's identification with intellectuals as "this splendid and oppressed class" is its "slave morality" sentiment, its *ressentiment*, willing to entertain the tyranny of Fascism to gain the recognition it felt its due.

We have seen that Jameson's contention "that, as an explanatory category, *ressentiment* is always itself the product of *ressentiment*" is at least true of Lewis's employment of it in *The Art of Being Ruled*, with exactly the political character that Jameson attributes to it. However, both Jameson and Girard fail to appreciate the scope of Nietzsche's own thinking about *ressentiment* and the "spirit of revenge." It is to Nietzsche and to those who have read him most carefully in this regard that we must turn in order to grasp the implications of Lewis's (self-) imprisonment within what Sugarman calls "the Hermeneutical Circle of Ressentiment."[46]

"For *that man may be freed from the bonds of revenge*: that is the bridge to my highest hope and a rainbow after protracted storms."[47] For Nietzsche, the bridge to Zarathustra's "highest hope," the Overman, is *deliverance from revenge*. "Revenge" is seen not as a mere "phenomenon," as Jameson would have it, but as *the* phenomenon that holds man in a bondage of the will. That revenge should not be a question of "ethics and morals" but one about the nature of man and of Being – that is, of metaphysics – is a condition of Nietzsche's notion of will as the will to power as "a name for the basic character of all beings."[48] When the will is not free, then man is not what he could be, and the healing of the will is a healing of man as he is, in his wholeness: "Truly, a great foolishness dwells in our will; and that this foolishness acquired spirit has become a curse to all human kind. The *spirit of revenge*: my friends, that, up to now, has been mankind's chief concern; and where there was suffering, there was always supposed to be punishment."[49]

The folly of revenge is rooted, Nietzsche says, in "suffering," and a particular response to suffering. That is, suffering is judged by man to be wrong: something or someone needs to be blamed and punished for it. Hence, Nietzsche's call for a "revaluation of all values," as rooted in a (metaphysical) judgement that life as it is is not good, and a (moral) judgement that seeks to protect the community from suffering by locating and punishing a scapegoat as the agent of contagion.[50]

Ressentiment, then, is a metaphysical condition in history as a whole rather than a particular historical phenomenon, even though it has, of course, historical manifestations of various types. The ethical and metaphysical dimensions are interdependent. Even though each has an autonomous ethos in European history as Judaic and Hellenic, respectively, they become blended in Christianity, becoming Heidegger's "onto-theo-logical tradition."[51]

The question clearly emerges, Why does suffering produce in man the response that Nietzsche claims, the spirit of revenge, of *ressentiment*? Nietzsche answers, "This, yes, this alone is *revenge* itself: the will's antipathy toward time and time's 'It was.'"[52] Heidegger observes that, if Nietzsche's definition of revenge as "rancor against time" is not to seem arbitrary, we must understand what he means by "time" here. Nietzsche himself specifies the sense of time that provokes the will's antipathy, "time and time's 'It was.'" But, Heidegger argues, "time's 'It was'" is not just a particular aspect of time, the "past" as opposed to the "present" and the "future": "Time is not a cage in which the "no longer now," the "not yet now," are cooped up together. How do matters stand with "time"? They stand thus: time goes. And it goes in that it passes away. The passing of time is, of course, a coming, but a coming which goes, in passing away. What comes in time never comes to stay, but to go. What comes in time always bears beforehand the mark of going past and passing away. This is why everything temporal is regarded simply as what is transitory" (96). This definition of time as the "It was," the transitory, is not peculiar to Nietzsche, Heidegger says; it goes back to Aristotle (95–101), and it shapes all subsequent philosophy to our own time. Indeed, it is "the idea of 'time' that is current throughout the metaphysics of the West" (97).

In conceiving the will metaphysically, says Heidegger, modern philosophy, and Nietzsche in particular, are able to demonstrate "that all metaphysics leaves something essential unthought: its own ground and foundation" (100). Heidegger explicates Nietzsche's thinking of the will to power as the eternal recurrence of the same, an attempt to discover a means of transcendence *immanent* to the world, a project which, we have seen, was shared by Lewis in his doctrine of "laughter." "Being" is that which is independent of time, the transitory, what "passes away": "Time persists, consists in pass-ing. It is, in that it constantly is not" (59). Because Being is conceived in metaphysics as independent of time, as the eternal "now," the fully "present" to itself, it is ruled "by the view of time, and of a time of such a nature as we could never surmise, let alone think, with the help of the traditional time concept … Must not one as much as the other, Being as much as Time … become questionable in their relatedness, first questionable and finally doubtful?" (103). Whence the title of Heidegger's seminal philosophical work, *Being and Time*.

It is out of this lacuna in the thought of metaphysics (and ethics) that *ressentiment* emerges, as voiced by Zarathustra: "The will itself is still a prisoner. Willing liberates; but what is it that puts even the liberator himself in fetters? 'It was' – that is the name of will's gnash-ing of teeth and most secret melancholy. Powerless against what has been done, he is an angry spectator of all that is past. The will cannot will backwards; and that he cannot break time and time's covetousness, that is the will's loneliest melancholy."[53] The will's anger against time's irreversibility is really anger against *its own powerlessness* to prevent the 'It was,' the suffering of loss: "Hence arises the existential guilt that derives from the absence of com-pleteness in which each deed is enveloped, and the companion demand for finality that must always fail of being met. Rather than striving for the release from the spirit of revenge occasioned by time's passing, *man strives for release from time* ."[54] The endless cycle of ever-deepening *ressentiment* produces an ever more isolating in-volvement of the will with its own inability to *be* will, eternal and self-complete.

The Art of Being Ruled is a product of Lewis's postwar interest in politics, in the historical and ideological forces that had led to Eu-rope, and Lewis himself, being engulfed in the dark "romanticism" of war. Familiar as he was with the implications of modern art and philosophy, that subjectivity was riven by the contradiction of dual-ism, Lewis's experience of the war was all the more threatening in that interior chaos was matched with exterior chaos, so that all reality was engulfed. There was no stable point from which the mind could view the interior or exterior world. Lewis's attempts to sound the depths of modern nihilism, as penetrating and challenging as they are in *Enemy of the Stars* and *Tarr*, were not a secure enough platform from which to absorb the implications of his war experience. In *The Art of Being Ruled*, Lewis turns firmly away from the interior concerns of his early work, and attempts to sort out the historical dynamics of modern thought, that is to say its "politics of revolution."

At the end of *Being Ruled*, Lewis is sufficiently the artist and intellectual to see modern politics as a "politics of the intellect." He is sufficiently the student of Nietzsche to see the dynamic of modern nihilism as worked by the spirit of revenge of the weak on the strong, but he is unable to prevent his own relation to Nietzsche from itself being caught in the regressive cycle of *ressentiment*. He does not penetrate beyond the historical and political dimension of Nietzsche's thought to its interior ethical and metaphysical implications, nor is he in any way self-critical about his employment of *ressentiment* as an explanatory category. Rather, the category, in the hands of Nietzsche (as thought through by Heidegger and explicated by Sugarman), can be seen to illuminate Lewis and the trajectory of his writing in subsequent years.

This is immediately demonstrated in the light of Nietzsche's location of the spirit of *ressentiment* in a "rancor against time." Lewis's next work after *The Art of Being Ruled*, published in the same year as Heidegger's *Being and Time* (1927), is *Time and Western Man*, described by him as "a comprehensive essay on the 'time'-notions which have now, in one form or another, gained an undisputed ascendancy in the intellectual world."[55] In fact, *Time and Western Man* is more. It is an attempt to defend the very possibility of art in the modern world by a traditional philosophical attack on time itself. SueEllen Campbell argues that the structure of the argument in *Time and Western Man* is an attack on the thought of Bergson:

Everywhere, Lewis's philosophical position is a sort of mirror image of Bergson's. *Creative Evolution* argues that intellect inverts the more natural intuition; *Time and Western Man* implies that Bergson and his followers invent – and pervert – everything that is valuable to our human experience, everything that results from our senses, our thoughts and our dreams. Noisily, Lewis reverses Bergson's values. Silently, at the same time, he appropriates Bergson's categories, constructing his central dichotomy of time and space to agree in almost every respect with that of his former teacher.[56]

The same structure of *ressentiment* is at work as in *The Art of Being Ruled*, with the same rancorous personal animus and as unable to recognize – or simply refusing to acknowledge – his indebtedness. (Bergson is described by Lewis as "the perfect philosophic ruffian, of the darkest and most forbidding description" [174].)

Underneath the surface arguments against the artists, scientists, and philosophers of the "time-cult," typified by Bergsonian *durée*,

Lewis is concerned with the impact of the flux of temporality on *individual identity*: "I will try next to give some compendious idea of the manner in which I regard the claims of *individuality* ... For our only terra firma in a boiling and shifting world is, after all, our 'self.' That must cohere for us to be capable at all of behaving in any way but as mirror images of alien realities" (5). This concern for "self," he acknowledges, puts him in an antagonistic position not only to Bergsonian *durée* and the philosophy of the self's immersion in time, but to the amorphous flow of time and of becoming itself:

But how can we evade our destiny of being 'an opposite,' except by becoming some grey mixture, that is in reality just nothing at all? Yet this fixation will be upon something fundamental, quite underneath the flux; and this will in no way prevent my vitality from taking at one time one form, at another another, provided, in spite of these occupations, on the surface, of different units of experience, the range of my sensibility observe the first law of being, namely to maintain its identity; and that the shapes it chooses for experiment shall agree with that dominant principle. (6)

Lewis senses an inherent contradiction in this position: that "sensibility" participates in the "flux" of time, while "observing the first law of being," identity; at the same time, it "chooses shapes that will agree with that dominant principle." If the "vitality" or "sensibility" "observes" and "chooses," in what sense can it be the incoherent and amorphous participant in time that Lewis claims it to be? It cannot be said to be mere "body" if it functions with such a coherent will and mind, choosing forms of becoming according to an abstract law of being. So he continues:

Yet how are you going about this fixation, you may ask; how will you tell offhand what is essential and what is not for the composing of your definite pattern ... since everyone includes, below the possibility of change, dispositions that war with one another? Well, the way I have gone about it is generally as follows. I have allowed these contradictory things to struggle together, and the group that has proved the most powerful I have fixed upon as my most essential ME ... I will side and identify myself with the powerfullest *Me*, and in its interests I will work. (6)

If the war of dispositions is truly "below the possibility of change," what in the personality stands above the conflict, "allows" the struggle, and then "fixes upon" the essential self as a "will to power"? The nature of the dualism of mind and body upon which Lewis insists is that "fixing upon" and "being fixed upon," imposing on the world and being imposed upon by it, endlessly alternate. By claiming the power to allow the struggle, Lewis assumes a self which is always beyond the flux of experience, the continuous stream of forms that come only to pass away. That is, he assumes a being that is always already beyond time, and for which becoming (the world of change and of suffering) will inevitably be resisted as an indignity. It is because such a self is "assumed" – that is, self-willed – that the suffering and loss of dignity inherent in experience are unrelieved. The resentment can have no satisfactory outlet. It smolders and "acquires spirit," as Nietzsche was the first to perceive, as *ressentiment*, the spirit of revenge.[57]

Time and Western Man is Lewis's attempt to meet the challenge of a modern philosophy which tries to think through the implications of science. In the dualism consequent on the death of God, man becomes less rational being than animal, and so must be seen from *within* the world of nature and experience – from within time. As a critic, Lewis understands that "body" can only be "seen" with "mind," and that consciousness of oneself in time implies a self which is not wholly submerged in it. Lewis's attempt to counter with a dynamic theory of self that "allows" the warring of temporal selves, however, does not escape the contradictions inherent in dualism. From his political and "interested" postwar perspective, Lewis has forgotten his thorough prewar grasp of the implications of dualism in his concern with exterior, historical, and political metamorphoses. The internal contradictions of the theory of subjectivity presented by Lewis in *Time and Western Man* are manifested externally in Lewis's being, in the 1920s, in open contradiction with himself as he was, for instance, between *Enemy of the Stars* and "Physics of the Not-Self." His claim to be able to maintain the identity of the self by always siding with the "powerfullest *Me*" is contradicted both by his former critical theory and by his ongoing literary practice.

As we have already seen, *The Apes of God* also demonstrates in its narrative structure a contradiction in its representation of "self." Pierpoint, as the central interpretive consciousness of the novel, though he stands apart from or behind the action, is very careful in his Encyclical not to stand *outside* it. He is not the supreme knower, the judge who hands down the true law from above. He is the "partizan," the scientific observer of phenomena from *within* the same social reality. At the end of the Encyclical, however, he sees the implication of his relativist standpoint: there is no absolute difference between observer and observed, Pierpoint and the Apes of God. They imply one another, so that, rather than constituting Pierpoint as a self, his stance "is a caricature of some constant figure in the audience" (125). His anxiety is exactly that expressed by Lewis in *Time and Western Man*: "For our only terra firma in a boiling and shifting world is, after all, our 'self.' That must cohere for us to be capable at all of behaving in any way but as mirror-images of alien realities" (5). Pierpoint's feeble disclaimer that the caricature is his "opposite" is a reversion to the position of absolute observer, the posture of "impartial and omniscient" judge, which he had just characterized as "a bluff or a blasphemy" (125).

Pierpoint's reversion from the relative to the absolute standpoint can now be seen to be the same contradiction in which we have observed Lewis, in his transition from the interior to the exterior exploration of dualism in the 1910s and 1920s. The earlier dualist theory of comedic "laughter" becomes the practice of political satire in *The Apes of God*. Although there is a meta-fictional subtlety in the parodic exaggeration of the satire, based as it is on the grasp of the implications of dualism for modern subjectivity, Lewis exploits these resources in the novel only for their political purposes. Neither in *The Art of Being Ruled* nor in *The Apes of God* does he explore the self-critical and ironic possibilities presented by his personal and political experience of dualism. Despite its virtuosity, *The Apes of God* does not absolve Lewis of the very problems he attacks with such energy, and the novel remains a massive and amorphous monument to literary *ressentiment*.

With *The Apes of God*, Lewis touched off "tremors in the literary world, and provoked violent letters, potential libel suits and madcap threats on [his] life."[58] Lewis responded with the pamphlet *Satire and Fiction* (1930), in which he vigorously defended his novel with a theory of satire as the simple, unvarnished truth about modernity: "But Satire is in reality often nothing else but *the truth*, in fact of Natural Science. That objective, non-emotional truth of the scientific intelligence sometimes takes on the exuberant sensuous quality of creative art: then it is very apt to be called 'satire,' for it has been bent not so much upon pleasing as upon being true."[59] Lewis carefully distinguishes this objectivist stance from the moralistic concerns of traditional satire.[60] He then expands this viewpoint into a full-scale defence of modern art as satire in *Men Without Art* (1934): "For all practical purposes, then, we may describe this book as a defense of contemporary art, most of which art is unquestionably satiric, or comic. And it is a defence against every sort of antagonist, from the deep-dyed Moralist, the public of Anglo-Saxony, down to that nationalist nuisance, which would confine art to some territorial or racial tradition; from the Marxist who would harness art to politics, up to the mystical dogmatism which would harness it to the vapours of the spirit-world."[61]

In *Men Without Art*, Lewis gathers together his aesthetic and political concerns in a theory of art as satire, by which he lays claim to a universal perspective on the human condition:

'Satire,' as I have suggested that word be used in this essay (applying to *all* art of the present time of any force at all) refers to an 'expressionist' universe which is reeling a little, a little drunken with an overdose of the 'ridiculous' – where everything is not only tipped but *steeped* in a philosophic solution of the material, not of mirth, but of the intense and even painful sense of the absurd. It is a time, evidently, in which *homo animal ridens* is accentuating – for his deep purposes, no doubt, and in response to adverse conditions – his dangerous, philosophic, 'god-like' prerogative – that wild nihilism that is a function of reason and of which laughter is the characteristic expression ... And that is why, by stretching a point, no more, we can without exaggeration write *satire* for *art* – not the moralist satire directed at a given society, but a metaphysical satire occupied with mankind. (288–9)

This is Lewis's earlier theory of the absurd, as presented in "Inferior Religions" and "The Meaning of the Wild Body," but it has been schooled by his wider political concerns of the 1920s and, most of all, it might be surmised, by the *particular* offence taken to *The Apes of God*. The personal spirit in which the novel was received, as well as the contradiction revealed in its structure, seem to have enabled Lewis to come to terms with his anxiety about the satirist's "god-like" stance. In the above passage, he accepts the inherent dualism of the human condition ("*homo animal ridens*"), the "'god-like' prerogative – that wild nihilism that is a function of reason and of which laughter is the characteristic expression," and he affirms it as an opportunity: "We may employ ... this verbal machinery, this dialectic, to *humanize* ourselves, or to *dehumanize* ourselves as we should say still further ... And there is, of course, only this alternative, for beings so very oddly placed: either to accept what we call our 'rational' equipment as a refinement, merely, of the mechanical animal condition – regard it as a 'word-habit,' which we certainly should have been better without: or else to look upon it as a *gift*, as we say in common speech" (289).

To my knowledge, this is the first time that Lewis admits the term "dialectic" into his treatment of the inherent dualism of the human condition. That he should do so in the context of a passage in which he so clearly presents the necessity of accepting that dualistic condition is significant in the light of the theory of art as a "game," which he says follows from this view of man: "This would 'class' the arts at once – to call them 'a game' – if it were not that life itself, the whole of the 'peculiar situation' in which we find ourselves should also be considered as a game – a game in the sense that no value can attach to it *for itself*, but only insofar as it is well-played or badly-played. Art in this respect is in the same class as ritual, as civilized behaviour, and all ceremonial forms and observances – a discipline, a symbolic discipline" (290–1). Here is Lewis's doctrine of arete translated into aesthetic terms. He identifies the "play" of reason, language, and art as an impersonal and symbolic activity which has no value "for itself." Art is not an identity but an activity, a dialectical play of opposites rather than a static oppositional dualism.

In other words, what distinguishes a humanized from a dehumanized approach to life has nothing to do with content. It is an attitude of acceptance, an act of will, a willingness to allow the absurdity of the human condition, to participate in the game of opposites. Lewis equates art here with an unconditional affirmation of symbolic value, so that art becomes, in his view, nothing else but a "will to power," an affirmation by the will of its own life, without dependence on a system of values outside this self-affirmation: "However this may be, the valuing of our arts is bound up with the valuing of our life and vice versa" (291). In this simple, almost tautological statement, Lewis lets go of the *tension* of his perception of dualism, accepting it as a contradiction which is valuable without having (transcendental) value. Rather than the agonistic stance of Tarr, who had to "betray the artist in him" so that "'Life' would be given a chance,"[62] Lewis affirms the meaninglessness, the lack of intellectual content and value, of both art and life in terms of transcendental value. He lets go of the role of art politician and philosopher-critic, of defender of the rational and morally responsible priority of art in culture, and affirms its more than rational symbolic and ritual value. He accepts that "dangerous, philosophic, 'god-like' prerogative – that wild nihilism," and in doing so, he embraces his own Nietzscheanism, even if still unacknowledged as such and motivated by *ressentiment* and a Bloomian "anxiety of influence."[63] But, of course, the discourse in which Lewis is speaking here is theoretical. We shall see that in the context of his art practice in the next novel, *The Revenge for Love*, his perception of the tension between free play and moral responsibility gains in subtlety, and his movement toward a formalist aesthetic of free-play is contained by his avant-garde political commitment.

Men Without Art is, then, a culmination of Lewis's postwar role of philosopher-critic and satirist. Having worked through his "political" preoccupations in *The Art of Being Ruled, Time and Western Man*, and *The Apes of God*, he was able in this work to unite his prewar interior and artistic concerns and his postwar exterior and political concerns, achieving a certain reconciliation of his static dualism in a more dynamic and dialectical theory of art. In *Men Without Art*, Lewis begins to think in terms of a reciprocity between subjective and objective experience, and between art and politics. This sense of a complex harmony becomes manifest in his major novel of the thirties, *The Revenge for Love* (1937). The first version of this novel was taking form at the time that *Men Without Art* appeared.[64] Linda Sandler compares an early version, which she calls *Jack's Tale*, with *Snooty Baronet*, a satiric novel that appeared in 1932. She treats these two as "novels of ideas," as "highly structural satiric parables," with "a series of dramatic episodes and scenes, and a developing action rather than a simple narrative sequence."[65] In fact, in both of these works Lewis merely employs fiction as a means to explore the violent implications of current social theories. "These fictions are," Sandler says, simply "philosophy lessons in vernacular form."[66]

Jack's Tale, like *Snooty Baronet* and *The Apes of God*, shows Lewis functioning in his capacity as political philosopher-critic. However, the form of *The Revenge for Love* published three years later displays a considerable evolution beyond the early "satiric parable." In *Jack's Tale*, the action is produced by a straightforward clash between representatives of two English social classes, with their respective demands and ambitions. *The Revenge for Love*, however, in addition to being a more complex treatment of the English social and ideological climate, is also set in Spain during the violent political strife prior to the Civil War. In fact, the novel begins and ends in Spain. Percy Hardcaster, the main character, is a professional communist agitator who, in the first section of the novel, is wounded in a bungled escape attempt from a Spanish prison. The middle sections of the novel are set in London and are taken up with the interaction among several sets of characters who receive Percy on his return to England. The dénouement features his return to Spain on a new mission, this time involving Victor and Margot, hapless figures on the fringes of London left-wing circles. The novel ends with the death of the couple and with Hardcaster's re-imprisonment in a Spanish jail.

Lewis added considerable structural complexity to his original version of the novel. Because the action begins and ends in Spain, the English scene is viewed in perspective, but it is also given a greater complexity in the final version through the inclusion of additional characters, with a more nuanced interrelation among them. The turn from quite static dualistic confrontation to a more dynamic dialectical reciprocity in *Men Without Art* is mirrored in the ethos of *The Revenge for Love*. The satiric parable of class conflict in *Jack's Tale* evolves into a novel of complex plot, setting, and character. The "logical enactment of an idea"[67] that is *Jack's Tale* becomes in *The Revenge for Love* an exploration of a complex dialectical play of opposing human drives and political ideologies.

As the novel opens, Percy Hardcaster is enjoying a privileged status among the inmates of a Spanish prison. Not only is he a political prisoner rather than a common criminal, but he is an Englishman and a trained, behind-the-scenes organizer of communist insurrection. Accorded a certain respect by Don Alvaro, the prison warder, Percy misjudges the urbanity of this "ex-Civil Guard," and is unwisely drawn into a quarrel about the nature of "freedom" and "law." Don Alvaro is offended by his anarchist views, and has some rueful thoughts about Percy's type of Englishman: "A new sewer variety of the English kind. Odd – or perhaps not! – that England should go the way of Spain. Two countries with a splendid past, of piratic achievement, of glorious blood and gluts of gold – yes, two countries going rotten at the bottom and at the top, where the nation ceased to be a nation – the inferior end abutting upon the animal kingdom, the upper end merging in the international abstractions of men – where there was no longer either Spanish men or English men, but a gathering of individuals who were *nothing* ."[68] England and Spain have fallen from a glorious past into a modern social and political morass, a polarization of rulers and ruled, in which, in Don Alvaro's eyes, the oppressed are animalistic, and the dominant are a new class of men without pride in their respective nations, and so seeming to lack a positive identity.

As an ex-Civil Guard, Don Alvaro was of "that legion of incorruptible police-soldiers" who "had never taken ... money as baksheesh": "He had belonged to a great kid-gloved military elite, with power to shoot all suspect citizens at sight, after a formal challenge. Once that, always that! One does not change. *Basta*! One does not become as other men once one has been *that*" (13). Alvaro harks back to the era of "great gentlemen" in whose name he wielded the life-and-death power of an élite military policeman, and has little taste for the present clash of abstract political forces: "All crimes of politics were potentially condoned as soon as committed – by *other* politicos of whatever colour, who understood that their own skins might not always be safe" (11). Hardcaster suggests to Alvaro that England, a "great nation, of portentously rich caballeros" (12), had "gone the way of Spain" in this regard. When he uncovers a plot to spring Hardcaster from his prison, he waits in ambush, killing one of his own guards as an accomplice and badly wounding Percy in the leg.

After recovering from the amputation of his leg in a Spanish hospital, Percy returns to England, where he is welcomed as a revolutionary hero by the artistic-intellectual élite of the Communist Party in London. The point of view is given over, for the five central sections of the novel, to several groups of characters within and on the fringes of London left-wing politics. As in the Spanish context of Part One, the issues determining characters' attitudes and actions are three: power, money, and love, but with an additional, non-materialistic factor: art and intellectual culture in general.

Victor Stamp, a mediocre Australian artist, has neither money nor talent, but he has a double measure of his companion Margot's love. Tristram Phipps, a successful artist, and his wife Gillian have the power, through his talent and their privileged backgrounds, to forgo both the pursuit of money and the conventionalities of love in the name of communist principles. Money matters, however, bring them into contact with Jack Cruze, whose financial expertise underwrites his single-minded dedication to sexual conquest. Sean O'Hara, a writer who marries for money and status, joins with Abershaw to exploit politics for financial gain, and is connected through him with Freddie Salmon, who uses art for a similar end.

Percy's working-class origins have produced in him a radical political commitment that embraces the cause of violent revolution. He rejects all traditional social, cultural, and religious as well as political values. Yet, oddly, his being shot in Spain comes as a rude shock. He had never thought of himself as vulnerable to the violence he fomented. The communist intellectuals in London are awed by his being wounded, and he is treated with near-religious reverence by those who prefer talking politics to practising them. Gillian Phipps' reverence for Percy takes an erotic form, but her attempt to seduce him turns sour when she discovers the implications of revolutionary propaganda for her own type of "mental communism" and commitment to "bourgeois honesty." Jack, who had been waiting his chance to tumble Jill, is summoned, and, out of sexual jealousy, administers a brutal kicking to Percy's still unhealed leg.

Percy, then, is a double victim in his service to the revolution, first on the Spanish and then on the home front. Despite the authenticity of his political commitment, however, both of his injuries are provoked by very dubious political motives. Don Alvaro, as it turns out, is also corrupt, his honour curiously offended by Percy's employment of his subordinate, Serafion, instead of himself to effect the escape. Gillian is discovered to have, in both senses, a completely "romanticized" communism, rooted in *haut bourgeois* disdain for the working class in whose name she is, as a communist, sowing sedition. She employs Jack, the son of a policeman and a financial advisor to her capitalist enemies, to teach Percy his place. This injury on top of an injury is doubly jarring to Percy's revolutionary commitment. Received at the instigation of fellow-travelling communists, in his own country and under embarrassing circumstances, it has all the rudeness but none of the heroic glamour of his Spanish exploits. In a dispirited state, Percy accepts the leadership of a dubious gun-running mission to Spain, a business deal that, despite its helpfulness to the Spanish left, he knows has no political sanction (288).

Percy's disillusionment renders him vulnerable to O'Hara and Abershaw's exploitation of his knowledge of Spain and its politics. He does not undertake the project for money, but for some more deep-seated and private reason. After hearing O'Hara and Abershaw's proposition, "Percy was left exhausted on the sofa, scowling into the twilight. In a few minutes he was sleeping soundly, the frown still on his face. Then, after an interval, the frown disappeared. A gratified smile flowered upon the lip of the dreaming Percy. Something had pleased him" (288–9). The satisfaction Percy takes in the plan is secret, even unconscious. These are the closing lines of Part Six and of the London sequence of the novel. We next find Percy at the Spanish border, accompanied by Victor and Margot, enmeshed in events that end in his own incarceration in a Spanish jail, a result that produces in him the following gratified reflections:

No illusions with regard to abstract justice disturbed the upright cynicism of his outlook ... To *himself*, at least, he never pretended that he was hardly used. He accepted, for his political opinions, the status of a game – a game, of course, of life and death ... There was even a certain crisp logic about finding himself back in a Spanish prison which appealed to him – it was so grim that it had a logical fitness ... Was it not in the last analysis his proper place? (375).

At the root, then, of his political commitment, Percy cherishes a highly romantic, quasi-religious view of himself as the political martyr. The indignity of the episode with Jack and Gillian is erased, and he is again within a setting that fits his self-image and for which he understands his role: "Heavily clamped upon his brick-red countenance, held in position by every muscle that responded to Righteous Wrath, was a mask which entirely succeeded the workaday face. It was the mask of THE INJURED PARTY (model for militant agents in distress)" (380). This is the final page of the novel. Percy, between his two Spanish imprisonments, has learned something essential about himself and has, we might say, brought his political vocation to a full realization. But into his consciousness of the "logical fitness" of events intrudes the knowledge that Victor and Margot, his unfortunate accomplices, have been killed trying to cross back into France. The accusing voice of Margot sounds in his conscience: "A strained and hollow voice ... tender and halting ... was talking in his ears ... denouncing him out of the past ... singling him out as a man who led people into mortal danger"(380). The final lines of the novel convey the effect of her words: "And the eyes in the mask of THE INJURED PARTY dilated in a spasm of astonished self-pity. And down the front of the mask rolled a sudden tear, which fell upon the dirty floor of the prison" (380). In this final vivid image, Lewis offers an image of the tortured modern mind imprisoned by the "logical fitness" of ideology. In Percy, he represents that mind as ruled by an unconscious drive whose hidden self-image is a romantic, secularized religious dream, rooted in a self-pitying *ressentiment* at injuries received.

Before exploring more closely how Lewis portrays this state of mind in *The Revenge for Love*, it would be well to observe that in writing it he has departed from the aesthetic he arrived at at the end of *Men Without Art*. To recall his position: both art and life should be "considered purely as a game" in that "no value can attach to it *for itself*, but only in so far as it is well-played or badly-played." Like other civilized observances, then, art is simply "a discipline, a symbolic discipline" (291). This notion of art and life as mere "proficient representation," untouched by any notion of ethical value, is an exact description of Lewis's portrayal of Percy Hardcaster. Percy plays the political game like an artist, "like a painter fond of self-portraiture" (377–8). He is the consummate ideological performer: "Swollen with an affected speechlessness, Percy proceeded to give a sculpturesque impersonation of THE INJURED PARTY. His cellmates watched him surreptitiously, with an admiration it was out of their power to withhold" (380). From this "sculpturesque" mask emerges the tear with which Lewis, in the final lines of *The Revenge for Love*, punctures both the "upright cynicism" of his character and the serene impersonality of his own, hard-won philosophy of art.

In the novel, the means for the overturning of Hardcaster's perception is the character of Margot, a pathetic figure despite, or perhaps because of, her passionate love for Victor Stamp. Victor is an unsuccessful – because a largely untalented – artist, an Australian condescended to by his London left-wing art circle because of his robust disrespect for authority and convention. Everyone "likes" Victor and Margot because they pose no threat, since they lack money, talent and social position. When Margot's job ends, the couple is destitute, since Victor can sell no paintings. He is forced to accept work from Abershaw's friend, Freddie Salmon, as an art "faker," a forger of paintings to be passed off as genuine by Salmon at a huge profit.

Victor is encouraged to do so because his friend Tristram is also involved in the racket. The most talented painter in London at the moment, Phipps is unable to make a living by his work, and his communist principles allow him to justify the forging. Victor, lacking both Tristram's talent and peculiar values, resents the job, destroying the "Van Gogh" self-portrait, he is working on: "Throwing the picture down against the wall, he trod into the centre of it, putting all his weight upon his foot, which tore through the canvas, the ragged edge of the gap gripping him about the calf" (266). This act somewhat disillusions his employer: "'"By their works ye shall know them." There is his!' Freddie indicated with his finger what first had been the work of Stamp's hand and had ended by becoming the work of Stamp's foot. '*Victor Stamp – his mark!*'" (271). Tristram tries to satisfy Freddie by explaining of Victor that "his is the religion of will," or, more plainly, "'His attitude towards the world is what, if he were not a Great Power, would be called typically that of the *Have-not*" (272–3). For Tristram, privileged by natural gifts and social background (son of a clergyman, Oxford-educated), Victor, the colonial mediocrity, is the quintessential underdog and victim of *ressentiment*. Abershaw, who had gotten Victor the job, reassures Freddie that "'Mr. Stamp, however, will come to regret his day's work'" (274).

It is precisely by using Victor's "mark" that Abershaw conspires with O'Hara to exploit him. Enlisting his Australian brawn in the arms-smuggling deal, O'Hara and Abershaw contrive to put letters into the hands of the Spanish police that indicate that Victor is the chief smuggler, letters on which Abershaw has forged Victor's signature. One of these letters is discovered by Percy as they wait on the French side of the Spanish border. Margot asks why Victor's name has been forged on the letter:

'I think, Victor, I must be very dense today,' said Margot. 'If it isn't a cheque -'

'Or a last will and testament,' suggested Percy, turning his head away as he made the remark, and staring at a Civil Guard, at whom he often stared, and who often contemplated him.

'Is it a will, Victor – have you made your will, or has somebody else forged one? Is that it?'

'No, it's about machine-guns,' said Victor. (319)

The forgery, is, in a sense, both a will and a cheque. It disposes of Victor, placing him in the hands of the Spanish authorities, and will make for O'Hara and Abershaw a tidy sum. Percy is subliminally conscious of its ominous implications; he jokes uneasily about wills and gazes at a Civil Guard, another of whom Victor will later kill in trying to escape, for which (because of his involvement with Victor) Percy will be treated as a criminal rather than a "politico."

The letter is about machine guns, euphemistically referred to in code as "typewriters." Abershaw and O'Hara do not deal in machines for creative purposes, but for war, their own creative abilities expended in the art of forgery.[69] As Margot reflected about these two, "They lay in wait, of course, for a man of Victor's stamp, until he was up against it ... Help him to work honestly they *would* not ... But they would give a leg-up on the ladder of *fraud* ... They hated his honesty. They hated all honesty so bitterly, because it countered all their plans ... that they might take it over and rule the roost, with a hand of iron" (182). It is Victor's "stamp," his antipodean energy and "will," of which O'Hara and Abershaw would defraud him. They, not Victor, are the true worshippers of will, because they have none themselves and are filled with envy and *ressentiment* toward those who have power, which in their "hands" would be "iron," that is, machine guns. Victor's identity is raw energy; a stamp of his foot is his signature; the "leg-up" they would give him is the sort with which Percy Hardcaster is intimate. When he has neutralized Margot's objections to the forged letter, he orders drinks, and then: "A mangy and vindictive cat had stealthily approached Victor's legs, and now it drove its claws through the trousers into the flesh with enthusiastic precision '... Its claws must be crawling with bacilli' said Percy, stroking it and offering it his wooden leg to scratch. He laughed. 'I'm safe! Have a scratch, pussikin!'" (332–3). The experienced Percy draws Victor farther and farther into mortal danger on the basis of Victor's and his own lack of sensitivity. When the two men try to dismiss the forged letter, Margot is not taken in:

'It does matter a great deal – I consider that it matters very much indeed! Margot retorted with such vigour that both Victor and Percy gave a slight start of surprise, as if something had pricked them in a sensitive spot …

Then Percy laughed a short and formal laugh, of bitter but indulgent finality. Margot had imported an attitude into the discussion that was so self-evidently confined to herself and to women in general that no response was required or indeed possible. (322–3)

Victor is equally resistant to Margot's alarming view of affairs: "She sought to impose [the objects of her fancy] upon the objective reality. To this, as an artist, he somewhat objected. Here was the *sur-real* – he had nourished it unawares in his own bosom! … Everything had become involved in this brutal invasion of the external plane by the internal plane" (324). Victor, like Percy, "was at a loss to cope with" (324) Margot's "Unconscious" (323), with such a "brutal invasion … by the internal plane." "For the two Margots in question had as it were coalesced" (323): what Percy had seen as Margot, the individual woman, and Margot, the representative of womankind. Victor finds security from Margot's challenge in Percy's masculine leadership: "[His eye] consorted with the latter's eye for that compartment of a *foot flashing* second during which Percy's had sought his. The calm message set Percy's mind at rest" (332; my emphasis).

Victor deceives Margot and heads into Spanish territory with his cache. She discovers the ruse and leaps a train to intercept him. She arrives before him, discovers that the police lie in wait, and warns him. As the two flee in a car back toward the border, Victor cannot understand why O'Hara and Abershaw would bother to betray him. As he says, befuddled, "'I'm *nobody*'" (358). Margot sees him differently: "And was not her Victor *the symbolic man*, as you might call it, to a fault? She grasped quite well the fact that he *stood for something*. Not for nothing, anything but that … She could not in any case have loved a nobody. But she could *love* a *symbol*" (358). In this she understands why Victor is in the position of the "hunted man": "But Victor, *he* poor chap did not know that he was *it* " (359). As Tristram had put it, Victor was, like "Cromagnon" and "Neanderthal" man, the "Kipling Man," "semi-extinct or … becoming so" (359). As Margot saw, "This sort of Man was in fact an outlaw …" (359). Margot was herself the faded remnant of the Victorian period, "the sigh of the last rose, and whisper of the last lily, when the Flower-haters have decreed the extinction of all luxury weeds'" (360).

The reflections come to Margot as they careen through the Spanish hills toward the border, but they are intercepted by a Civil Guard, planted in the road. She shouts, "'Stop!' It was *her* duty, too, to halt him. But it was quite unavailing to shout at *events* – at events three seconds off. As well talk to Time and tell it where to stand! ... But why would not Victor stop? He would not stop because he *could* not. It was this machine – *it* would not stop: he was attached to a plunging twenty-ton magnet, which rushed to meet the lifted gun" (361). Margot was caught in "this telescopic closing-up of the time – of all that separated the man that was a gun, and the man that was a car" (361). These two were "compelled by their natures to clash": "This was a fatality that came into play the moment it was machines, not men, that mattered. But she could see the end of it as plain as two and two make four. And her teeth came out grinning against the shock, like a cat's at bay" (362). That "Victor was a boy who was fond of cars she had always known," but with this one he countered Margot's "bacilli" in his system and "tromped her with a machine" (364).

By associating her with cats, Lewis suggests Margot's spiritual, even witch-like qualities: "Nature had enabled her to see a symbol, where another would just see a pair of trousers ... by second sight. That was how she had surprised his secret" (359). She was aware that her love for him had a noxious effect: "It was because *she* was there that no pleasant thing ever happened. It was *the revenge for love*! This, on the part of fate ... There was no way out, unless she could kill love. And to do that she must first kill herself. But even then love would not die! Once to have been loved as she did Victor was enough ... He was a marked man ... *the man who had been loved* ... she *knew*!" (70). The clear-sightedness of Margot's love is envied by "the gods" themselves, who "had a hatred for love," for "it was *the way* that she loved that was at the bottom of the matter" (70). It enabled her to see the unreality of everything but love, since it was the only thing that could not be killed. As such a permanent possession, it provoked the envy and smoldering resentment of those who had everything but love: power, privilege, money, talent. She could see it in the attitude toward her and Victor of their London political friends: "It was a mad notion, but it was just as if they had engaged in a battle of wills, to decide who should possess most *reality* – just as men fought each other for money, or fought each other for food" (177).

It is this clear vision of things that particularizes Margot and at the same time makes her into a representative woman. Both Percy and Victor resort to denial and deception in order to avoid acknowledging her. Significantly, Victor drives her from their hotel room by bringing out his largest painting, in order to sneak across the border with the arms (333). Victor's painting is a matter of empty technique, "of pure chance," of "tossing red blocks with the Devil for his life," rather than of "any personal skill on his part" (90). In the end, Victor makes his mark with the car; he "trompés" Margot "with a machine," killing the Civil Guard. As Margot knew, when it is mere technique, "machines, not men" (362), that matter, death is inevitable.

Percy, however, is half-awake, at least subliminally aware of the authenticity hidden within Margot's attenuated frame. He follows her on the train to intercept Victor, and deliberately gives himself up to the police to allow Victor and Margot to escape. Though satisfied with the grim "logical fitness" of his second Spanish imprisonment, he casts a hard critical eye over his mistake in landing there: "Mateu was right! … Perhaps after all he did somewhat suffer from a weakness that was very common. Women after all were perhaps his weak spot! It looked uncommonly like it. For why had he followed Margot as he had?" (378). Looking back, we can indeed see that Percy's hard knocks have each, in some way, involved women. If he had been more attentive to the Spanish peasant girl, he would have avoided Don Alvaro's bullet and saved his leg (and Serafion's life). Gillian, of course, was a more genuine affair of the heart, for which incaution he paid dearly. ("'All for nothing' … 'All for love!'" [281]) In Margot, he meets a woman who sees "something" rather than "nothing" in what she loves, even if it is only a "symbol." It is her "strained and hollow voice" that echoes behind the mask of "THE INJURED PARTY": "It was denouncing him out of the past, where alone now it was able to articulate; it was singling him out as a man who led people into mortal danger, people who were dear beyond expression to the possessor of the passionate, the artificial, the unreal, yet penetrating voice, and crying to him now to give back, she implored him, the young man, Absalom, whose life he had had in his keeping, and who had somehow, unaccountably, been lost, out of the world and out of Time!" (380).

Margot's voice is able to "single Percy out" and reveal to him his true nature, as a man possessing heart and conscience, behind the mask of the ideologue, the professional martyr and agent of revenge and *ressentiment*. Life as seen by Margot is not a battle of abstract wills, a game of chance, whose stakes are *nothing* – a "false bottom" in a machine.[70] In the opening lines of the novel, Don Alvaro pronounces that "'we are only free once in our lives'": "'That is when at last we gaze into the bottom of the heart of our beloved and find that it is false – like everything else in the world!'" (7) At the end, Percy is staring into the bottom of his own heart, knowing it to be false. If the whole world is unjust to "THE INJURED PARTY" it is his doing, responsible as he is for the loss of the innocent "out of the world and out of Time."

Although by no means all of the structural and thematic issues of *The Revenge for Love* have been touched on here, it is clear that in this novel Lewis displays a command of both character and plot that far surpasses other works of his discussed already. The reconciliation with dualism and the acceptance of a dialectical play of opposites in art and life in *Men Without Art* seems to have freed Lewis to actually *perform* as a novelist. He says in that work, "I am a performer. It is as a performer that I shall speak" (10). In *Revenge*, perhaps more than in any other of his works, he does not even speak, but rather performs. The evolution of this novel from the early form of *Jack's Tale* into its published version is a striking illustration of how the work was shaped as it was being written, by the very process of writing. In *Blasting and Bombardiering*, after observing that he had developed from a novelist into a philosopher-critic, he could say, "I have now married the novelist to the philosopher" (5). We can see in *Revenge* how he takes his theory of art as symbolic discipline and thinks it through, not as philosophy or art theory, but, to use his term, as "life," the world.

In *The Revenge for Love*, Lewis thinks fully with his imagination. This is corroborated by the fact that his theory of art and life as game is systematically satirized in the novel in the characters of Victor and Percy. The acceptance of duality in *Men Without Art* seems to release his capacity to imagine the practical consequences of the notion of art as symbolic discipline for living in the world. These are indeed Lewis's terms in *Men Without Art*: "All forms of art of a permanent order are intended not only to please and excite ... but to call into play the entire human capacity – for sensation, reflection, imagination, and will. We judge a work of art, ultimately, with reference to its capacity to effect this total mobilization of our faculties. The novel is no exception to this rule" (8–9). The "total mobilization of faculties" effected by Lewis in *Revenge* fundamentally changes his art theory. Victor, the art technician, and Percy, the ideologue, are both dangerous and fragmented persons, in league with each other against Margot, with no regard for the welfare of themselves or those involved with them.

In short, the "god-like prerogative" of "wild nihilism" that they exercise is seen in its very nature as destructive. Here, some of the subtlety of Lewis's insight in the novel emerges. Percy and Victor are both perceived to be dominated by *ressentiment*. They are have-nots and injured parties. They naïvely draw upon themselves, as a result, the *ressentiment* of such as O'Hara, Abershaw, Freddie Salmon, Gillian, and Jack Cruze, who hate Victor and Margot's "honesty" (182) and Percy's political commitment. Their own *ressentiment* functions as a weakness, as primarily *self*-destruction, and as a tool for the violence and greed of the merely self-interested. In this, we can see Lewis reflecting on the implications of treating art and life like a game, and discovering in such an attitude, even in those who are sincerely investing themselves, as do Victor and Percy, in art and politics, a moral culpability that he had earlier sought to exclude from all consideration.

Where we can see Lewis functioning freely, however, not only as a thinker but as an artist, is in the character of Margot. She presents a perspective on events and characters – and on the principles they represent – that is not anticipated in the theory itself. Insofar as she is the character who actively knows and sees in the novel, and in doing so learns and becomes an integrated thinker and doer,[71] she is able to speak, to "articulate" with a "penetrating" voice the question of value. She sees a symbolic, cultural, and artistic value in Victor and a moral value in Percy, a capacity to take active responsibility,[72] simply because she is animated by love.

Margot is that point of view in the novel where interior and exterior, thought and action, art and politics, coalesce. The drive that forces her beyond her own very obvious limitations is experienced by Victor and Percy as a "brutal invasion of the external plane by the internal plane" (324). By her affective and intellectual interiority (her love and her "second sight"), she effects the "total mobilization of faculties" that Lewis demanded from a work of art. But Margot, moved by her love, is responsible for the deaths of herself and Victor (and of a Civil Guard), as well as the capture of Percy. She is "love" in a world of "machines," and so fails to see the consequences. Lewis embodies in Margot a critique of the aesthetic theory of *Men Without Art*.

By uniting feeling and intellect, subjectivity and objectivity, Margot represents a perspective beyond the dialectical play of opposites arrived at in *Men Without Art*. She represents a principle which transcends art and life as game. Her love for Victor gives him a symbolic value of which he was not himself aware. It makes him a person, as it were, despite himself, in the very midst of his destruction of both their lives. Her love for Victor leads Percy, in and through his delusive martyr-complex, to see that he is not only the innocent sufferer, but the cause of innocent suffering. In *The Revenge for Love*, Lewis is performing a thought which he never formulated theoretically.

There is a complexity to Lewis's representation of these ideas and principles which, indeed, is difficult to fully articulate. He allows the strange and halting quality of Margot's love only within a context of failure, death, and imprisonment. Indeed, this love is presented as the force that attracts to itself destruction, by exciting the spirit of *revenge* – but it also brings down vengeance on those who are loved: "Once to have been loved as she did Victor was enough – it was compromising to the *n*th degree. He was a marked man!" (70) This is *"Victor Stamp – his mark"* (271) rather than the faked Van Gogh through which he put his foot. It is his being "compromised" and "stamped" by Margot's love that makes him, along with her, the "mark" for the ill will of such as Abershaw and O'Hara: "But she had the strongest feeling that their intentions ... were *not* charitable ... It was *their* reality, that of Victor and herself, that was marked down to be discouraged and abolished" (176–7).

Motivated by her love and the greater insight that accompanies it, Margot interferes in events as they unfold at the Spanish border. After the Civil Guard is killed, "She saw that the very worst had happened. And after that, last of all, she perceived ... that it was herself that had been to blame! She, Margot, was at the bottom of this adventure!" (368). Margot wonders is she "possibly a more dangerous sort of Ophelia – one who did *not* go away? One who, on the contrary, blundered into action, with her ill-judged and untimely interference?" (369).

Lewis does not spare Margot. The principle of value she represents is seen to function completely within the contingency of her weak, timid, and artificial character. Her capacity to love Victor and to see him as a symbolic value "was at the bottom of his adventure" (368). Her love itself has the character of *ressentiment*. She saw that she and Victor were engaged with the likes of those at O'Hara's party "in a battle of wills, to decide who should possess the most reality ..." But what if everyone, including Victor, were unreal? "Her love would be a passion of her brain: with no more stuff to it than the rest of the rigmarole – if nothing in time *could* be real, as Victor so often would say, when he ... started explaining to her all about *Time* – about 'becoming' which was not *being*: and she could quite follow that of course – for your self of last week ... did not really exist in the way you existed in the moment you were thinking. And yet it had existence, and in so for as it *had*, it took away from what you possessed of reality at any selected moment" (177). Victor and

Margot too, then, were engaged in a "battle of wills" over "who should possess most reality." Was it Victor's self of the moment, or Margot's atemporal identity? Margot was not going to be defeated: "The mere notion of a Victor as a shadow-person distressed her so much that she grappled him to herself, so that he, at least, should not be outside herself among the unreals" (177). Victor is the innocent, susceptible to the fashionable arguments about art and identity that were being used by those bent on political destruction and financial self-interest. Margot is prepared "to use violence if necessary" (177) to secure Victor for her "reality": "As his muscles played about like fishes under his skin, she tried to catch them with her ever-timid fingers ... as if to arrest life, and its reality as well, if she could only catch one and hold it still *in her hand*, extracting it from its bloody element" (177). "This, yes, this alone is *revenge* itself: the will's antipathy toward time and time's 'It was.'"[73] Margot's "ever-timid fingers" harbour an ill will toward time, that "bloody element" in which everything appears only to pass away. Her "love" for Victor imposes on him her "second sight," in which he is seen as a "symbolic man," a character in a narrative history of which he, "poor chap" has no idea. Margot's love, then, as an act of will imposes and "marks" Victor from the outside, stamping itself on him and functioning as an irritant in the smooth, undifferentiated flow of his hapless becoming: "It was *the way* that she loved that was at the bottom of the matter" (70). It is another forgery. For "Victor Stamp," we should read "Margot."

Thus, at the most fundamental level of *The Revenge for Love*, the apparent distinction between the forces of selfishness and destruction and those of love is seen, in fact, to be relative. Lewis carries his exploration of *ressentiment* to remarkable lengths, allowing us to envision a transcendent love that synthesizes and lends ethical value to the dialectical play of feeling and intellect, art and politics, self-interest and ideology. But at a more profound level, love is itself seen as conditioned by the desire and will that manifest it. The dialectic is not transcended, but maintained with a fundamental reorientation. Its relativity – its non-ethical, purely "symbolic play" – is impregnated with seriousness and value.[74] Going beyond the static dualistic distinction between symbolic and ethical values in *Men Without Art*, Lewis has represented the truly *artistic* values of tragedy and comedy in *The Revenge for Love*. He has done so by demonstrating that, as in Margot's "unreal, yet penetrating, voice" (380), even the highest values devalue themselves, and the mechanism of this self-devaluation is *ressentiment*.

5 The Logic of Representation: *Self Condemned*

From 1918 to 1936, Lewis was occupied in sorting out the impact of the First World War on his artistic career. The war forced on him a wholesale revaluation of his original artistic and philosophical concerns, in the light of the "political education"[1] initiated by his active service as an artillery officer. In *The Revenge for Love*, Lewis managed to reconcile the two strains of his career – art and politics – in a unified work of art which explored the interrelation of subjective and objective, personal and historical reality. On the basis of the objectification of these forces achieved in *The Revenge for Love*, Lewis was able to turn, in *Blasting and Bombardiering*, to a subjective revaluation of the war's impact on his career. "This book," he says in *Blasting and Bombardiering*, "is about what happened to me in the Great War": "The War is such a tremendous landmark that locally it imposes itself upon our computations of time like the birth of Christ. We say 'pre-war' and 'post-war,' rather as we say B.C. or A.D. This book is about the war, with a bit of pre-war and post-war sticking to it fore and aft" (1). Later in the book, however, he asserts, "My life as an artist and my life as a soldier intertwine, in this unaffected narrative. I show, too, going from the particular to the general, how War and Art in those days mingled, the features of the latter as stern as – if not sterner than – the former. This book is Art – War – Art, in three panels. War is the centre panel. But for me it was only a part of Art: my sort of life – the life of the 'intellect' – come to life. A disappointing imitation. I preferred the real thing: namely Art" (63). We have already noted his observation of "how like art is to war, I mean 'modernist' art," and how he wished he could "get away from war": "Writing about war may be the best way to shake the accursed thing off by putting it in its place, as an unseemly joke" (4).

On the one hand, war is that "tremendous landmark" from which Lewis would like to get away, and on the other it is an epiphenomenon, a lesser "imitation," within and subordinate to art. "With me war and art have been mixed up from the start" (4), he says, so that *Blasting and Bombardiering* is clearly itself a kind of battleground in which he re-examines the impact of the Great War in an attempt to secure the hegemony of art in his life.

In *The Revenge for Love*, Lewis gained a confidence in his capacity to achieve artistic control, a confidence which asserts itself in the first paragraph of *Blasting* when he declares that "a good biography is of course a sort of novel" (1). It springs from the same objectivity and control that the artist exerts over his material: "Don't you often feel about some phase of your existence that it requires going over with a fine comb and putting in order?... It is desirable to establish a principle of order as we go along in this chaos of instinct called 'living,' is it not? That is the principle upon which this self-history is composed. I rope in a given area ... With this selected area or section I deal as would a tidy god" (6). In this passage, we can see Lewis leaping from an immanent to a transcendent relation to his past.

To begin with, he says, we are immanent in our experience. Experience is a "chaos of instinct" within which it is "desirable" to establish a principle of order. That is, we need to discover a unity or pattern *within* our experience. But Lewis uses the word "establish," as if the principle of order came from outside the chaos and was imposed on it. The result of this view is an unbridgeable gap between instinct and intellect, experience and reflection, which carries Lewis forward to claim that he "ropes in" an area of his life (roughly 1914 to 1926) toward which he has the completely extrinsic and transcendent relation of a "tidy god": "The god was of course mortal at the time he experienced the events in question. Having gained immortality, he feels he had better go back and have a look around – like a week-end trip to a Flanders Battlefield, more curious than sentimental" (6).

For Lewis to describe this return to his war experience in *Blasting and Bombardiering* as "curious" is bravado, dissimulation, or weak irony masking the underlying seriousness (and even aggression) of the work. He had already admitted how the war "imposes itself on our computations of time" (1), and how depressing it was "to con-

sider how as an artist one is always holding the mirror up to politics" (4). His ambivalence is embedded in his metaphors. Writing
about war is the attempt "to shake the accursed thing off." Lewis
wants his subject to seem worthy of serious attention, but he also
wants to maintain a breezy objectivity and irony, "by putting it in
its place as an unseemly joke" (4). He says that "the War and the
'post-war' are over long ago. They can be written about with detachment, as things past and done with" (2). Rather, it is clear that
for him they must be written about because they are *not* past and
done with, but still, in 1937, forces that have imposed on his persona
and raised fundamental questions of art and identity. The ambivalent tone of *Blasting and Bombardiering* indicates a reluctance on Lewis's part to give over the control that a thorough acknowledgement
of these questions would entail. At the same time, this reluctance
expresses itself in a style whose lightness of touch gives to *Blasting*
a readability, and also a humane power to move, that rank it among
Lewis's more readable works.

In "The Observer Observed: Distancing the Self in Autobiography," Shirley Neuman demonstrates how in *Blasting and Bombardiering* Lewis has "sidestepped" what she calls "the paradox of
alterity":[2] "The genre posits an autobiographer who presents himself
from the point of view of the self and *not* the *other*; it demands an
autobiographer who must use conventions and, in so doing, treat
himself as *other* in order to make the self accessible to readers" (323).
Neuman effectively documents Lewis's successful use of the
metaphor of the "observer observed" as a "series of displacements
away from the first person" (329), displacements that overcome the
paradox of alterity by joining the readers and the narrator in a subjective "we":

Successfully used, the ruse places the autobiographer beyond the paradoxes
of alterity and veracity by incorporating a number of genuine embodiments
of alterity *into* the text rather than splitting the self ... He concludes on just
this familiar note which simultaneously makes him *external* to himself and
suggests that the *reader* should have *internalized* the experiences of the text:
"And I hope that ... as my sight is keen ... by following my body round,
as we have done, some portion of my experience may have passed over
into you." (329)

In other words, Lewis's "ruse" has the effect of placing his readers
in the same subjective relation to their own experience that he *appears*
to have taken to his.

However, as I have already suggested, while this strategy may be
technically successful, it dissimulates the true purpose of Lewis's

autobiography: to engage in battle the two personae of "blaster" and "bombardier," the art-warrior and the war artist, and to achieve a victory for the "real thing: namely Art" (63). Neuman does not pursue Lewis's avoidance of the "paradox of historicity," in which the autobiographer "describes his past selves because they provide a developmental continuity with his present self; at the same time, he makes those past selves the object of mature description, retrospective analysis, judgement and irony, that is, he treats them as separate from his present self and defines himself *against* them" (322). By declaring that "a good biography is of course a sort of novel" (1), Lewis sidesteps the temporal paradox by simply resolving it in his own favour – that is, in favour of the narratorial persona's "observational," god-like objectivity, as if he were the omniscient narrator of a novel.

As an instance of Lewis's effective use of metaphor of the observer observed, Neuman cites a passage treating his days as an artillery officer, in which, in attempting "to reach his observation post (or O. Pip), he finds himself first observed then fired upon by enemy observers in a sausage balloon above him": "What was the matter with this O. Pip was obviously that it was *itself* observed by another O. Pip – but one above it, suspended in the air … An expert Observer, vertically above him, was observing any Observer who might take it into his head to use this particular spot for his so-called observations" (327). The narrator, Neuman says, enlists the reader to join him in the *metaphorical* position of the observers in the sausage-balloon and to share their "god-like advantage" (162) over Lewis's past self as "observer." In other words, the spatial metaphor (of alterity) is displaced toward the temporal metaphor (of historicity) in order to dissimulate the paradox inherent in Lewis observing his past selves as if from outside (i.e. as if from *above*) in the text of *Blasting and Bombardiering*.[3]

Neuman's focus on Lewis's metaphor of the observer observed is a central insight, and it can help us to go beyond technique to the intention behind *Blasting and Bombardiering* as a whole, so that the significance of technique in this work can be grasped in the context of Lewis's evolving career.

Particularly noteworthy in Lewis's experience of the observer in the sausage-balloon is the contrast between the impersonal scale of the military technology and the personal nature of this attack: "I should think you could count on the fingers of your hands the soldiers who have been fired at in this *personal* way by weapons of such dimensions – and a whole battery of them … Men have been hunted with rifles ... But what men before or since have been hunted by a how-itzer?" (164; 166–7). Within the context of the war, then, Lewis's metaphor of the "observer observed" points to the loss of ordinary identity of the autonomous citizen, who is forced into uniform, into military discipline and group identity, and made a participant in destructive mass action. Within this alienation, Lewis – the avant-garde "observer" and critic of peacetime culture – experiences the role of "observed" as if the massive machine of war were aimed directly at him personally. As the militant artist of *Blast*, he had seen himself as the guardian of the spiritual freedom and identity of the person in modern mass culture. As the artist-military officer, he is the "hunted." The impersonal machine of war is directed against him as if he represented "personality" itself, the single element that could not be assimilated by the war machine, and the principle against which it is violently directed.

Lewis survived his term as a bombardier and, while on leave in London, had himself transferred to the Canadian forces as a war artist. Military procedure forced him to return to his unit at the front to be "seconded" as a British officer: "This episode was not without its grimness. The sensation of a desertion came back to me with redoubled force, more as regards the men than the officers" (194). Lewis was wary of his good fortune in being born with the talent to paint, and, by curious circumstance, as a Canadian citizen able to benefit from Lord Beaverbrook's endowment of war artists: "Destiny, I felt, might regard it as a joke in excellent taste to blow my head off, just as I was receiving my formal Godspeed from my o.c." (194).

Reflecting on his release, Lewis expands on the metaphor of the observer observed: "I am never sure that there is not an Observer up above us, like the Observer in the sausage-balloon, but yet more advantageously placed: one who is quite capable of setting a battery on to one, and in a word, causing the fire to be more *personal* than otherwise it would be. If that is the case, and if he was watching me, he did not on that occasion molest me" (194). Lewis's war experience turns his perspective as an artist inside out. Far from declaring and representing the freedom and creativity of the human condition, the artist as military officer becomes conscious of the great Observer, of the possibility of a higher-than-human power which holds all things, and the artist himself, in its power. Lewis gains an ultimate experience of himself as *object*, as an "observed" whose actions, far from original and creative, are subordinate to a will higher than his own.

His sense of himself as artist is curiously challenged in this process: "Perhaps I am *half* a romantic. Half my mind was elated at the congenial prospect of twirling my brush once more and bringing to life upon the canvas the painted battery. But half my mind was forlorn as I said good-bye to my untidy little batman. I was the heartless young squire bidding a last farewell to the simple village maid he has betrayed, beside the cottage gate" (195). The circumstances bring home to him a natural injustice and élitism in art, and uncomfortably demonstrate in a subtle duality the inherent romanticism of his own view of the artist's role. The very capacity through which, in *Blast*, he sought to liberate modern culture[4] becomes a means, in war, for a "betrayal," a "romantic" indulgence of self which is at the same time demonstrated as delusive, because it is not "original" or "creative." It is "permitted" by the great Observer, and so is robbed of autonomy. (The paradox is also literal: he is creating paintings of scenes of destruction.)

This complete reversal, in the context of war, of the significance of art and artist constitutes the fundamental challenge that Lewis attempts to meet in *Blasting and Bombardiering*. As a "phase" of his existence, it requires "going over" and "putting in order"; it cries "out for inspection perhaps. Yes, and *revision*" (6). *Blasting* is an attempt to reassert the divine creative imperative of the romantic artist. The war, Lewis says, "imposes itself on our computations of time like the birth of Christ" (1). As an advent of the divine, it must be put in its place by writing about it (4). Neuman refers to the metaphor of the observer observed as a ruse which sidesteps the structural paradoxes of autobiography. We can now see clearly that these structural paradoxes in *Blasting* overlay a more fundamental autobiographical paradox of content. Is Lewis the "observer" or the "observed"? As prewar artist, he was observer. As warrior, he was observed, by the enemy and by "destiny." Is Lewis the subject of his own consciousness or the object of others' – or, ultimately, of an Other?

As Neuman demonstrates, Lewis's choice and employment of structural metaphor is wonderfully apt, but there is a question as to whether it succeeds on the level of intention or content. In contending with the war's impact on his identity in *Blasting*, Lewis needs to demonstrate that, in the postwar period, he is able to *transform* that experience of himself as object into a more complete vision, one that subjectively *contains* it. As he says: "This book is Art–War–Art, in three panels" (63). His assertion that war "was only a part of Art" needs to be demonstrated in *Blasting* if the work is to succeed.

The third part of Lewis's triptych in *Blasting and Bombardiering*, which according to his schema is devoted to postwar art, should, then, attempt a synthetic transformation of the dualism of prewar art and its displacement by war itself. But his characterization of the dualism fails to transform it into the necessary dialectical play of opposites. Looking back at the halcyon days of nascent pre-war modernism, he says,

What I think history will say about the 'Men of 1914' is that they represent an attempt to get away from romantic art into classical art, away from political propaganda back into the detachment of true literature ... And what has happened – slowly – as a result of the War, is that artistic expression has slipped back again into political propaganda and romance ... The attempt at objectivity has failed. The subjectivity of the majority is back again, as a result of that great defeat, the Great War ... And as there are more Wars ... to come, that is that, I believe we must regretfully conclude. (250)

Lewis takes in this passage a clearly defensive stand against any notion of dialectical relation between art and war. He asserts their mutual exclusivity, their entrenched duality, maintaining a puritanical aesthetic idealism that forces on him, as "half a romantic," the role of pessimist, insofar as the Great War was not "the war to end war."

The third panel of *Blasting*'s triptych looks across the abyss created by the war at the irretrievable days of vorticism: "The period of *Blast*, of *Ulysses*, of *The Waste Land* will appear an island of incomprehensible bliss, dwelt in by strange shapes labelled 'Pound,' 'Joyce,' 'Weaver,' 'Hulme' ... Yes ... and, for I said my piety was egoistic, the Enemy, as well – the Chiricos and Picassos ... will be the exotic flowers of a culture that has passed. As people look back at them ... the critics of that future day will rub their eyes. They will look, to them, so hopelessly *avant-garde*! so almost madly up-and-coming!" (254). "The men of 1914," as Lewis terms these avant-garde heroes, believed in "the future of the world" (255), but the postwar is a period of political and cultural compromise, thwarting heroic action: "Martial law conditions have come to stop. The gentler things of life are at an end" (256). The great modernists are suspended in history: "*We are the first men of a Future which has not materialized*" (256).

Lewis's identification with this group and this condition is complete, and *Blasting and Bombardiering* is the vehicle used to project his voice: "I will fix for an alien posterity some of the vain features of this movement. No one is better fitted than I am to do so, in all humility I may asseverate. I was at its heart. In some instances I was it" (255). This is a significant discursive manoeuvre. The most troubling revelation undergone by Lewis in the war was the degree of inherent romanticism in his own commitment to art. By wholly identifying himself with the prewar modernist movement, which repudiated romanticism and subjectivity, and, at the same time, by identifying that pure objective art movement with himself ("I was *it*"), Lewis both sidesteps the compromising nature of his war-time insights and embraces an objective persona. Vorticism was (as was modernism at large) a movement, an action, a "work" of art that entailed no compromising artistic subjectivity, no egoistic personality. Lewis's subjectivity in *Blasting* is the "egoism" of a persona, the mask of "the Enemy."

Lewis remains, in *Blasting and Bombardiering*, the observer, observing himself from outside and above. He does not enter into the dialectic of art and war and the implications he observes through his participation in the latter. The subjectivity that he observes in himself in the context of battle, excited by the experience of himself as the *object* of perception, manifesting itself as a personal choice of art over conventionally responsible involvement in the fighting, is circumvented by means of the text of *Blasting* itself. The dialectical play that he was able to admit in *Men Without Art* as the structure of the objective world is refused in *Blasting*, when he is concerned with his own subjectivity. The reciprocity perceived within the world is clearly inadmissible between himself and the world, insofar as a dialectic of self and world, subject and object, inevitably moves toward a necessary synthesis and, therefore, according to Lewis's somewhat pedestrian logic, a confusion of mind and body, self and other.[5]

The aesthetic at work in *Blasting and Bombardiering* clearly reflects this brush with and refusal of dialectic: "That the artist of 1914 was no seer is of little general importance, since it would have made no difference if he had been. Yet the artist is, in any society, by no means its least valuable citizen. Without him the world ceases to see itself and to reflect. It forgets all its finer manners. For art is only manner, it is only style. That is, in the end, what 'art' means. At its simplest, art is a reflection: a far more mannered reflection than that supplied by the camera" (259). Lewis confuses the physical and intellectual metaphor of "reflection" here. Reflecting or pondering *on* what we see through art (i.e., ourselves) is an intellectual act, a reflexive relation. But artistic seeing itself, Lewis says, is "simple reflection," a mimetic mediation. Reflexivity actively takes up the subject-object relation, while mimesis, in silently residing within it, renders it transparent, invisible.

Lewis's use of the metaphor of the observer observed in *Blasting* is mimetic rather than reflexive. But this is a doubly significant moment in Lewis's development, because of the inherently reflexive

structure of autobiography itself, a property that he amply acknowledges in the opening pages. In *The Revenge for Love*, Lewis achieves
a high degree of complexity within the traditional parameters of the
realistic novel. As "the possessor of the passionate, the artificial, the
unreal, yet penetrating, voice," Margot is able to produce that reflection that humanizes Percy behind the mask of "THE INJURED
PARTY." But Margot's voice is able to reach him only "out of the past,
where alone now it was able to articulate."[6] It is only with her death
and removal from active dialectical and dialogic relation to the action
of the novel that she can be used by Lewis as an agent of reflection.
There intrudes no dialectical complexity between the characters and,
therefore, between the omniscient narrative voice and the immediate
thoughts of the characters.

The very structure of autobiography introduces the complexity of
a narrator relating his own subjectivity as if it were an object. Lewis's
claims "to establish a principle of order … as would a tidy god" (6),
which he attempts through the metaphor of the observer observed,
are clearly refuted by the very content of the narrative. Rather than
being "the best way to shake the accursed thing off by putting it in
its place, as an unseemly joke" (4), his writing about war merely
confirms a naïve, idealistic opposition to an objective reality which,
as he himself reveals, throws an embarrassing light on the inade-
quacy of his prewar aesthetic principles. And yet, rather than ab-
sorbing the lessons of war in a genuinely reflexive and dialectical
relation to his experience, Lewis uses his autobiography as a nostalgic lament for a lost artistic paradise: "Expressionism, Post-
impressionism, Vorticism, Cubism, Futurism … were the heralds of
great social changes. Then down came the lid – the day was lost,
for art, at Sarajevo … a 'war to end war.' But it merely ended art"
(257, 258).

In 1936, just prior to *Blasting and Bombardiering*, Lewis published *Left
Wings Over Europe: or How to Make a War About Nothing*, in which he
discussed, in the frankest possible terms, the politics that were leading Europe directly into the Second World War. The uncompromising idealism of *Blasting and Bombardiering*, in which art and war were
sharply opposed, grew out of a deep pessimism about a political
atmosphere that threatened to submerge all cultured activity in a
second inundation of mass violence, even more pervasive and destructive than the one that thwarted Lewis's early career as an avant-
garde leader in 1914. His attempt to reconstruct that career in the
1920s received a fatal blow from within – his disastrously naïve

approbation of early Hitlerism in *Hitler* (1931). Lewis had allowed himself to be implicated in the machinations leading toward a second war, and his attempt to publicly extricate himself in *Left Wings* and *The Hitler Cult* were unsuccessful. The latter was an energetic repudiation of Hitlerism as it had emerged since the publication of *Hitler*, but it appeared three months after the outbreak of war in 1939, too late to affect the public mind.[7]

Blasting and Bombardiering, then, begun as a personal attempt to affirm the spiritual priority of art over political reality, ended as a private retreat on Lewis's part into an idealist artistic isolation, for he was overwhelmed by historical forces that, as he clearly saw, were gathering themselves for a second onslaught. On September 2, 1939, a day before England's declaration of war against Germany, Lewis sailed for North America in the belief that, in wartime, it would provide greater opportunities for support to a painter and writer. In this, he was proved wrong. He received few painting commissions. His novel *The Vulgar Streak*, an attack on the English class system, begun in England and finished in the United States, was refused by American publishers, who thought it inappropriate while England was at war.[8] This was the only novel that Lewis was to publish between 1936 and 1954. In 1939–40, Lewis spent one of the worst years of his life trying to establish himself in New York: "I feel as if I were in a stony desert, full of shadows, in human form. I have never imagined the likes of it, in my worst nightmares."[9] In November, 1940, he moved to Toronto, again taking up in wartime the prerogatives of his Canadian citizenship. But his three-year stay in Toronto was an even worse experience than New York. He was isolated, unknown, and penurious in a colonial city in wartime, a scarifying experience that slowly gestated and, in 1954, emerged as his next – and one of his best – novels, *Self Condemned*.

Blasting and Bombardiering (1937) and *Rude Assignment* (1950), as autobiographies, and *America, I Presume* (1940) and *Rotting Hill* (1951), as fictional travel narrative and autobiographical short stories, respectively, attest to the pervasive autobiographical turn in Lewis's work after *The Revenge for Love*. In *Blasting* and *Rude Assignment*, Lewis's motive was to create, through autobiography, a persona that would set the record as he saw it straight. That is, he laboured to give his life as artist (in *Blasting*) and controversialist (in *Rude Assignment*) a consistency which he felt it lacked in the public eye.[10] In *Self Condemned*, however, we have a sustained and penetrating work of self-examination and revelation. Just as in *The Revenge for Love*, where Lewis had "wedded the philosopher and the novelist" and joined hitherto separate life concerns in a powerful synthesis, so in *Self Condemned* Lewis joins the autobiographer to the philosopher-novelist, escapes the ruses and circumlocutions imposed, in Neuman's terms, by the autobiographical paradoxes of alterity, historicity, and veracity, and successfully engages a fictional talent that (with the minor exception of *The Vulgar Streak*) had lain largely fallow for fifteen years.

Like Lewis, the hero of *Self Condemned*, René Harding, leaves England at the outbreak of the Second World War for Canada, where he lives, with his wife, Hester, in agonizingly drab exile in a hotel in a small mid-Canadian city. Lewis critics have unanimously acknowledged the novel's autobiographical roots.[11] At the same time, as Rowland Smith emphasizes, "René Harding is not Wyndham Lewis. He is a created character who shares characteristics with his creator but who is also observed with detachment and irony throughout the book."[12] It is the form of the realistic novel that provides Lewis the vehicle for generating this "detachment and irony." No longer constrained by the historical veracity conventional to autobiography, he is able to explore his own experience intimately, and yet with the liberty and objectivity of fiction. The fruit of this synthesis of the autobiographical impulse with the analytic power of the philosophical novelist is, as Smith goes on to observe, a new development in Lewis's work: "The pain that René and his wife endure as exiles in Canada, as well as their intimacy in the worst days of their loneliness, are created from the inside in *Self Condemned*. Lewis knew what he was writing about. To a large extent the agony was his own. For most of his life he advocated the external view ... What is so striking about the Canadian section of *Self Condemned* is its recreation of an inner hell."[13]

In *Self Condemned*, René Harding is a professor of history and the author of controversial "popular" works which gain a wide public audience. As the novel opens (it is 1939), he has decided to resign his chair of history and emigrate to Canada in expectation of the outbreak of war. In a too lengthy set piece, the reader is treated to an extensive analysis of René's ideological stance in the form of a review, by his friend "Rotter" Parkinson, of René's recent book *The Secret History of World War* II. The review, intended for an American journal, is titled "A Historian who is Anti-History."[14] Rotter's review is an apologia for his friend, intended "to discourage the misconception, so often met with in connection with a thinker of this kind; namely, that his is a purely destructive intelligence" (82). His defence of René's work turns on his description of him as "a perfectionist, or, if you prefer it, an idealist" (95), a condition which sets him apart from the contending ideologies of his milieu, whether traditional or

revolutionary, Christian or Marxist, both of which look to an apocalyptic or utopian solution to the chronicle of failures that is termed
by them "history."

Both traditional and revolutionary utopianism look on history as
a unified process whose goal is beyond history itself, either in a
heaven or in a classless society: "Instead of this what Professor
Harding suggests is more like a description of the activities of two
races of men, one destructive, the other creative. The destructive
always wins in the end: just as we see, in this century, miraculous
technical inventions, which could have set men free from senseless
and wasteful toil, being seized on by the destructive race, so that,
at last, things are a hundred times as bad as they were to start with,
instead of a hundred times as good" (88). "History à la René
Harding," then, "is an essentially pessimistic narrative. Man is
shown as an uncivilizable animal; the inferiority and destructive
character of his appetite forbids attempts by the civilized minority
to establish a civilized order" (88–9). René's supposed "perfection-
ism," as Rotter sees it, resides in this exclusive character of the forces
of creativity and destruction. They are in no way synthetically or
dialectically related, or in any way possessed, even *in potentia*, by
all people. Harding's historical pessimism derives, Rotter observes,
from the fact that the "creative mind" is "a mind not possessed by
man in general" (89).

Despite Rotter's relationship to René of disciple to master, he is
led, in his very attempt to explicate René's work, to uncover the
flawed assumptions on which it is built. In characterizing its idealistic
and perfectionistic tendencies, he uncovers the dualistic logic that
underlies its uncompromising opposition of creative and destructive
forces in history. René's assumption of the superiority of destructive
forces, taken to its ultimate conclusion, simply makes inevitable the
end of the world, an outcome more than once alluded to as present
in René's mind (105). But Rotter cannot follow him the whole way:
"This, of course, is all very well: but in life nothing is taken to its
ultimate conclusion, life is a half-way house, a place of obligatory
compromise; and, in dealing in logical conclusions, a man steps out
of life – or so it would be quite legitimate to argue" (96).

Rotter points unerringly to the "compromising" nature of René's
position as a philosophical or apocalyptic historian, switching from
the objective study of facts to the recommendation of values: "He
feels that his is a function of authentic value, as a counsellor of
perfection; in spite of the fact that it would be quite impossible to
convert most historians to his standpoint, as it would mean the end
of their careers" (96). René advocates "not merely a reform in the

writing of history ... but an implicit proposal for revaluation, moral and intellectual, throughout society. Which is absurd. Men do not turn their lives upside down in response to the summons of a professor of history" (95). The reasons for René's resignation and exile are clearly anticipated in Rotter's review: Harding has committed himself to the absurdity of a logical adherence to utterly pessimistic and unprovable values. On hearing of René's plans to leave the university and England, his mother's response is somewhat more succinct than Rotter's: "You are not by any chance *a fool*, my son?" (26).

René's decision to turn his own life "upside down" and to leave his post as a professor of history is taken entirely without consultation with others, least of all his wife. He tells his mother and sister of his plans before he tells Hester. Intending finally to reveal to her his resignation and their imminent removal to Canada (in the relative public safety of a restaurant), René demurs, orders a lavish meal with copious wine, and behaves like an "amorous student" on their way home: "When, some time later, his glands emptied and his head as clear as a bell, this hairy faun in a jack-knife jump sprang into his own pillowless bed, it was without a shadow on his conscience" (32). For René, sexuality is less human than bestial. Coitus is "an embrace that is not objectively edifying and is accompanied by pants and grunts and expressions of ridiculous and unmerited approval" (30). Though his mother, like his sister, was "typically stupid ... at least as ... concerned the matter in hand" (28) (his resignation), she was "not such a brute as Essie" (30), insofar as she could recognize in René "how frivolous she had been ... and today she had, with disgust, even believed that she had given birth to a fool, into the bargain, *pauvre chérie!*" (30). But with Hester, who, "though smart enough ... had not a fraction of Mary's or of his mother's judgement," sex was "unpleasantly prominent" (31).

Hester's "exultant freshness" on the morning after the abortive confrontation in the restaurant merely annoys René. A casual reference by Essie to money gives him the opportunity to announce that he has "just sent in my resignation to the University," and that, in view of impending war and "as I no longer have my job, I propose to go to Canada" (35). He offers her no explanation beyond: "It is history itself I am displeased with" (37). Hester's attempt to reason with him provokes anger: "'It is not in the marriage contract that wives should hold the same political views as their husbands,' he told her harshly. 'Nor is it necessary for them to display more intelligence than a domestic cat. But they *do* have, on certain occasions, to keep their big silly mouths closed'" (39). His response to her query as to why she was not consulted is unyielding: "What was involved could only be settled by myself, not in discussion with others" (36).

Clearly, René's attitude toward women in general, and Hester in particular, is haughty and uncompromising. There is no accommodation, no recognition of mutuality or of the least reciprocity: "Being a man of great natural severity, an eroticism which did not live very easily with it was instinctively resented: and the mate who automatically classified under the heading 'Erotics' was in danger, from the start, of being regarded as a frivolous interloper by his dominant intellectuality" (41). Yet René was "still very attached to her upon the sexual level." His resignation, as "the first occasion on which disagreements between them had taken the form of a 'row,'" was the scene of a confrontation within René of spirit and flesh, eroticism and "dominant intellectuality," for the first time overcoming a "training" that "had led to his locking up any irascibility in a frigid silence" (41). This first challenge to his serene intellectual self-centrol is quickly examined by René in solitude. He quiets his anxiety with the satisfaction that "he experienced no pang at the thought of Hester's departure" (42). By such rigid means does René manage to maintain his sense of autonomy in the midst of his social and domestic life.

Hester yields to René's autocratic decision to move to Canada, a decision apparently vindicated by the declaration of war with Germany during their voyage out. The Hardings take up residence in a residential hotel in "Momaco," a small central Canadian city. The second of the novel's three parts is devoted to their life in the "Room," a space "twenty-five feet by twelve," "lit by six windows" (169). This "lethal chamber," flooded by the "violent light" (186) of Canada, becomes for "three years and three months" (169) a literal hothouse of an intense, forced intimacy which changes René's attitude toward Hester. He realizes "how his belief in blood, in the Family, had taken him, in the crisis of his life, to a lot of strangers beginning with his mother ... But here, all the time was the person he should have gone to" (238): "'I, no more than you, *would seek hardship*,' he said ... 'But honestly, being imprisoned, as we have been, here, has its compensations. This barren life has dried out of me a great deal that should not have been there. And you have become integrated in me. This tête-à-tête of ours over three years has made us one person'" (239).

René's awakening to what a "grand woman" (238) Hester is is achieved at the cost of Hester's own sense of self: "She had been a violently self-conscious woman – she was a cow in a field excessively conscious of being observed; and for whom to be observed was *to be*. But it was so long now since she had been under human observation – for she did not regard her present environment as human – that self-consciousness had left her" (197–8). Despite their integration in the Room, there remains a crucial sense in which René cannot permit the "sight" of Hester: "It was René's habit to place an upended suitcase upon a high chair and drape it with a blanket. He stood this between his wife and himself, so blotting her out while he wrote or read" (169). This "minimum of privacy," René's "substitute for a book-lined study" (169), allows him to generate a subsistence income by journalism, but it is more than Hester has. She comes to feel increasingly estranged and exposed: "She felt like some wild animal not accustomed to be looked at" (238).

In fact, René's awakening to Hester's importance to him is an invasive act. They have become "one person" because, as he says, "you have become integrated in me" (239). René has removed her against her will from all that sustained her, placed her in an alien environment in utter dependence on himself. Their intimacy is artificial, imposed by the fiat of his resignation. Despite his disclaimer, he has indeed *sought* "hardship" as an expression of his own creed of antagonism between spirit and flesh: "No one could imagine why man abstracted himself and acquired consciousness; why he had gone sane in the midst of a madhouse of functional character. – And History: with that, René's central tragedy was reached. History, such as is worth recording, is about the passion of men to stop sane. Most History so-called is the bloody catalogue of their backslidings. Such was René's unalterable position" (212). René's attempt to abstract himself, to step out of the stream of "History" and "stop sane," is an act of antagonism toward nature and natural relations, toward the piety of the hearth: "The fact was that René Harding had stood up to the Gods, when he resigned his professorship in England. The Gods had struck him down. They had humiliated him, made him a laughing-stock, cut him off from all recovery; they had driven him into the wilderness" (406).

Lewis's narrative voice euphemizes the condition of his character here. Harding has, more accurately, directly challenged the gods, rather than merely defying them in a Promethean sense. René has simply declared, in Zarathustrian fashion, that they do not exist, that human intellect is itself divinely self-sufficient, and that a man can "stop sane" by merely stepping outside any commerce with the flux of nature or history. But René carries with him the source of and witness to his own continual commerce with and "backslidings" into nature, his own "madhouse of functional character," Hester, whose understandable reaction to their forced exile is antagonism toward Momaco. Her increasing sense of alienation from her life in England will end in suicide, an act of despair at the changes produced in René by his decisions.

René's decision to leave his job and England is justified by his analysis both of the politics of scholarship and of international relations. For the historian to betray "the guilty secrets he has learned is more than his place is worth. As the servant of the ruling class, he cannot but become privy in the course of his researches to the dark secrets of his masters" (56). The "dark secret" to which René saw himself as privy was that England "would see to it, according to plan, that a war should occur, but they would see to it that England was in a condition of glaring inferiority. It was 'the English way': provoke an enemy, but never be ready to meet him on equal terms. This was intended as an alibi" (42–3). This canny analysis on René's part is never seen by him to apply to his own condition. In withdrawing himself and Hester to the "sanctimonious ice-box" of Momaco, he attempted to seal himself off from compromising involvement with a compromised world. The Hotel Blundell, however, he is to discover, is no refuge. The hotel is a "microcosm," containing "everything belonging to human society." It is "the State," "the world" (190): "'How extraordinary, when one shuts oneself up in a little segment of the world like this hotel, it is brought home to one what a violent place the world is'" (231). This violence breaks out in a murder and a fire that destroys the hotel.

René's attempt to silence Hester by forcibly integrating her into himself is abruptly ended by the fire. Just as he was "almost reconciled to the hardship," it is interrupted: "Even, he had developed an appetite for this negation of life, and a sort of love for this frightful Room" (245). "The Room was him, it was them, they might never be so happy again" (281). René had counselled Rotter, despairing in the midst of England at war, that the "taper" of enlightenment "would not be extinguished by the tornado if it were secreted in the mind" (244). René's attempt to secrete himself in his own private enlightenment was invaded from within by tensions in the microcosmic society of the hotel, which hoarded secrets. The behind-the-scenes owner of the hotel, Mr. Martin, murders his manageress, Mrs. McAffie, when he finds her spying on him, and attempts to cover the crime with a fire.

René's forcible parting from the "barren abstraction of the Room" (211) produces in him a derangement, an estrangement from himself, "something did find its way into his manner of thinking which was insane" (304). "The destruction of the hotel by fire divided their life at Momaco into two dissimilar halves." Just as the war and the hotel were outer reflections of René's life and psyche, so is this division of his life in Momaco: "There was a growing dissimilarity, owing to a psychological factor, a tension, becoming more acute month by month, between René and Hester, and, independently, within both René and Hester" (307). The hotel fire is the objective correlative of René's attempt to secrete the "taper" of his so-called enlightenment in his own mind. By isolating Hester and "integrating" her into himself, he had tried aggressively to subdue his consciousness of the compromise between intellect and sensuous life which Hester embodied. The inherent violence of his appropriation turns him out into Momaco and forces him to compromise with it in a way that is impossible for Hester. That her suicide results in her decapitation is again an objective correlative of René's treatment of her as a mindless body, forcing her to choose between her love for him and London, the environment in which their life had made sense to her.

René's post-fire alliance with Momaco begins with a friendship with a fellow expatriate professor at the University of Momaco, the Scottish metaphysician MacKenzie. MacKenzie is an acute reader of Harding's books, and on their first meeting he raises an objection to *The Secret History of World War II*, in effect that René has "cut [himself] off from mankind" in becoming "a Member of the Party of Superman" (314): "'Everywhere we have seen from the teachings of Nietzsche ... onwards, a dissatisfaction with life as it has so far been lived, and is still lived by everyone except a very few: a demand that man should remake himself and cease to live upon the paltry, mainly animal plane we know. – And now you, Professor Harding, wish to supermanize the writing of history.'" "'Always, Professor,'" René replies, "'I have made it my business to keep clear of what you call the Superman party'" (315). But his attempt to demonstrate this serves to jog into action his "rusty dialectical machine" (324). René's mind awakens from its three-and-a-half-year Canadian slumber, and he begins to write another book, in which he confronts the question "at the root of all his type of thinking": "This problem of problems can be compressed as follows: if one condemns all history as trivial and unedifying, must not all human life be condemned on the same charge? Is not human life ... too hopelessly compromised with the silliness involved in the reproduction of the species, of all the degradations accompanying the association of those of the opposite sex to realize offspring?" (351). René's confrontation with the "problem of problems" clarifies the springs of his own actions. Criticism of History as a discipline makes it "necessary to attempt to expunge from our daily life, as far as possible, the things we condemn in history" (355). This attempt at intellectual integrity was, of course, at the root of René's resignation and emigration, against the austere logic of which his friend Parkinson had warned him. Having now seen clearly the implications of his philosophical position, René "then proceeded to go over, lock, stock and barrel, into what Professor MacKenzie had called the Party of the Superman": "[Humanity] would obviously perish ignominiously if we continued as we were at present. We must train and compress ourselves in every way, and breed an animal superior to our present disorderly and untidy selves" (356).

René's final acceptance of the logical implications of his theoretical position is a crucial turning point in the novel. As he realizes, his historical theory clearly requires that we "would reflect forward ... to how we all acted today" (355), which is to say, that history should become a moral and intellectual teacher and guide to present action.[15] While René has himself been consistent insofar as opposition to quantitative historiography has called forth his resignation from the university, his own eventual clearer understanding of the élitist and pessimistic implications of his own qualitative historiology is not able to teach him a more humane view or instigate any fundamental revaluation of his intellectualist isolation.

At the very point at which René appears most capable of critical insight into the implications of his thoughts and actions, a fatal breakdown in his "dialectical machinery" occurs: "Here it must be observed that the violence of thought which was characteristic of René received everywhere an additional edge because of the mental instability developing in him just then ... One might even go a step further, and find in his adoption of the Superman position a weakening; the acceptance of a solution which formerly he would have refused" (356). That is, when René finally realizes the incompatibility between his philosophical method and its supposed ethical motivation, and might therefore be capable of redressing the balance, the fatal dominance of his intellectualism asserts itself all the more inexorably. In the very adherence to the strict logic of his position, René is seen to betray the ethical principles which he imagines himself supporting. Now, "in everything expediency counted more for him ... He was writing a book ever so slightly too much as part of his new plan of life, from which the integrity and belief were missing" (356).

The strict logic of René's critique of the world, as a place of what Rotter describes as "obligatory compromise" (96), has driven him to the margins – from his position in the world as professor to a hand-to-mouth existence as a journalist in a provincial outpost. But René's critique of the "world" had sheltered his own compromise with the "flesh" in his marriage to Hester, and the enclosure with her in "the Room," while it reveals to him his need of her, reveals also the "bad faith" of their relationship – René's inability to admit any reciprocity, any dialectical "play" (not to mention any synthesis) into the static dualism of his worldview.

René's "intellectual life" is, of course, a sham. His claim to Olympian transcendence of what he sees as the merely sensuous life of ordinary mortals is openly contradicted by his continuous recourse to the "logic of copulation" (341) in his relationship with Hester. Yet, when he openly acknowledges in his new book "the degradations accompanying the association of those of the opposite sex" (351), he is driven to the "compromise" and "expediency" of a new intellectual career in Momaco, in the form of a book that rejects faith in the common run of humanity in favor of a supposed "Nietzschean" élitism. René's bad faith finally penetrates to its own ground within René himself. His return to the writing of his idealist historical critique is compromised by a pragmatic motivation. He openly repudiates the very principle of his "relationship" to Hester, and every word with which he champions heroic autonomy is repudiated by the "expediency" of his desire for material survival, and the renewed public recognition on which it depends.

Hester, not surprisingly, acts on her utter superfluity in René's life, locked as he now is in irretrievable contradiction with himself. After her suicide, René has a complete breakdown and goes into hospital, where he attempts to come to terms with her death and his role in it. His image of Hester becomes "as much a part of his physical being as if they had been born twins, physically fused – or better, one might say, for physical amalgamation would be unpleasant, identical twins … Could he ever be forgiven? No, forgiveness was of course impossible" (376). René tries to restore his sense of spiritual unity with Hester, broken by their conflict of wills over return to England and her resultant death:

At the time this communion of the dead and the living started, it was only the decapitated Hester who was present to him. His impulse in the police mortuary to seize and to carry off her head was realized in the imagination. In trembling horror he grasped the decapitated head, and pressed her dear face against his. And then the lifeless lips moved and grew warm. With amazement and soon with delight, he felt the warming lips glueing themselves against his. His entire body responded, for she was no longer merely a head. Love had brought her to life again. He imagined, in a sort of delirium this miracle. (376)

Here, again, René tries to ignore Hester's separateness, now accentuated by death. His attempt to absorb her into his psyche is in some ways, however, made more successful by her simply spiritual existence. His "imagination" can restore her to life in an ideal form, in his image, as it were, in which he can enjoy a communion with her undisturbed by the "absurdity" of their sexual relationship. René sustains this ideal communion by repairing, appropriately enough, to the College of the Sacred Heart, where he dons a cassock in a "second withdrawal and suspension of intellectual processes, the giving up of being himself." It was "as much a negation as the Hotel Blundell," but whereas his first withdrawal, his resignation of the professorship, "had for its rationale a great moral issue, ... his second exit was not a martyrdom but a sacrifice, an emotional act of propitiation and to assuage a phantom" (385). René even contemplates conversion to the "old faith": "This was irrational, but he had buried his reason in the tomb of his wife" (386).

René sacrifices his reason in remorse for his role in Hester's death, and in doing so enjoys, through his imaginative union with a spiritualized Hester, a nearness to "God" supposedly greater even than that of the celibate priests with whom he is now living (388). But, through his lecturing in the college, René's reason begins to assert itself against this "spiritist degeneration," this "Hesteria" (389). René begins to ponder the fatal question: "Why did Hester kill herself?" Once asked, he cannot avoid the fatal conclusion that ends their communion, that her desire to return to England, insofar as it conflicted with his own to stay in Momaco, must stem from "purely selfish reasons" (390). The strict dualism of René's logic reasserts itself. The law of non-contradiction can allow no compromise of the intellect's strict autonomy from the body, from the merely sensuous concerns of women: "A woman is always on the side of the lousy world" (329). As René reflects, "For had she not placed her private wishes in competition with everything he desired? ... Her will did not prevail" (390).

So far, René's conclusions are strictly in line with his habitual cast of mind, at work in the novel from the beginning. But he goes on to ask a question which is provoked not merely by Hester's opposition (also a habitual element), but by its form as suicide: "He now understood why Hester had taken her life. It was with hatred that he brought his analysis to the point at which he declared, 'Hester's suicide was an act of insane coercion. My cold refusal to do what she wanted crazed her egoistic will ... She was acting vindictively'" (390–1). His attitude toward the sacred image of her mutilated body changes dramatically: "Was any pity due from him to this mutilated corpse – it was death militant. *This* dead body was there with a purpose. It was designed to upset his applecart, violently to interfere with his life. It was a Japanese-like suicide, a form of vengeance" (395).

Self Condemned is Lewis's exploration of the interior dimension of "the revenge for love." As Nietzsche so forcefully and paradoxically asserted, "God is dead ... And we have killed him."[16] Modern man's sense of himself as autonomous demands the sacrifice of all transcendental value, of all interpretation of life and its suffering as a moral judgement on man's lack of wholeness.[17] Lewis pursues this logic into the realm of human relationships, first in the context of social institutions – politics and marriage – in *The Revenge for Love*, then in more strictly psychological and spiritual terms in *Self Condemned*. So long as René buries his reason, Hester can function as a transcendental value through which he can achieve reconciliation, drawing on the peace and stability of the college, and its study of "the Summa of all philosophies (providing a static finality in which the restless intellect might repose)." But René's "intelligence was too dynamic, his reason was too bitterly bruised, for static bliss" (380). Even as a purely transcendental centre, Hester cannot hold for René, and his "dialectical machine" (324) reasserts its inexorable polarizing force.

As René explains on departing the college, "But there is no peace for me, I should tell you. I see a fiery mist wherever I direct my eyes. But the fire is not outside me, the fire is in my brain" (397). The Hotel Blundell has burst into flame inside René himself, and he is reduced to "The Cemetery of Shells" (as the closing chapter is titled). The fire is ignited by the confrontation of wills between himself and Hester. But once Hester removes herself, René loses his last external impediment. There is no longer anything or anyone outside himself which he can accuse of obstructing him – neither his profession, nor his mother (and her pride in him), nor his wife (and her dependence upon him). René's polar swing, from imagining the dead Hester as transcendental value to thinking of her as vengeful obstructionist, is necessary to his sustaining the belief that he is whole and complete in himself, that any interior conflict must arise from others' attempts to render him as absurd as they appear in his eyes.

In René's post-mortem attitude to Hester, Lewis captures the hidden structure of *ressentiment* so concisely rendered by Jameson, that "the bitterness with which the 'phenomenon' of *ressentiment* is inevitably involved ... suggests that, as an explanatory category, *ressentiment* is always itself the product of *ressentiment*."[18] The "hatred" with which René concluded his "analysis" (390) of Hester's "Japanese-like suicide," and his portrayal of it as "a form of vengeance" (395) – that is, as *ressentiment* – is a Nietzschean response, itself full of characteristic vituperation and *ressentiment* against the self-martyring slave morality of the weak. Lewis is exploring the interior landscape of *ressentiment*, here, its phenomenology as an "explanatory category," a conscious and critical perspective on the world. But, while René is conscious of *ressentiment* in others, he is not aware of it in himself. He is satirist, not ironist.

René's return to the world from the College of the Sacred Heart is a return to an apparently new life, chiefly signified by the unqualified success of his new book. But MacKenzie makes the innocent mistake of congratulating René on the book's reception. The reply: "'I feel a tremendous nausea of my tremendous success ... and I am *bored* ... I am bored, no, I am not bored, I am butchered ... I'm split down the middle with dreary horror'" (403–4). MacKenzie does not know what to make of René's state of mind, only that "to speak of *that* [René's new book] meant that one had to think of René as he had been, and as he now was – had to speak of his decadence: of his *death*" (405–6). Cut off from Hester, René is cut off from his body and from life. Hester is "Essie," as René calls her, or "Ess," as she signs her suicide note (392). She is René's being, his *esse*, insofar as she sustains the polar tension of his Cartesian dualism of mind and body, intellect and sensuousity (*René* Descartes),[19] which after her death "splits" within him. But as Hester puts it in her suicide note, "I cannot leave you physically – go away from you back to England. I can only go out of the world" (392). René explains to MacKenzie that "it seemed to be a matter of her life or mine, almost" (390). Hester had to become impossibly submerged in René or else disappear. René has no such alternative. He can make no concession to dialectics in his insistence that the tension of mind and body should be resolved solely in favour of mind.

Self Condemned enshrines what appears to be an exemplary master-slave dialectic, in which two consciousnesses, desiring identity and value, are driven to contend for one another's "recognition."[20] The transition from the animal and appetitive desire of merely natural existence to the human and psychic desire of cultural and historical life, according to Hegel, is initiated as a "desire of desire," a desire to be the object of others' desire, and for their recognition of one's more than material existence and value. The emergence of such human desire (as desire for recognition) takes the necessary initial form, says Hegel, of a fight to the death, since desire, to confirm its more than appetitive nature, must prove that it is willing to forgo material survival for the sake of recognition as an "identity" (rather than as a mere entity). Thus, the first stage of culture is a society of masters and slaves, in which the slaves, in choosing survival over death, through submission to the aggression of the masters, render service and recognition to the superiority of the conquering class. Within this first, highly polarized stage of culture there exists, by necessity, a degree of reciprocity. If the master does not spare the life of the conquered, and the latter choose submission to the master, then there is neither survival nor, obviously, the desired recognition. On the other hand, insofar as the recognition accorded by the en-slaved of the master's superiority is forced and secured by merely appetitive desire (instinct for survival), it does not provide the higher, non-material recognition that can truly appease the moti-vating desire of the master. The violence of the master's enforcement of recognition fails to acknowledge the necessary reciprocity of a thorough desire for recognition, and so creates a reactive and élitist social structure, the energy of which will reside largely in the slave class's inevitable impetus toward reciprocating recognition, realiz-able only through revolutionary change.

It is the uncompromising logic of René Harding's élitist intellec-tualism, denying all reciprocity between himself and the world, him-self and Hester, that in the end "split[s him] down the middle with dreary horror" (403–4). Hester, in coming to recognize the monolithic nature of René's conviction, can only abandon him to his own de-vices. That René consoles himself at her death with the imagined possession of her decapitated head is a representation of the attempt to coerce her consciousness, her will, and her recognition while alive. True to form, he reverts to anger at her assertion of autonomy and right to recognition through suicide, since she has wilfully removed herself as mediator of the essentially violent and coercive demands of his remorseless "dialectical machine." René's mind functions like that of a machine and not a person because he refuses the complexity of genuine dialectic, the reciprocity of thesis and antithesis that results in a sublation and synthesis of their opposition. Hester's suicide removes René's last point of compromise and dialectical re-lation with the world, and so delivers him up to the abstract and inhuman purity of his own logic.

But, of course, implicit in René's rationalism is the instability of its motivation. The strict monologism of his self-understanding denies reciprocity with the world. And this denial of interdependence is rooted in *ressentiment*, the "rancor against time" that for Nietzsche is the desire to punish, the search for a scapegoat that arises from the experience of suffering.[21] When René loses Hester, he loses the ability to displace the contradictions of his dualistic existence as both mind and body. The recognition by the world of his book now becomes a challenge to his claim of autonomy. He can no longer blame the world for wrongly valuing him, or Hester for compromising him. His *ressentiment* turns into "horror" at his un-mediated hunger for recognition and mastery, and his existence becomes a "cemetery of shells."

We have seen how, in the caricatural extremity of his portrayal of Tarr, Lewis achieves a critical (if not an entirely controlled and re-flexive) edge in his art. *The Apes of God*, in its strict externality and focus on "objective" satire, indicates the absence of concern for re-flexivity and self-criticism in Lewis's early career. Indeed, he takes considerable pains to condemn interior and psychological explora-tion in fellow writers such as Joyce, Eliot, and Woolf in *Time and Western Man*, clearly stating the principle in "The Meaning of the Wild Body": "Fundamental self-observation … can never on the whole be absolute. We are not constructed to be *absolute observers*."[22] We can see an evolution in Lewis's exploration and application of this principle, from *Enemy of the Stars* through *Tarr* to *The Apes of God* and *The Revenge for Love*: a steady move away from reflection on self toward observation of others, and so to a perception of inauthenticity and *ressentiment* in *The Revenge for Love*.

But, as we have observed, the objective insight into human char-acter and psyche is followed by reflection – by a significant turn toward autobiography, explicitly in *Blasting and Bombardiering* and *Rude Assignment*, but in more complex form in *Self Condemned*. Lewis becomes aware that, as Jameson puts it, "*ressentiment* is always itself the product of *ressentiment*."[23] Though René Harding is not Wyndham Lewis, the autobiographical specificity of *Self Condemned* is impossible to ignore. In so thoroughly taking up his personal experience in his art, Lewis allows himself to be closeted in an intimacy with himself which is directly analogous to René and Hes-ter's sojourn in "The Room" in Momaco. He risks the same loss of clear lines of demarcation and delineation between his life and his art that he makes the undoing of his characters, and that he had rigorously avoided in his earlier work. Lewis is clearly conscious of the presence of *ressentiment* within his own satirical representation of it. The scrutiny of his own personal history and the failure to achieve a synthesis of the art-war-art dialectic in *Blasting and Bombardiering* compelled him to create in the realm of art what he was unable to achieve in autobiography: a vantage point enabling reflection on the very motivation of satire and critique.

René's uncompromising intellectualism is analogous to Lewis's own insistence on externality and mind/body dualism dominating his thinking through *The Apes of God*. We saw him modify that dualism in the direction of dialectical play in *Men Without Art*, a strategic containment of formalist interiority within the political critique of *The Revenge for Love*. *Self Condemned* is Lewis's admission of the obligation to view himself in the "hard and exquisite light"[24] of his own satirical and objectivist aesthetic. The strict dualism of his externalist satire had necessarily to become dialectical and self-critical in the process, and in doing so it enables him to make the transition in *Self Condemned* from the dualism of critical observation of others to the dialectic of self-criticism, from satire to irony.

But it should be no surprise that such an elegantly simple (and dualistic) formulation of the import of Lewis's achievement in *Self Condemned* is inadequate. Lewis does not simply pass beyond the dualism of satire to the dialectic of irony, and so achieve through self-criticism a Hegelian reconciliation and sublation of the restless, agonistic, and disquieting moments of his work. Certainly, as we argued in relation to *Tarr*, the sheer extremity of Lewis's characterizations has the effect of critical *caricature*, of a deliberately exaggerated satire that achieves ridicule rather than condemnation. Likewise, there is a poignancy about René's shell-like existence at the end of *Self Condemned*. René has condemned himself, and because of that very severity our condemnation becomes superfluous.

But the self-critical and ironical element of *Self Condemned* is strictly contained. René Harding is not only not Wyndham Lewis, he is incapable of becoming a Wyndham Lewis. The dialectic of self-scrutiny that Lewis admits through his art is never allowed to be entertained by René. Lewis was no more interested in than he permitted René to be capable of an ordinarily discursive scrutiny of his artistic persona. *Blasting and Bombardiering* demonstrates that.[25] But the objectification through fictional representation that is available to Lewis in the form of *Self Condemned* is not made available to his character within the novel, so that Lewis, at the same time as he explores the limitations of his former strict dualism, maintains a distance between himself and his main character, and so contains the critical and reflexive dialectic of autobiography within the objectivist and dualistic structure of the realistic novel and the omniscience of third-person narration. *Self Condemned* is the achieved poise for Lewis between satire and irony, tragedy and comedy, dualism and dialectic. The strategic, controlled dualism of the *Blast* manifesto "VORTEX: BE THYSELF" has been internalized and rendered complex, such that dualism is itself seen dualistically, as both a necessary and a potentially destructive objectivism, and is at the same time sustained in a dialectical relation to (a necessarily dialectical and reflexive) subjectivism.

Lewis's progression from satire to irony, then, moves behind irony itself. More specific than the dialectical self-criticism of irony is this reflexive grasp of the perception of *ressentiment* as itself rooted in *ressentiment*. Lewis is driven to get in behind the spirit of critique itself, whether of others or of self, satiric or ironic. His principle that "fundamental self-observation ... can never ... be absolute," that "we are not constructed to be *absolute observers* "[26] is concretely validated here. If analytic thought, whether dualistic or subtly dialectical, is motivated by this hunger for the absolute, for mastery of the contingencies of temporal existence, then another strategy of perception than observation and "speculation" must be negotiated. Lewis's grasp of the contingencies of rational discourse, however reflexive, is inscribed in his commitment to the primacy of art and representation over reflection and analysis. Lewis confirms what Eric Gans articulates: "Literary epistemology demonstrates here, as throughout the history of high culture, its anteriority to theoretical reflection in uncovering the critical categories of human interaction."[27] Lewis makes his most authentic contribution as an artist. In the realm of intellect he is a strategist and politician only, and his willingness to adopt merely polemical positions consistently undermines his artistic credibility. But at the same time it is precisely his grasp of the political and material implications of art practice in modernity that makes of him the most significant English-speaking representative of what, after Peter Bürger, I have called the avant-garde.[28] Lewis's pursuit of a "politics of the intellect"[29] led him, by a long and circuitous route, to an art practice more radical than any politics of which he could conceive.

Notes

1 Richard Quinones, "Previews and Provocations," in *Modernism*, ed. Chefdor, Quinones, and Wachtel, 6.
2 Quoted in Monique Chefdor, "Modernism: Babel Revisited?" in ibid., 5.
3 Jameson, *Fables of Aggression*, 3.
4 Bürger, *Theory of the Avant-Garde*.
5 Lewis, *Blasting and Bombardiering*, 5.
6 I have chosen not to discuss either *The Human Age* trilogy or the stories in *The Wild Body* (though I refer to some of the essays in the latter collection). With respect to *The Human Age*, the view of this study is that, after *Enemy of the Stars*, the leading edge of Lewis's development is along the line of his more realist works – that is, *Tarr*, *The Revenge for Love*, and *Self Condemned*.
7 It is all the more important that Lewis be read, for the same reasons that Philippe Lacoue-Labarthe argues, in "Transcendence Ends in Politics," in *Typography: Mimesis, Philosophy, Politics*, ed. Christopher Fynsk (Cambridge, Mass.: Harvard University Press 1989), for the careful study of Heidegger, while at the same time holding to "a necessary ethical condemnation" of what is "absolutely irreparable" and "unpardonable" in Heidegger's complicity with Nazism:

> One will recognize [Heidegger's] famous remark: "Whoever thinks greatly must err greatly." Let the error, or rather the *fault*, of Heidegger be what it may; I persist in believing that it removes ab-

solutely nothing from the "greatness" of his thought, that is to say, from its character – today, for us – as decisive. A thought can be less than infallible and remain, as we say, "impossible to avoid." *Its very fallibility, furthermore, gives us to think.* This is why I persist in believing that it is also this thought itself that poses to us, out of its weaknesses, as out of its most extreme advances, the question of politics. (269–70; my emphasis)

8 Jameson, in *Fables of Aggression*, notes "some striking similarities between Lewis' undertaking and the contemporary poststructuralist aesthetic, which signals the dissolution of the modernist paradigm ... and foretells the emergence of some new, properly postmodernist or schizophrenic conception of the cultural artifact" (20). See also Lafourcade, "Metaphor–Metonymy–Collage," 6–11.

CHAPTER ONE

1 Lewis, *Caliph's Design*, 129–83.
2 Lewis, *Wyndham Lewis the Artist*, 69.
3 Ibid., 87.
4 Lewis, *Rude Assignment*, 135.
5 Lewis, *Caliph's Design*, 133–4.
6 Ibid., 130.
7 Ibid., 129.
8 Ibid., 130.
9 Ibid.
10 Ibid.
11 Ibid.
12 Ibid., 131.
13 Ibid.
14 Ibid.
15 Lewis outlined the theoretical basis for this in a series of four articles, which appeared in *The Athenaeum* from November, 1919, to January, 1920, under the title "Prevalent Design"; see Michel and Fox (eds.), *Wyndham Lewis On Art*, 117–28.
16 Lewis, *Caliph's Design*, 169.
17 See Lewis, *The Writer and the Absolute*, 132–3, for a striking instance of this nostalgia for eighteenth-century mind and manners.
18 Lewis, *Caliph's Design*, 169.
19 "The back of his talent is too broad to suffer from even an avalanche of criticism ... But it is the uncertain and mercurial quality of his genius that makes him *the symptomatic object* for your study and watchfulness." Ibid., 170, 171.
20 Ibid., 174.

21 Ibid.
22 Ibid., 169.
23 Lewis, "A Review of Contemporary Art," 39; my emphasis.
24 Edwards, "Afterword," in Lewis, *The Caliph's Design* (1986), 148.
25 Bürger, *Theory of the Avant-Garde*.
26 Ibid., 17.
27 Ibid., 19.
28 As Jameson puts it, in *Fables of Aggression*: "Any historicizing approach must reckon our own situation, our own present as observers, judges and actors, back into our evaluation of the past; and the approach of a postindividualistic age argues powerfully for the discovery of Lewis' kinship with us" (20).
29 See, for example, Poggioli, *Theory of the Avant-Garde*; Weightman, *Concept of the Avant-Garde*; and Howe, *Literary Modernism*.
30 Schulte-Sasse, "Foreword," viii.
31 Quoted in ibid.
32 Ibid.
33 Schulte-Sasse, "Foreword," xiii.
34 Ibid., and Bürger, *Theory of the Avant-Garde*, 20.
35 Quoted in Schulte-Sasse, "Foreword," xiv.
36 Ibid.; my emphasis.
37 Bürger, *Theory of the Avant-Garde*, 22. Note that for Bürger, here, "objective understanding" is not ahistorical, "does not mean an understanding that is independent of the place in the present of the cognizing individual; it merely means insight into the overall process insofar as this process has come to a conclusion in the present in the cognizing individual, however provisional that conclusion may be."
38 Ibid., 18.
39 Jameson corroborates this view of Lewis's "style" in *Fables of Aggression*: "So Lewis' style, the only true English futurism, an immense hangar in which we may still learn to tap the almost extinct sources of language production, does not in the clattering, deafening noise of its own mechanical processes seek to be preserved as an icon in its own right, but rather consents to its own abolition in time, freeing us in turn from the fetishistic spell of style itself" (86).
40 In "Modernity and the Avantgarde in Wyndham Lewis's *Tarr*," an article which appeared after my own text was written, Peter Bürger observes the same oppositional stalemate represented in the two main characters in Lewis's *Tarr*: "In Lewis's novel the modern and the avantgarde positions correspond to two equally aporetic forms of life in the crisis period of bourgeois society, the defensive armoured self of the working citizen on the one hand and the diffused identity of the proto-fascist character on the other" (17).

41 Lewis, *The Caliph's Design*, 174.

42 Ibid., 175.

43 Jameson, *Fables of Aggression*, 5.

44 Ibid., 17.

45 Ibid., 18.

46 For the Cantleman "Crowd" material see Lewis, *Blasting and Bombardiering*, 66–83; *Art of Being Ruled*; *Revenge for Love*; *Left Wings Over Europe*; and *The Writer and the Absolute*.

47 Lewis, *Caliph's Design*, 131.

48 Lewis, *Rude Assignment*, 135.

CHAPTER TWO

1 Neither Chapman, *Wyndham Lewis: Fictions and Satires*, Materer, *Wyndham Lewis as Novelist*, nor Jameson, *Fables of Aggression*, mentions the work, and Hugh Kenner, *Wyndham Lewis*, Timothy Materer, *Vortex*, Pritchard, *Wyndham Lewis*, and Meyers, *The Enemy*, do so only in passing.

2 Wagner, *Wyndham Lewis*, 116.

3 Only a handful of short stories appeared in print prior to *Enemy of the Stars*. These were revised and later collected in *The Wild Body*. *Tarr*, of course, was being written between 1909 and 1915 (more on this in chapter three); see O'Keeffe, "Afterword."

4 Lewis, "Note" to *Enemy of the Stars* (1932) in *Collected Poems and Plays*, ed. Alan Munton, 221.

5 Lewis, *Filibusters in Barbary*, *The Doom of Youth*, and *Snooty Baronet*.

6 Of the only two articles devoted to *Enemy of the Stars*, both are excellent: Beatty, "'Enemy of the Stars'," and Flory, "*Enemy of the Stars*." Book-length studies of Lewis have mentioned it only briefly, with the exception of Kush, *Wyndham Lewis's Pictorial Integer*, 78–86, whose focus is on the visual – literary relations, and Dasenbrock, discussed below.

7 Pound and Grover, in *Wyndham Lewis*, 32–3, include an illustration of a page from the manuscript of *Enemy of the Stars*. Copious corrections, deletions, and additions are made directly on a copy of the 1914 *Blast* text.

8 Lewis, "Physics of the Not-Self," 68. Lewis included a revised version of the essay in the 1932 *Enemy of the Stars*.

9 Flory, "*Enemy of the Stars*," 92; Flory's essay has been invaluable in penetrating the obscurities of *Enemy of the Stars*.

10 Materer, *Wyndham Lewis as Novelist*, 50.

11 Ibid., 51, 52.

12 Dasenbrock, *Literary Vorticism*, 135.

13 Ibid., 150.

14 Ibid., 135.

15 Ibid., 131.

16 Flory, *"Enemy of the Stars"*, 92–3.

17 Ibid., 105; my emphasis.

18 Ibid., 105–6.

19 Ibid., 93–4.

20 Lewis, *Enemy of the Stars*; all subsequent references are cited parenthetically by page number in the text.

21 Levenson, in *A Genealogy of Modernism*, ix, remarks on "the strength of the modernist urge towards dualistic opposition and radical polarities."

22 Lewis, ed., *Blast I*, 147, 148.

23 Flory, *"Enemy of the Stars,"* 93.

24 Simpson, *Cassell's*.

25 Martin Esslin remarks, in "Modernity and Drama," in *Modernism*, ed. Chefdor, Quinones, and Wachtel, on the crisis in modern drama in the light of attempts analogous to Lewis's to overcome alienation: "Have we not reached the limits, the point at which even the definition of what drama, what theater is, has been almost totally dissolved by the tearing down of the distinction between actor and spectator, audience and participant-in-the-action?" (64).

26 Stirner, *The Ego and His Own*, trans. S.T. Byington 1907; this translation forms the basis of John Carroll's *Max Stirner: The Ego and His Own*, from which references are cited parenthetically by page number in the text.

27 Löwith, in *From Hegel to Nietzsche*, observes, "Stirner's book ... has usually been considered the anarchic product of an eccentric, but it is in reality the logical consequence of Hegel's historical system, which – allegorically displaced – it reproduces exactly" (103).

28 Carrithers, *The Buddha*, 45, defines *anatman* as "the absence of an eternal, independent Self, whether in ordinary consciousness, in meditative states or anywhere else."

29 Arghol's designation as "enemy of the stars" is the descriptive equivalent of his formal designation as a mask. It is a comment on "Max Stirner," the pseudonym of Johann Caspar Schmidt. As Carroll observes in his introduction to *The Ego and His Own*, "His unusually high forehead gained him the nickname of *Stirner* at school, and, with his individualistic fancy tickled and his romantic ambitions stirred by the allusion to the stars (*Stirn* = *forehead*, *Gestirn* = star), the plebeian name of Schmidt was abandoned" (18). Arghol is "enemy" of the stars both as symbols of Stirner himself and as what he represents, the ego as the last refuge of transcendentalist aspirations.

30 Lewis, "Physics of the Not-Self," 68.

31 Burnet, *Greek Philosophy*. It is this work, rather than Burnet's *Early Greek Philosophy* (London, 1892), as Munton, *Collected Pœms and Plays*, suggests (223), that Lewis quotes from in the essay. See Walter Michel, "Books 'From One of Lewis's Libraries,'" 37, where Lewis's copy of Burnet is noted among books of his now in the Humanities Research Center of the University of Texas at Austin. Michel's annotation for *Greek Philosophy* notes that the Socrates chapter only is marked and annotated (but which one of chapters eight (through ten on Socrates he doesn't say); curiously, "most of the annotations though made in ink, are efficiently erased – one of only two examples of such erasures I can recollect in this collection."

32 Burnet's position on the faithfulness with which Socrates' views are presented by Plato, called by Guthrie, in *Socrates*, "'the argument from outraged propriety,'" receives "little if any support today" (31). Burnet thought it "an offence against good taste and an outrage on all natural piety" (31) that Plato should put his own ideas into the mouth of Socrates, particularly in the context of the *Phaedo*, when Socrates is awaiting the effects of hemlock. After Burnet, Lewis assumes that Socrates speaks for himself in Plato's work.

33 Deussen, *The Philosophy of the Upanishads*, 74. Subsequent references are cited parenthetically by page number in the text.

34 Hiriyanna, in *Outlines of Indian Philosophy*, 148, describes the difference between the two views: "Nor is it here [in Buddhism] … as in the Upanishads, ignorance of the unity of all existence, but the failure to recognize the hollowness of the so-called self."

35 See David Loy, "The Paradox of Causality in Madhyamika": "What is most significant … is that it is no longer a disagreement over the nature of non-dual *experience*. Since Brahman is qualityless and imperceptible, there is no phenomenological difference between a Madhyamika [Buddhist] interpretation … and an Advaitic [Hindu] one" (72).

36 Burnet, *Greek Philosophy*, 175.

37 Ibid., 156.

38 Ibid.

39 Dasenbrock, *Literary Vorticism*, 171.

40 Clearly, the "Wild Body" stories (and their commentaries) and *Tarr* are also important expressions of the mind/body theme, but *Enemy*, as more sustained than the former and earlier than the latter, has the prior claim on our attention.

41 Sfox is Lewis as the Socrates whose "critics called him 'sly,' using a word (*eiron*), which is properly applied to foxes" (Burnet, *Greek Philosophy*, 132). Sfox's featureless mask no doubt refers to the authorial indifference and impersonality which Lewis advocates in "Physics."

42 Lewis, *Rude Assignment*, 139. For an overview of Nietzsche's ongoing influence on Lewis's thought, see Edwards, "Wyndham Lewis and Nietzsche," 203–17.
43 Nietzsche, Birth of Tragedy, 39.
44 Arghol, as a Prometheus figure, is a response to Nietzsche's casting of Aeschylus' Prometheus in the role of archetypal Dionysian tragic figure: "The story of Prometheus is an original possession of the entire Aryan race, and is documentary evidence of its capacity for the profoundly tragic," Nietzsche, *Birth of Tragedy*, 997.
45 Though Nietzsche never mentions Stirner in his work, he is the product of the same intellectual milieu: "And so, historically considered, the coincidence that Stirner's book appeared in the year of Nietzsche's birth seems as necessary as the connection between Nietzsche's attempt at a new beginning and the Nothing which is reached in Stirner" (Löwith, *From Hegel to Nietzsche*, 176). Carroll, in his introduction to *The Ego and His Own*, observes, "Overbeck's final conclusion ... was that Nietzsche had read Stirner, was impressed, and worried that he should be confused with him" (25); he cites Leszek Kolakowski's comment: "'Stirner's grounds are irrefutable ... Even Nietzsche seems inconsequential in comparison to him'" (15).

CHAPTER THREE

1 Lewis, *Rude Assignment*, 139.
2 Revised in the same way as *Enemy of the Stars*, *Tarr* (originally serialized in *The Egoist* [vol. 3, April 1916, to vol. 4, May 1917] and published in book form in 1918) was reissued in 1928. As with *Enemy*, the more finished version of 1928 will be used. Subsequent quotations are cited parenthetically by page number in the text.
3 Lewis, *Rude Assignment*, 139.
4 Lewis, *Enemy of the Stars*, 15.
5 Ibid., 191.
6 "The new vortex plunges to the heart of the present." "The vorticist is at his maximum point of energy when stillest." Lewis, *Blast*, 1:147, 148.
7 Wyndham Lewis, "Beginnings" (1935) in *Wyndham Lewis on Art*, ed. Michel and Fox, 291.
8 Ibid.
9 Ibid., 295.
10 Ibid., 294 (Lewis's emphasis).
11 Lewis, *Blast*, 2:196.
12 See McFarland, *Originality and Imagination*.
13 Lewis, *Rude Assignment*, 136.
14 Lewis, "Beginnings," 296.

15 Ibid., 295.

16 As O'Keeffe observes, it may have been "with the intention of estab-lishing a balance between the two characters that Lewis wrote the first three chapters of Part I," in which Tarr's character is established inde-pendently of Kreisler's. O'Keeffe gives evidence that these chapters were added later than December, 1913. Indeed, O'Keeffe observes two distinct strains associated with the characters, a "psychological" ele-ment with Kreisler and a "philosophical" one with Tarr: "The work might therefore be seen as a novel within a novel: Tarr's summation of Kreisler ... as a 1914–15 gloss on the 1909 character." See O'Keeffe, "Afterword," 363 and 379–80. I would argue that the transition from "psychological" to "philosophical" concerns during the composition of *Tarr* (over the years 1909–10 to 1914–15) finds autonomous expression in the more philosophical *Enemy of the Stars* (written very likely in 1913–14, a period which Jeffrey Meyers calls "his most extreme phase of abstract art" in *The Enemy*, 64), and that *Tarr* actually contains the philosophical impulse and subordinates it to the more concrete exi-gencies of narrative.

17 Lewis, *Blast*, 2:91.

18 Bertha represents the lifeless opposition of tragedy and humour: "Tarr's idea of leisure recognized no departure from the tragic theme of existence: pleasure could take no form that did not include death and corruption – at present Bertha and Humour" (39).

19 Meyers, *Wyndham Lewis*, 108–9.

20 Ibid., 118.

21 Ibid., 117.

22 From *The Will to Power*, quoted in Heidegger, *Nietzsche*, 1:3.

23 See Walter Kaufmann, "Translator's Introduction" to Nietzsche, *The Gay Science*, 11.

24 I am indebted in the following discussion to Heidegger, *Nietzsche*, vol. 1, and "The Word of Nietzsche: 'God is Dead'" in *The Question*, 53–112; and to Deleuze, *Nietzsche and Philosophy*.

25 Nietzsche, *Gay Science*, 181.

26 Heidegger, "Word of Nietzsche," 61.

27 Ibid., 62.

28 Ibid., 65.

29 Ibid., 66.

30 Nietzsche, *Will to Power*, quoted in ibid.

31 Nietzsche, *Will to Power*, quoted in ibid., 70.

32 Nietzsche, *Gay Science*, quoted in Heidegger, *Nietzsche*, 1:41.

33 Heidegger, ibid.

34 Ibid.

35 Heidegger, "Word of Nietzsche," 96.

36 Nietzsche, *Will to Power*, quoted in ibid., 71 (Nietzsche's emphasis).

37 Heidegger, ibid., 85.
38 Nietzsche, *Will to Power*, quoted in ibid.
39 Nietzsche, *Will to Power*, quoted in ibid., 86.
40 Nietzsche, *Will to Power*, quoted in Heidegger, *Nietzsche*, 1:75.
41 Ibid., 73.
42 Ibid., 74.
43 Nietzsche, *Will to Power*, quoted in ibid.
44 Ibid.
45 See Martin Heidegger, "The Onto-Theo-Logical Structure of Metaphysics," in *Identity and Difference*.
46 Heidegger, *Nietzsche*, 42.
47 Nietzsche, *Will to Power*, quoted in ibid., 70.
48 Ibid., 40.
49 Ibid., 72.
50 Nietzsche, *Will to Power*, quoted in Heidegger, "Word of Nietzsche," 85.
51 Deleuze, *Nietzsche and Philosophy*, 9.
52 Heidegger, *Nietzsche*, 71.
53 Lewis, *Rude Assignment*, 128.
54 Heidegger, "Word of Nietzsche," 69.
55 Ibid., 88.
56 Lewis, "Beginnings," 295.
57 Flory, *"Enemy of the Stars,"* 105–6.
58 Perhaps the most authoritative response from this point of view is Northrop Frye's review of Geoffrey Wagner's *Wyndham Lewis: A Portrait of the Artist as Enemy*, "Neo-Classical Agony," 592–8.
59 Lewis, *Rude Assignment*, 128.
60 See Lewis, "The Meaning of the Wild Body," in *The Complete Wild Body*, ed. Bernard Lafourcade, 57–60.
61 Lewis, "Physics of the Not-Self," (1932) in Lewis, *Collected Poems and Plays*, 202, 203.
62 Emmanuel Levinas, *Collected Philosophical Papers*, 3. Subsequent references are cited parenthetically by page number in the text.
63 Toby Foshay, "Wyndham Lewis: Between Nietzsche and Derrida."
64 See Levinas, *Totality and Infinity*, and *Otherwise than Being*; for a central article-length statement, see "The Trace of the Other."
65 In "Différance," Derrida says, "The thought of différance implies the whole critique of classical ontology undertaken by Levinas" (152). See also Derrida, "Violence and Metaphysics: An Essay on the Thought of Emmanuel Levinas," in *Writing and Difference*, 79–153.
66 See Heidegger, "Letter on Humanism," 189–242; and Derrida, "Structure, Sign, and Play in the Discourse of the Human Sciences," in *Writing and Difference*, 278–93.
67 Derrida, "Deconstruction and the Other," 108.

68 Ibid., 109.

69 Ibid., 113.

70 See Derrida, *Of Grammatology*, and "Semiology and Grammatology: Interview with Julia Kristeva," in *Positions*, 15–36.

71 As Jameson puts it, in *Fables of Aggression:* "Such impulses [to the ugly or the ideologically offensive] are freed to acquire their figuration; [Lewis's] artistic integrity is to be conceived, not as something distinct from his regrettable ideological lapses (as when we admire his art, *in spite of* his opinions), but rather in the very intransigence with which he makes himself the impersonal registering apparatus for forces which he means to record, beyond any whitewashing and liberal revisionism, in all their primal ugliness" (21).

72 In Lewis, "The Meaning of the Wild Body," 158.

73 Bürger, in "Modernity and the Avantgarde," comments, "Even before the Dadaists and Surrealists attempted to bring art back into life-praxis, Lewis describes the failure of such an attempt. He exposes the destructive and self-destructive forces within the avantgarde project, forces which Breton, for example, was only able to control because he broke off the process of radical surrender to instinctual potential as soon as it threatened to become dangerous" (15).

CHAPTER FOUR

1 Lewis, *Blasting and Bombardiering*, 4.

2 Ibid.

3 Ibid.

4 Ibid., 5. Though *Tarr* was published in book form only in 1918, it was finished by 1914–15, before the war.

5 Ibid., 186.

6 Wyndham Lewis, "VORTEX: BE THYSELF", in *Blast* 2:91.

7 Meyers, *The Enemy*, 158.

8 Lewis, *Rude Assignment*, 57.

9 Ibid., 56.

10 Lewis, *Satire and Fiction*, 46.

11 Ibid.

12 Ibid., 48.

13 Lewis, *The Art of Being Ruled*, 16. All subsequent quotations are cited parenthetically by page number in the text.

14 Lewis, *The Apes of God*, 117. All subsequent quotations are cited parenthetically by page number in the text.

15 Lewis, "The Meaning of the Wild Body," in *The Complete Wild Body*, 158.

16 Lewis, "Inferior Religions," in *The Complete Wild Body*, 151.

17 Lewis, "Meaning of the Wild Body," 157–8.
18 Ibid.
19 This disclaimer of bombast by Pierpoint is puzzling and gratuitous given the quite dispassionate tone of the Encyclical; this supports the claim that it is the narrator breaking through the Pierpoint mask.
20 Lewis, "Meaning of the Wild Body," 158.
21 Ibid.
22 Lewis, "Inferior Religions," 151.
23 See MacFarland, *Originality and Imagination*.
24 "First, to assume the dichotomy of mind and body is necessary here, without arguing it; for it is upon that essential separation that the theory of laughter here proposed in based." Lewis, "Meaning of the Wild Body," 157.
25 Ibid.
26 Ibid., 158.
27 Lewis, "Inferior Religions," 151.
28 Lewis, *Rude Assignment*, 139.
29 Ibid., 57.
30 Lewis launched *Blast* at London from his base in the Rebel Art Centre; see Meyers, *The Enemy*, 54.
31 Levinas, "Reality and Its Shadow," 1–13.
32 For the reasons behind Nietzsche's appropriation of the name of the prophet Zoroaster, or Zarathustra, see Hollingdale's introduction to his translation of Nietzsche, *Thus Spoke Zarathustra*, 30–7.
33 Kaufmann, *Nietzsche*, 371. For an explanation of Nietzsche's retention of the French term, see Sugarman, "*Rancor Against Time*," x–xi. The French term includes a sense of "time-lag" in the working of *ressentiment*, between offenses suffered and displeasure expressed, that is not included in the meaning of "resentment."
34 Kaufmann, *Nietzsche*, 371–2.
35 Nietzsche, *The Gay Science*, quoted in ibid., 374–5 (Kaufmann's interpolation).
36 Nietzsche, "Of the Tarantulas," quoted in ibid., 373–4.
37 Heidegger, *Nietzsche*, 1:42.
38 Heidegger, "The Word of Nietzsche: 'God is Dead,'" in *The Question Concerning Technology*, 85.
39 See Heidegger, *Nietzsche*, vol. 2.
40 Heidegger, *What is Called Thinking?*, 97. All subsequent quotations are cited parenthetically by page number in the text.
41 Heidegger, *Nietzsche*, 1:42; see also Kaufmann, *Nietzsche*, 221–7.
42 For a forceful analysis of the role of *ressentiment* in Nietzsche's madness, see René Girard, "Strategies of Madness: Nietzsche, Wagner, and Dostoevski," in "*To Double Business Bound*," 61–83.

43 Jameson, *Fables of Aggression*, 131.

44 Kaufmann, *Nietzsche*, 371–2.

45 Lewis, *Hitler*, Meyers, *The Enemy*, 187: "Lewis first became interested in Hitler while working on *The Art of Being Ruled*."

46 Sugarman, *"Rancor Against Time,"* 79.

47 Nietzsche, *Thus Spoke Zarathustra*, 173.

48 Heidegger, *Nietzsche*, 1:31.

49 Nietzsche, *Thus Spoke Zarathustra*, 162.

50 In *Violence and the Sacred* and *Things Hidden*, Girard develops a persuasive theory of the origins of culture in such a scapegoating mechanism. See Gans, *The End of Culture*, for an important critique and extension of Girard's hypothesis.

51 See Heidegger, "The Onto-Theo-Logical Structure of Metaphysics," in *Identity and Difference*.

52 Nietzsche, *Thus Spoke Zarathustra*, 162. In Sugarman, *"Rancor Against Time,"* "antipathy toward time" is rendered "rancor against time"; in Heidegger *What is Called Thinking?*, "revulsion against time."

53 Nietzsche, *Thus Spoke Zarathustra*, 161.

54 Sugarman, *"Rancor Against Time,"* 79.

55 Lewis, *Time and Western Man*, 3. All subsequent quotations are cited parenthetically by page number in the text.

56 Campbell, "Equal Opposites," 366.

57 Nietzsche, *Thus Spoke Zarathustra*, 162.

58 Meyers, *The Enemy*, 181.

59 Lewis, *Satire and Fiction*, 48.

60 Ibid., 43.

61 Lewis, *Men Without Art*, 10. All subsequent quotations are cited parenthetically by page number in the text.

62 Lewis, *Tarr*, 213.

63 See Bloom, *Anxiety of Influence*.

64 See Sandler, *"The Revenge for Love,"* ch. 5, *passim*.

65 Ibid., 203.

66 Ibid., 204.

67 Ibid., 203.

68 Wyndham Lewis, *Revenge for Love*. All subsequent quotations are cited parenthetically by page number in the text.

69 This inversion of art is reflected in Abershaw's forging technique, which he performs "upside-down" (166).

70 Victor's car is carrying a false cargo – bricks rather than guns. "False Bottoms" was Lewis's original title for the novel; see Materer, *Wyndham Lewis as Novelist*, 121, 130.

71 "For the two Margots in question had, as it were, coalesced" (323).

72 "And I think you, Percy, should protect us too. After all *you* are responsible for what happened!" (323).

73 Nietzsche, *Thus Spoke Zarathustra*, 162.

74 Jameson presents a more uniformly negative view than I do of Margot and her role in the narrative: as she is "passive and victimized," she "marks no transcendence of the mature narrative system." And yet Jameson acknowledges, "it may be taken as something of a dialectical 'negation of the negation' in the way in which the externality of the dominant satiric portraiture in Lewis is [with Margot] systematically undermined." See Jameson, *Fables of Aggression*, 146. My analysis of the role of *ressentiment* in *The Revenge for Love* adds specificity and a corrective positivity to the structural accuracy of Jameson's analysis.

CHAPTER FIVE

1 Lewis, *Blasting and Bombardiering* (London: John Calder 1982), 189. All subsequent quotations are from this edition and are cited parenthetically by page number in the text.

2 Neuman, "The Observer Observed," 329. All subsequent quotations are cited parenthetically by page number in the text.

3 Insofar as Lewis employs a metaphor, invoking autobiography as "biography ... a sort of novel" (1), and thus disguises the paradox of veracity, all three of Neuman's paradoxes are seen to be interdependent.

4 As is said in *Blast*, "*Blast* will be popular essentially. It will not appeal to any class ... The moment a man feels or realizes himself as an artist, he ceases to belong to any milieu or time. *Blast* is created for the timeless, fundamental Artist that exists in everybody." "Long Live the Vortex!" in Wyndham Lewis, ed., *Blast* I, 7.

5 Jameson too refers, in the context of a discussion of *Time and Western Man*, to Lewis's "insufficiently reflexive position, the failure of Lewis' situational self-consciousness to become genuinely dialectical." See Jameson, *Fables of Aggression*, 126.

6 Lewis, *Revenge for Love*, 380.

7 See Meyers, *The Enemy*, 245.

8 Ibid., 259.

9 Quoted in ibid., 247.

10 Lewis makes no bones about his defensive intentions in *Blasting*: "And I fully realize what, when I shall no longer be here to defend myself, is in store for me. Who would not, in my position, and seeing the execution done amongst our dead peers daily by the little bows and arrows of the passerine intelligentsia?" (13) In *Rude Assignment*, 13, he implies that he has been thwarted by the legal concerns of his publisher in his attempt to "set the record straight" regarding his political stances in the 1930s and the persecution they attracted from the literary and publishing establishment.

11 These are most comprehensively rehearsed by Jeffrey Meyers, "*Self Condemned*," in Meyers, *Wyndham Lewis*, 226–37; and by Smith, "Introduction," v–x, and "Afterword," 411–21.

12 Smith, "Afterword," 411.

13 Ibid., 412.

14 Lewis, *Self Condemned*, 81. All subsequent quotations are from this edition and are cited parenthetically by page number in the text.

15 Lewis gives to René the position taken by Nietzsche in *Use and Abuse*, 22:

> Every man or nation needs a certain knowledge of the past, whether it be through monumental, antiquarian, or critical history, according to his objects, powers, and necessities. The need is not that of the mere thinkers who only look on at life, or the few who desire knowledge and can only be satisfied with knowledge; but it has always a reference to the end of life, and is under its absolute rule and direction ... The knowledge of the past is desired only for the service of the future and the present, not to weaken the present or undermine a living future.

As Nietzsche reveals in the preface to this work, "I have tried to describe a feeling that has often troubled me: *I revenge myself* on it by giving it publicity" (3; my emphasis). René is animated by Lewis with a like revenge and *ressentiment* against the intellectually established historians. But Lewis shows how the spirit of *ressentiment* is rooted in René's psyche and pursues him into his personal life, conditioning all his outward relations.

16 Nietzsche, *The Gay Science*, 95.

17 Nietzsche, *Thus Spoke Zarathustra*, 162: "And because there is suffering in the willer himself, since he cannot will backwards [i.e., cannot change the past] – therefore willing itself and all his life was supposed to be – punishment!"

18 Jameson, *Fables of Aggression*, 131.

19 On mind/body dualism in Descartes, see Kenny, *Descartes*, 79–95 and 216–26.

20 See Hegel, *Phenomenology of Spirit*, 111–19, and the commentary on this passage by Kojève, *Introduction*, 3–30.

21 Nietzsche, *Thus Spoke Zarathustra*, 162.

22 Lewis, *The Complete Wild Body*, 158.

23 Jameson, *Modernist as Fascist*, 131.

24 Lewis, "The Meaning of the Wild Body," 158.

25 Lewis, in *Rude Assignment*, as "narrative of his career" as critic, is discursive to the point of self-indulgence.

26 Lewis, "The Meaning of the Wild Body," 158.

27 Gans, *The End of Culture*, 246.

28 Bürger, *Theory of the Avant-Garde*.
29 The title of the final chapter of Lewis's *The Art of Being Ruled*.

Bibliography

PRIMARY SOURCES

[Where more than one edition of Lewis's work is available, the edition cited is preceded by an asterisk.]

Lewis, Wyndham. *America and Cosmic Man*. London: Nicholson & Watson 1949.
– *America, I Presume*. [New York:] Howell, Soskin 1940.
– *The Apes of God*. London: Arthur Press 1930. *Santa Barbara: Black Sparrow 1981.
– *The Art of Being Ruled*. *London: Chatto & Windus 1926. Edited by Reed Way Dasenbrock, Santa Rosa: Black Sparrow 1989.
– *Blast*. Vols. 1 and 2. London: John Lane 1914–15. *Santa Barbara: Black Sparrow 1981.
– *Blasting and Bombardiering*. London: Eyre & Spottiswoode 1937. *London: John Calder 1982.
– *The Caliph's Design*. London: Egoist 1919. Rev. ed. in *Wyndham Lewis the Artist, From Blast to Burlington House*. London: Laidlaw 1939. In *Wyndham Lewis On Art*. Edited by W. Michel and C.J. Fox, 129–83. London: Thames & Hudson 1969. Edited by Paul Edwards, Santa Barbara: Black Sparrow 1986.
– *Collected Poems and Plays*. Edited by Alan Munton. Manchester: Carcanet 1979.
– *Count Your Dead: They are Alive!* London: Lovat Dickson 1937.
– *The Demon of Progress in the Arts*. London: Methuen 1955.

– *The Doom of Youth*. London: Chatto & Windus 1932.
– *Enemy of the Stars*. In *Blast* I. London: John Lane 1914, 87–97. Rev. ed. London: Desmond Harmsworth 1932. Both eds. rpt. in *Collected Poems and Plays*. Edited by Alan Munton, 93–119 and 141–91. Manchester: Carcanet 1979.
– *Enemy Salvoes: Selected Literary Criticism*. Edited by C.J. Fox. London: Vision 1976.
– *Filibusters in Barbary*. London: Grayson 1932. Rpt. as *Journey into Barbary: Morocco Writings and Drawings*. Edited by C.J. Fox, Santa Barbara: Black Sparrow 1983.
– *Hitler*. London: Chattus & Windus 1930.
– *The Hitler Cult*. London: Dent 1939.
– *Left Wings Over Europe*. London: Jonathan Cape 1936.
– *Letters*. Edited by W.K. Rose. London: Methuen 1963.
– *The Lion and the Fox*. London: Grant Richards 1927. London: Methuen 1955.
– *Men Without Art*. London: Cassell 1934. *Reprinted, New York: Russell & Russell 1964. Edited by Seamus Cooney, Santa Rosa: Black Sparrow 1987.
– *One-Way Song*. London: Faber 1933; rev. ed. 1960.
– *Paleface: The Philosophy of the The Chapbook* 40 (1925): 68–77. Rev. ed. in *Enemy of the Stars*. London: Desmond Harmsworth 1932. Latter rpt. in *Collected Poems and Plays*. Edited by Alan Munton, 195–204. Manchester: Carcanet 1979.
– *The Red Priest*. London: Methuen 1956.
– *The Revenge for Love*. London: Cassell 1937. *Harmondsworth: Penguin 1983.
– *The Roaring Queen*. Edited by Walter Allen. London: Secker & Warburg 1973.
– *Rotting Hill*. London: Methuen 1951. Edited by Paul Edwards, Santa Barbara: Black Sparrow 1986.
– *Rude Assignment*. London: Hutchinson 1950. *Edited by Toby Foshay, Santa Barbara: Black Sparrow 1984.
– *Satire and Fiction*. London: Arthur 1930.
– *Self Condemned*. London: Methuen 1954. *Santa Barbara: Black Sparrow 1983.
– *Snooty Baronet*. London: Cassell 1932. *Edited by Bernard Lafourcade, Santa Barbara: Black Sparrow 1984.
– *Tarr*. London: Egoist 1918. Edited by Paul O'Keefe, Santa Rosa: Black Sparrow 1990. Rev. ed. London: Chatto & Windus 1928. *Harmondsworth: Penguin 1982.
– *Time and Western Man*. London: Chatto & Windus 1927. *Boston: Beacon 1957.

– *Unlucky for Pringle: Unpublished Short Stories*. Edited by C.J. Fox and R.T. Chapman. London: Vision 1973.
– *The Vulgar Streak*. London: Robert Hale 1941. Santa Barbara: Black Sparrow 1985.
– *The Wild Body*. London: Chatto & Windus 1927. Rev. ed. rpt. as *The Complete Wild Body*. Edited by Bernard Lafourcade. Santa Barbara: Black Sparrow 1982.
– *The Writer and the Absolute*. London: Methuen 1952.
– *Wyndham Lewis the Artist, From 'Blast' to Burlington House*. London: Laidlaw 1939.
Michel, Walter, ed. *Wyndham Lewis: Painting and Drawings*. London: Thames & Hudson 1971.
Michel, Walter, and C.J. Fox, eds. *Wyndham Lewis on Art*. London: Thames & Hudson 1969.
Morrow, Bradford, and Bernard Lafourcade. *A Bibliography of the Writings of Wyndham Lewis*. Santa Barbara: Black Sparrow 1978.
Pound, Omar, and Philip Grover. *Wyndham Lewis: A Descriptive Bibliography*. Folkestone: Dawson 1978.

SECONDARY SOURCES

Armstrong, T.I.F. *Apes, Japes and Hitlerism. A Study and a Bibliography*. London: Unicorn 1932.
Barthes, Roland. "Whose Theater? Whose *Avant-Garde*?" In *Critical Essays*, translated by R. Howard, 67–70. Evanston: Northwestern University Press 1972.
Beatty, Michael. "'Enemy of the Stars': Vorticist Experimental Play." *Theoria* 46 (1976): 41–60.
Blanchot, Maurice. "The Limits of Experience: Nihilism." In *The New Nietzsche: Contemporary Styles of Interpretation*, edited by David Allison, 127–27. New York: Delta 1977.
Bloom, Harold. *Agon: Towards a Theory of Revisionism*. New York: Oxford University Press 1982.
– *The Anxiety of Influence*. New York: Oxford University Press 1973.
Bradbury, Malcolm, and James MacFarlane. *Modernism*. Harmondsworth: Penguin 1978.
Bridson, D.G. *The Filibuster: A Study of the Political Ideas of Wyndham Lewis*. London: Cassell 1972.
Bürger, Peter. *The Theory of the Avant-Garde*. Translated by Michael Shaw. Minneapolis: University of Minnesota Press 1984.
– "Modernism and the Avantgarde in Wyndham Lewis's *Tarr*." *News From Nowhere: The Politics of Modernism* 7 (Winter 1989): 9–18.
Burnet, John. *Greek Philosophy*. London: Macmillan 1914.

Campbell, SueEllen. "Equal Opposites: Wyndham Lewis, Henri Bergson, and Their Philosophies of Space and Time." *Twentieth Century Literature* 29 (1983): 351–69.

Carrithers, Michael. *The Buddha*. Oxford: Oxford University Press 1983.

Carroll, John, ed. *Max Stirner: The Ego and His Own*. New York: Harper & Row 1971.

Chapman, Robert T. *Wyndham Lewis: Fictions and Satires*. London: Vision 1973.

Chefdor, Monique, Richard Quinones, and Albert Wachtel, eds. *Modernism: Challenges and Perspectives*. Urbana & Chicago: University of Illinois Press 1986.

Cianci, G., ed. *Wyndham Lewis Letteratura/Pittura*. Palermo: Sellerio 1982.

Cooney Seamus, ed. *Blast 3*. Santa Barbara: Black Sparrow 1984.

Dasenbrock, Reed Way. *The Literary Vorticism of Ezra Pound and Wyndham Lewis*. Baltimore and London: Johns Hopkins University Press 1985.

Davies, Alistair. "*Tarr*: A Nietzschean Novel." In *Wyndham Lewis: A Revaluation*, edited by J. Meyers, 107–19. Montreal: McGill-Queen's University Press 1980.

Deleuze, Gilles, *Nietzsche and Philosophy*. Translated by Hugh Tomlinson. New York: Columbia University Press 1983.

Derrida, Jacques. "Différance." In *Speech and Phenomena: And Other Essays on Husserl's Philosophy of Signs*, translated by David B. Allison, 129–60. Evanston: Northwestern University Press 1973.

- "Deconstruction and the Other." In Richard Kearney, *Dialogues with Contemporary Continental Thinkers: The Phenomenological Heritage*, 107–26. Manchester: Manchester University Press 1984.

- *Of Grammatology*. Translated by Gayatri Chakravorty Spivak. Baltimore and London: Johns Hopkins University Press 1976.

- *Positions*. Translated by Alan Bass. Chicago: University of Chicago Press 1981.

- *Writing and Difference*. Translated by Alan Bass. Chicago: University of Chicago Press 1978.

Deussen, Paul. *The Philosophy of the Upanishads*. Translated by A.S. Gedden. London: T & T Clark 1906.

Edwards, Paul. "Wyndham Lewis and Nietzsche: 'How Much Truth Does a Man Require?'" In *Wyndham Lewis Letteratura/Pittura*, edited by G. Cianci, 207–17. Palermo: Sellerio 1982.

Eliot, T.S. *Selected Prose*. Edited by J. Hayward. Harmondsworth: Penguin 1953.

- "Wyndham Lewis," *Hudson Review* 10 (1957): 167–70.

Flory, Wendy Stallard. "*Enemy of the Stars*." In *Wyndham Lewis: A Revaluation*, edited by J. Meyers, 92–106. Montreal: McGill-Queen's University Press 1980.

Foshay, Toby. "Wyndham Lewis: Between Nietzsche and Derrida." *English Studies in Canada* 16 (1990): 339–53.

Freed, Lewis. *T.S. Eliot: The Critic as Philosopher*. West Lafayette: Purdue University Press 1979.

Frye, Northrop. "Neo-Classical Agony." *Hudson Review* 10 (1958): 592–8.

Gadamer, Hans-Georg. *Reason in the Age of Science*. Translated by Frederick G. Lawrence. Cambridge, Mass.: MIT Press 1981.

Gans, Eric. "The Culture of Resentment." *Philosophy and Literature* 8 (1984): 55–66.

– "Differences." *Modern Language Notes* 96 (1981): 792–808.

– *The End of Culture: Toward a Generative Anthropology*. Berkeley and Los Angeles: University of California Press 1985.

Gasché, Rodolphe. *The Tain of the Mirror: Derrida and the Philosophy of Reflection*. Cambridge, Mass.: Harvard University Press 1986.

Girard, René. "Dionysus versus the Crucified." *Modern Language Notes* 99 (1984): 816–35.

– *Things Hidden Since the Foundation of World*. Translated by Stephen Bann and Michael Metteer. Stanford: Stanford University Press 1987.

– *"To Double Business Bound."* Baltimore and London: Johns Hopkins University Press 1978.

– *Violence and the Sacred*. Translated by Patrick Gregory. Baltimore and London: Johns Hopkins University Press 1977.

Guthrie, W.K.C. *Socrates*. Cambridge: Cambridge University Press 1971.

Harrison, John R. *The Reactionaries: A Study of the Anti-Democratic Intelligentsia*. New York: Schocken 1967.

Head, Philip. "Ego and Object: Lewis and the Theory of Art in the Twenties." *Enemy News* 23 (1986): 15–18.

Hegel, G.W.F. *The Phenomenology of Spirit*. Translated by A. V. Miller. Oxford: Oxford University Press 1977.

Heidegger, Martin. *Identity and Difference*. Translated by Joan Stambaugh. New York: Harper & Row 1969.

– "Letter on Humanism." In *Basic Writings*, edited by David Farrell Krell, 189–242. New York: Harper & Row 1977.

– *Nietzsche*. Vols. 1, 2, and 4. Translated by David Farrell Krell. New York: Harper & Row 1979–84.

– *The Question Concerning Technology and Other Essays*. Translated by W. Lovitt. New York and London: Garland 1977.

– *What is Called Thinking?* Translated by J. Glenn Gray. New York: Harper & Row 1968.

Hiriyanna, M. *Outlines of Indian Philosophy*. London: Allen & Unwin 1932.

Howe, Irving. *The Decline of the New*. London: Gollancz 1971.
– ,ed. *Literary Modernism*. New York: Fawcett 1967.
Hyde, Lewis. *The Gift: Imagination and the Erotic Life of Property*. New York: Random House 1979.
Jameson, Fredric. *Fables of Aggression: Wyndham Lewis, the Modernist as Fascist*. Berkeley and London: University of California Press 1979.
John, Augustus. *Finishing Touches*. London: Jonathan Cape 1964.
John of the Cross, St. *The Collected Works*. Translated by K. Kavanagh and O. Rodriguez. Washington: ICS 1973.
Kaufmann, Walter. *Nietzsche: Philosopher, Psychologist, Anti-Christ*. 3d ed. Princeton: Princeton University Press 1968.
Kearney, Richard. *Dialogues with Contemporary Continental Thinkers: the Phenomenological Heritage*. Manchester: Manchester University Press 1984.
Kenner, Hugh. *Gnomon*. New York: McDowell, Obolensky 1958.
– *Wyndham Lewis*. Norfolk, Conn.: New Directions 1954.
Kenny, Anthony. *Descartes: A Study of His Philosophy*. New York: Random House 1968.
Kojève, Alexandre. *Introduction to the Reading of Hegel*. Edited by Allan Bloom; translated by James H. Nichols. New York: Basic Books 1969.
Kristeva, Julia. *Desire in Language: A Semiotic Approach to Literature and Art*. Edited by Leon S. Roudiez; translated by Alice Jardine, Thomas Gora, and Leon S. Roudiez. New York: Columbia University Press 1980.
Kurrik, Maire Jaanus. *Literature and Negation*. New York: Columbia University Press 1979.
Kush, Thomas. *Wyndham Lewis's Pictorial Integer*. Ann Arbor: University of Michigan Press 1981.
Lafourcade, Bernard. "Metaphor-Metonymy-Collage: Post-Modernist Aspects of Lewis's Style." *Enemy News: Journal of the Wyndham Lewis Society* 25 (Winter 1987): 6–11.
Levenson, Michael H. *A Genealogy of Modernism: A Study of English Literary Doctrine 1908–1922*. Cambridge: Cambridge University Press 1984.
Levinas, Emmanuel. "Beyond Intentionality." In *Philosophy in France Today*, edited by Alan Montefiore. Cambridge: Cambridge University Press 1983.
– *Collected Philosophical Papers*. Translated by Alphonso Lingis. Dordrecht: M. Nijhoff 1987.
– *Ethics and Infinity: Conversations with Phillippe Nemo*. Translated by Ralph A. Cohen. Pittsburgh: Duquesne University Press 1985.
– *Otherwise than Being or Beyond Essence*. Translated by Alphonso Lingis. The Hague: Martinus Nijhoff 1981.
– "Reality and Its Shadow." In *Collected Philosophical Papers*, translated by Alphonso Lingis, 1–13.
– *Totality and Infinity: An Essay in Exteriority*. Translated by Alphonso Lingis. Pittsburgh: Duquesne University Press 1969.

– "The Trace of the Other." In *Deconstruction in Context: Literature and Philosophy*, edited by Mark C. Taylor, 245–59. Chicago: University of Chicago Press 1989.

Löwith, Karl. *From Hegel to Nietzsche*. Translated by David E. Green. New York: Holt, Rinehart, Winston 1964.

Loy, David. "The Clôture of Deconstruction: A Mahayana Critique of Derrida." *International Philosophical Quarterly* 27 (1987): 59–80.

– "The Paradox of Causality in Madhyamika." *International Philosophical Quarterly* 25 (1985).

McCabe, Colin. *James Joyce and the Revolution of the Word*. New York: Barnes & Noble 1979.

McFarland, Thomas. *Originality and Imagination*. Baltimore and London: Johns Hopkins University Press 1985.

Magliola, Robert. *Derrida on the Mend*. West Lafayette: Purdue University Press 1984.

Materer, Timothy. *Vortex: Pound, Eliot, and Lewis*. Ithaca, N.Y.: Cornell University Press 1979.

– *Wyndham Lewis as Novelist*. Detroit: Wayne State University Press 1976.

Meyers, Jeffrey. *The Enemy: A Biography of Wyndham Lewis*. London: Routledge & Kegan Paul 1980.

– "Wyndham Lewis." In *The Craft of Literary Biography*, edited by Jeffrey Meyers, 118–32. New York: Schocken 1985.

– , ed. *Wyndham Lewis: A Revaluation*. Montreal: McGill-Queen's University Press 1980.

Michel, Walter. "Books From One of Lewis's Libraries." *Enemy News: Journal of the Wyndham Lewis Society* 19 (Summer 1984): 37.

– "On the Genesis of *Tarr*." *Enemy News: Journal of the Wyndham Lewis Society* 22 (1986): 38–41.

Morrow, Bradford, and Bernard Lafourcade. *A Bibliography of the Writings of Wyndham Lewis*. Santa Barbara: Black Sparrow 1978.

Munton, Alan. "Wyndham Lewis: the Transformations of Carnival." In *Wyndham Lewis Letteratura/Pittura*, edited by G. Cianci, 141–57. Palermo: Sellerio 1982.

Navickas, Joseph L. *Consciousness and Reality: Hegel's Philosophy of Subjectivity*. The Hague: Martinus Nijhoff 1976.

Neuman, Shirley. "The Observer Observed: Distancing the Self in Autobiography." *Prose Studies* 4 (1981): 317–36.

Nietzsche, Friedrich. "The Birth of Tragedy From the Spirit of Music." In *The Philosophy of Nietzsche*, translated by Clifton D. Fadiman, 949–1088. New York: Modern Library 1954.

– *The Gay Science*. Translated by Walter Kaufmann. New York: Random House 1974.

– *On the Genealogy of Morals*. Translated by Walter Kaufmann and R.J. Hollingdale. New York: Random House 1967.

– *Thus Spoke Zarathustra*. Translated by R.J. Hollingdale. Harmondsworth: Penguin 1969.

– *The Use and Abuse of History*. Translated by Adrian Collins. Indianapolis: Bobbs-Merrill 1957.

Nishitani, Keiji. *Religion and Nothingness*. Translated by Jan Van Bragt. Berkeley: University of California Press 1982.

O'Keefe, Paul. "Afterword." In Wyndham Lewis, *Tarr: The 1918 Version*, edited by Paul O'Keefe, 361–85. Santa Rosa: Black Sparrow 1990.

Paterson, R. W. K. *The Nihilistic Egoist: Max Stirner*. London: Oxford University Press for University of Hull 1971.

Poggioli, Renato. *The Theory of the Avant-Garde*. Translated by G. Fitzgerald. Cambridge, Mass.: Harvard University Press 1968.

Porteus, Hugh Gordon. *Wyndham Lewis: A Discursive Exposition*. London: Desmond Harmsworth 1932.

Pound, Omar and Philip Grover. *Wyndham Lewis: A Descriptive Bibliography*. Folkestone: Dawson 1978.

Pritchard, William H. *Wyndham Lewis*. New York: Twayne 1968.

Rajchman, John. *Michel Foucault: The Freedom of Philosophy*. New York: Columbia University Press 1985.

Rose, Margaret A. *Parody/Meta-Fiction*. London: Croom Helm 1979.

Rose, William K. *Wyndham Lewis at Cornell: A Review of the Lewis Papers*. Ithaca, N.Y.: Cornell University Press 1961.

Sandler, Linda. *"The Revenge for Love* by Wyndham Lewis: Editorial, Genetic and Interpretive Studies." Ph.D. Diss. University of Toronto 1974.

Schulte-Sasse, Jochen. "Foreword: Theory of Modernism versus Theory of the Avant-Garde." In Peter Bürger, *The Theory of the Avant-Garde*, vii–xlvii. Minneapolis: University of Minnesota Press 1984.

Simpson, D.P. *Cassell's New Latin-English, English-Latin Dictionary*. London: Cassell 1968.

Smith, Rowland. "Afterword." In Wyndham Lewis, *Self Condemned*, 411–21. Santa Barbara: Black Sparrow 1983.

– "Introduction." In Wyndham Lewis, *Self-Condemned*, v–x. Toronto: McClelland & Stewart 1974.

Stirner, Max. *The Ego and His Own*. Translated by S.T. Byington. New York 1907; London 1912.

Sugarman, Robert Ira. *"Rancor Against Time": The Phenomenology of "Ressentiment"*. Hamburg: Felix Meiner 1980.

Toews, John E. *Hegelianism: The Path Toward Dialectical Humanism*. Cambridge: Cambridge University Press 1980.

Tomlin, E. W. F. *Wyndham Lewis*. London: Longmans 1955.

Wagner, Geoffrey. *Wyndham Lewis: A Portrait of the Artist as Enemy*. New Haven: Yale University Press 1957.

Weightman, J. *The Concept of the Avant-Garde. Explorations in Modernism*. Lesalle: Open Court 1973.

Woodcock, George, ed. *Wyndham Lewis in Canada*. Vancouver: Publications Centre, University of British Columbia 1971.

Zimmerman, Michael E. *Eclipse of the Self: The Development of Heidegger's Concept of Authenticity*. Athens and London: Ohio University Press 1981.

Index